J.P.G.

For love of chivalry.

Table of Contents

AUTHOR'S INTRODUCTORY NOTE TO THE TRILOGY

William Marshal, or William the Marshal (1146 – 1219), is the first commoner in European history to have had a memoir of his life written; it was set down shortly after his death. What follows in these pages is the first of three books loosely based upon this and the several biographies that the discovery of the *History of William Marshal* (in 1861) subsequently inspired. It seems to me that William Marshal's life had a well-defined formative period followed by an extraordinary maturity during which he retained his vigour into his seventies.

However, this is a work of the imagination not history, a fictional representation of the man behind the legend, intended to discover perhaps why, even to his contemporaries, William Marshal acquired the soubriquet 'the Greatest Knight'. Although my story relies heavily on the principal incidents in William's life, and, of course, many of the powerful characters who shared his lifetime, a number of the lesser players are my own invention, chief among these is Robert de Salignac. Such a presumption is necessary to develop a narrative that seeks a speculative answer to questions that remain open about William. What made him the man he was, coming as he did from a troubled childhood of parental repudiation – at least on the part of his father? How, in a brutal age, did he earn that peerless reputation among many of his contemporaries when the hands of some were firmly set against him? What made him serve five kings, not always with unblemished loyalty, and among whom was 'Bad' King John? Why is there a statue of him - a powerful magnate - in the Palace of Westminster suggesting he was an architect of English liberties?

Who knows for certain? All I can do is offer the reader what I consider a plausible enough evocation of a great Anglo-Norman, a self-made man who lived in an era when one's descent mattered, the Church was all-powerful, when Heaven and Hell were very real and life hung by a thread; when Kings were anointed of God's good Grace and called thereafter in the Almighty's name – not Majesty in their own. Under the invigilation and spiritual jurisdiction of Holy Church, the politico-military system of his day was feudalism, a structure of apparent simplicity until dynastic ambitions, treacheries and sexual confusions made it a horror, riven by the lust for power, ruthless ambition, disloyalties, repudiations, murders and a complete disregard for those at the bottom of the social pile. It was an era when most women were mere pawns and the vast majority of people were held in the thrall of serfdom. Without land a man was nothing and while William was not intellectual or over-gifted with political nous, he succeeded – often against the odds and despite falling from grace on more than one occasion – in establishing himself and his family as a major force in the realm. As is often the case from such origins his dynasty did not last long.

*

Beyond the fact that William Marshal's life coincided with the first tentative stirrings of what would much later mature into our form of democracy, in that he lived at the time of Magna Carta, it was also contemporaneous with what would develop into medieval chivalry and the full flowering of heraldic symbolism. The tournaments mentioned herein were not the colourful jousts in the lists of a later era, but full-blown war-games played over vast tracts of border lands that one historian compares with today's Formula One racing circuit. The analogy is apt enough; death by the principals was rare because fortunes could be made from the ransom of captives; there was a value attached to the war-horses known as destriers and their equipage; prestige was accrued from displays of valour and that cherished attribute, 'prowess'. By such means even a relative nobody - and in early medieval terms William was not much more – might rise as William did to an Earldom and a surrogate King as Regent of England.

Moreover, of course, England's fate was indissolubly linked with that of France to whose Kings the Kings of England owed allegiance as Dukes of Aquitaine and the lords of other duchies and counties of western France that made up the great Angevin Empire. Such an unbalanced polity was bound to be governed chiefly by the quarrels of the handful of powerful men, and at least one woman, who vied for supremacy therein.

Though born in England, William Marshal was thus part of this feudal Anglo-Norman Ascendancy imposed a century earlier upon his own conquered territory by his namesake, King William I – the Conqueror. This upper stratum of the social order, in which his father was of minor importance and his mother rather better born, spoke Norman-French. With this in mind I have occasionally used words familiar to him without italicising them; destrier is one example, mesnie (the knights attached to a great nobleman's household) another. As for knighthood and chivalry, the former was a far less socially elevating affair then than later. It conferred the acceptance of a squire or un-dubbed fighting gentleman (and 'gentleman' derives from this period, though few were characterised by gentleness) as a competent warrior by his peers. Hence, off stage in these pages, it is William who 'knights' his vastly social superior, the 'Young King' Henry. The ceremony, such as it was, consisted of a girding on of a sword and belt, dubbing actually being a blow to the shoulder with the fist of he who bestowed the honour. As for chivalry, this too was embryonic, developing as part of the emerging ritual and eventual refinement of the tournament (as a later, limited spectator sport confined to lists, lists in William's day being the meeting points in the wider-ranging tourney), and an important aid to identification on the battlefield. Even in full-blown war capture and ransom rather than death was the easy fate of a cornered and outnumbered baron, though the same could not be said for their common soldiery. Moreover, 'chivalry' (a word deriving from horsemanship) had few of the connotations we attach to it today. Like notions of 'honour' – usually a peevishly dangerous self-esteem – a knight of William's time was never the 'parfait gentle knight' that Chaucer attempted to peddle. He might pray but he readily killed, maimed and murdered in his or his overlord's name. It was in such dutiful conduct that 'loyalty' was to be found and William's story must be read in this light.

Because Angevin England and Capetian France were so intertwined and the use of the same names was so common, I have occasionally resorted to the French spelling of a name for a person originating in what we now call France – Guillaume for the Lord of Tancarville, for example – to differentiate from their English cousins. The greatest difficulty arises in making the distinction between the 'Old' King Henry (Henry II, nicknamed 'Curtmantle') and his heir who was crowned within his father's reign as was then the fashion, and generally known as the 'Young King'. The title Prince of Wales had not then been coined and I hope that the reader is spared confusion by the somewhat repetitious use of 'Old' and 'Young'. Furthermore, to emphasise the contemporary importance – not to say dominance - of feudal precedence, I have capitalised all titles and ranks. Although the English Kings of this era are best known to history as early Plantagenets, their contemporaries referred to them as of the House of Anjou.

Finally, though he would have been bound to an overlord, a Knight Banneret bore his own 'device' – an early form of coat of arms – and employed his own household knights in his mesnie. Few were unlanded, as was William during the years covered by this tale (1146 – 1183).

*

One of the great unanswered questions about William Marshal's life is what happened to him in the Holy Land and in the second of this trilogy, *The King's Knight*, I take a slightly different view to several of his modern biographers who lay understandable emphasis on some sort of spiritual awakening. On his return to the Court of Henry II in 1186 we certainly see a different William. He was, by medieval standards, approaching old age and his mission to Jerusalem was an obligation contracted at the death-bed of his patron, liege-lord and friend, the so-called 'Young King'. I suggest, however, that the change in William was more complex than a mere morbid contemplation of mortality, though that undoubtedly played its part. Although I do not go into details, which lie in the margins of my tale, the consequences of this transformation are played out in this second book.

It is in the period covered by the third book, *Guardian of the Realm*, that it seems to me that William more justifiably established a name for greatness in the sense history understands and this too marks a shift in his values. He had the good fortune to live a long life and his political outlook changed with the years. Perhaps he could see that those to whom he left his fortune might not sustain it but, whatever *his* motives, it is from these perceived alterations in his conduct that the process of imaginative recreation has derived.

CHAPTER ONE: THE IMP OF SATAN, 1146

'What is wrong?'

The Lady Sybil raised her head from the pillow. Her brow was still gleaming with perspiration, curls of her dark hair stuck to her pallid skin and her fine brown eyes were sunk in sockets dark with sleeplessness and fatigue. She stared at the lying-in woman at the end of the bed who was startled at the vehemence of the question.

The lying-in woman had assumed her charge had fallen asleep; indeed but a moment before she *had* been asleep, her eyes closed and her breast rising and falling regularly, exhausted with the business of giving-birth. She had been relieved that the baby had been a boy and had cried for a few moments as the lying-in woman wrapped the infant in a linen cloth. Then the child had fallen silent and in that briefly blissful moment the lady had closed her own eyes.

'What is wrong?' her Ladyship asked again, her voice strained with tiredness but taut with a sudden expectation of obedient answer.

The lying-in woman seemed caught-out and flustered. Her Ladyship must have sensed all was not well, for instead of bending to place the boy in the prepared cot, the lying-in-woman had been peeling back the swaddling cloth to show the mark to the Lady's handmaid. Perhaps the sound of the sharply indrawn breath of the maid had woken her, but whatever had revived her did not matter now. She was awake and aware of something amiss.

'Why, 'tis nothing my Lady,' the lying-in woman temporised foolishly, provoking a second indrawn breath, this time from the maid who anticipated her mistress's reaction.

It came quickly, with a flash of fire from the pain-ringed eyes. 'Something cannot be nothing,' her Ladyship snapped, betraying, besides her frustration at being brooked, the keenness of her intelligence.

' 'Tis but a little mark, Madam,' put in the lady's handmaid with a clumsy attempt at mediation.

'Mark! What mark! Show me!' The Lady Sybil was struggling to sit up. 'Show me…' She was gasping for air and perspiring again from the effort. 'I shall…not tell you…again,' she managed. The lying-in woman came nervously forward, bent over the bed and showed the boy-child's exposed right shoulder. A red naevus of raised and granular tissue disfigured the perfection of the soft pink skin just beside the shoulder-blade.

' 'Tis nothing, my Lady, but a birth-mark g…given by God to…' she began, but was cut short.

'Holy Christ!' exclaimed the Lady Sybil, her pale features drawn into a rictus of horror. ' 'Tis no mark of God! 'Tis that of the Devil!' She crossed herself and, waving the child away fell back on her pillow. 'Look to it, confound you, do you not see it has the very form of Satan, tail and all!'

The lying-in woman, her face a mixture of fear and credulity, turned to the maid for help. The maid motioned her aside and came forward to her mistress who was now wracked with deep and tearless sobs of anger and despair.

'My Lady, 'tis not so, not so at all. I do not see the Devil, my lady, but,' and here she hesitated for a moment, casting about for some placatory image before hurrying on. 'I see nothing more than the shape of a noble lion.' She tried a smile as she laid a tentative hand upon the arm of the Lady Sybil.

Her Ladyship did not open her eyes but withdrew her arm sharply. 'Do not presume to console me Angharad! When did you

15

ever know the shape of a noble lion? You have beguiled me in the past with your faerie notions. Understand the Devil comes in disguises, even that of a lion, to deceive eyes that cannot see the truth…'

'Madam, it is a fancy… your condition and long labour…'

The Lady Sybil opened her eyes and withered Angharad with a baleful stare. 'You have not had the child within you these nine months, girl! You know not of what you speak.' Then she lowered her voice and, speaking more calmly, terminated the horrid intimacy of the incident. 'I know the Devil's work when I see it. Go tell my lord that he has a son who bears an image of Satan'.

'Madam…' the handmaid Angharad drew back uncertainly, exchanging glances with the now trembling lying-in woman.

'Go!' The Lady Sybil had closed her eyes again and lay back upon the damp pillow.

'Wait here,' the maid Angharad ap Gwyn commanded the lying-in woman and, opening the door, ran from the chamber.

Shoving aside the waiting priest she descended the ladder to the bottom of the wooden tower, emerging into the great hall of the motte-and-bailey castle of Hamstead Marshal, seat of John, the King's Marshal and his wife, Sybil of Salisbury. Here Angharad found her master sitting at a trestle-table with his steward, Geoffrey du Bois, standing alongside him, a glass of wine and an open book before him. Further down the hall, beside a fire in a brazier, two men half-clad in mail sat on a low bench; one desultorily sharpened a long and wicked knife, the other fondled the soft ears of a boar-hound.

Angharad's entry drew all eyes and the man all called 'the Marshal' rose expectantly to his feet, followed by the three other men in the hall. The boar-hound also stood with a low growl. Angharad met her master's one eye and felt – as she always did –

the sharp, intuitive tug of disgust and pity for the severely disfigured face that looked at her expectantly.

'Well?'

'My Lord, will you come? Her Ladyship…'

'Is it born?'

'Aye, my lord…'

'Well, is it a boy?'

'Aye, my lord…'

'Jesu Christ be praised,' the Marshall said piously, crossing himself before throwing out a joyous laugh. 'I knew it!' Then he assumed a serious mien, asking, 'is the priest here?'

'Aye, my lord he waits, but her Ladyship wishes you first to come…'

'Is something amiss?' the Marshal asked, perceiving for the first time that the maid was flustered and she wore an anxious expression. Her silence and downward glance told their own story. 'By the bones of Christ,' the Marshal muttered, drawing his right hand down over the scar-tissue of his face and moving towards the tower stairs with such abruptness that he upset the upholstered stool upon which he had been sitting. As he disappeared his steward bent and restored the stool to its upright position and looked at the half-armed men.

'What means this?' the younger asked.

' 'Tis a birth, and a birth among the great is always to be fossicked over until all is known,' the man who had been fondling the hound remarked, reseating himself. 'Perhaps her Ladyship has not come well through it'.

'That would go very ill with the master,' Geoffrey du Bois muttered half to himself before they all fell silent, listening for any noises from above.

The Marshal entered his wife's chamber and, pushing the insistent priest back into the tiny ante-chamber, closed the oak door behind him and took in the scene before him. The chamber was the only room in the castle finished to John Marshal's satisfaction. Besides the two iron-bound chests, the spread furs and an arras of strange working, it was dominated by a French bed.

His wife lay upon her pillow, eyes closed. At the foot of the bed lay the cradle beside which the lying-in woman stood trembling. John Marshal crossed the small room in a stride and stood looking down at his son. The baby stared upwards at him, an expression of perfect equanimity upon his squashed features which somehow, in his father's imagination, possessed some innate wisdom whilst reflecting his own ugliness. The impression was powerful and shocked the father; he looked then at his silent wife and at the lying-in woman, not fully comprehending what – if anything - was wrong.

'What is it?' he asked, thinking it some foolish woman's concern.

'Why, my Lord... I, er...I...' The lying-in woman was plainly terrified.

'For the love of God...' Marshal began, exasperation in his voice. He half turned as Angharad ap Gwyn slipped into the room behind him and then swung round as the Lady Sybil called to him from the bed.

'He bears the mark of the Devil, husband,' she said wearily.

'*What*?' The Marshal frowned, then looked again at the boy who wrinkled his face and seemed about to cry. 'For the love of Christ will someone enlighten me?'

'He has a birth-mark, my lord,' explained Angharad, moving forward and displacing the lying-in woman who was peremptorily waved out of the chamber by the Marshal.

'Where? What manner of birth-mark...?'

'It is blood-red and has the appearance of Satan,' said the Lady Sybil.

'Show me.'

The handmaid reached down and drew the boy from the cradle, uncovering his shoulder and presenting his father with the contentious marking.

'Do you see the tail...Satan's tail?' asked the Lady Sybil from her bed, her eyes still closed.

'We see a lion, my Lord,' offered the handmaid placatingly, greatly daring but trespassing upon John Marshal's liking for her.

For a long moment John Marshal stared at the evidence of Satanic intervention in the birth of his son. He knew, as did Angharad better than he, that the child had kicked in the womb with a fury that was unusual. So unusual had it been that it had convinced them all that a boy was on the way. He shot his eyes sideways at the maid.

'What do you make of it?' he asked quietly, aware that there were some who considered Angharad had inherited her mother's second-sight. 'He is unnaturally silent and, it seems to me, has a knowing look about him...'

'I am still in your presence, my Lord,' the Lady Sybil said with heavy sarcasm, opening her eyes. 'The wench knows nothing of such things.'

'I think him an old soul, my Lady,' Angharad ventured, boldly addressing her mistress, though intending the information for her master.

'You presume too much...'

'No, no, the girl should be heard for she has some wisdom...'

'Methinks 'tis a lion, my Lord,' Angharad said hurriedly before drawing the cloth back over the child's exposed shoulder and lowering him back into the cradle.

'You have milk?'

'Aye, my lord…'

'John!' The Lady Sybil had extended her right arm, her hand shaking, motioning her husband to come to her, her eyes blazing with anger. 'I am not just your brood-mare, I am your wife!'

'Of course you are, my love.' Marshal moved beside his spouse and took her hand and she frowned up at him. 'And what name shall we give him, this imp of Satan,' he asked almost facetiously.

' 'Tis no laughing matter, my lord.'

'I am not laughing. Do you not wish him to be baptised and saved in the love of Christ? Or shall I have him cast upon the midden without further ado, eh?'

'Call him what you will,' she responded peremptorily, turning towards Angharad who was gathering up the swabs used at the child's birth and casting them into an iron bowl. 'And you, you may have him taken at once to the wet-nurse…'

'You will not suckle him?' the Marshal asked. 'You suckled our first-born…'

'And you mis-liked my breasts thereafter.'

John Marshal sighed, well-knowing the uncongenial mood of a woman after child-birth. Turning to the handmaid he said, 'do as my lady asks and tell the lying-in woman to await my pleasure below.'

Angharad bobbed her obedience and left the chamber. The Marshal turned back to his wife who had again closed her eyes, raising her cold hand to his lips. 'He may come in useful, Sybil,' he murmured, 'so I shall call him William after your late brother. They said *he* was an imp and Angharad thinks the new-born an old soul. Perhaps,' the Marshal added with a chuckle, 'he has come back to us, sent from the fiery pit complete with a brand…'

20

He stopped abruptly as his wife squeezed his hand hard. 'Do not jest over such matters,' she hissed. 'This is not a woman's silly fancy! The child is marked…' Her voice rose, ignoring the index finger he raised to his lips. 'Marked, d'you hear? Have him removed from my presence. Have him baptised by all means but not here. Thereafter, keep him in ignorance, use him as you will. You already have an heir. He may, as you say, come in useful.'

Her husband nodded. 'Very well; Angharad shall have the nurturing of him.'

And so, late in the afternoon of the day of his birth, the second son born to John the Marshal and the Lady Sybil, sister to Patrick, Earl of Salisbury, was baptised William by a priest who knew not then that he held in his arms a child marked by the Great Lucifer.

*

It was long after dark when the Marshal reeled to the palliasse laid at the foot of the French bed. The Lady Sybil breathed the breath of deep sleep and he lay for a while staring up into the darkness, aware that he had partaken of too much wine yet unready for slumber himself as his mind whirled. What was he to make of the day's events? He had no doubt that the new-born boy possessed some quality he did not recall observing in his other children, and he had sired several, including one by his first wife, Adelina, whom he had set aside to cement a difficult alliance with Patrick of Salisbury amid the turbulence of a civil war. He belched quietly into the night, his hand clamped over his mouth to stifle the sound and feeling the appalling mess the molten lead falling from the roof of Wherwell Abbey had made of his visage some six years earlier. He had held off the pursuers of the Empress Mathilda after the disastrous siege of Winchester, packing her off riding astride like a man so that she did not compromise her escape and could ride like the wind with her small escort.

21

John Marshal had covered her departure by giving her pursuers grounds for thinking her mewed-up in the sanctuary of the nunnery at Wherwell where he and another knight pretended Mathilda's defence. Unable to enter the church under the rules of sanctuary, King Stephen's men set the place ablaze to smoke their quarry out and when they entered the blackened ruin they found only the charred body of John Marshal. In pursuit of Mathilda, they left him alone for a corpse; but he came round, hideously disfigured, half his face melted, his left eye a liqueous mess – but alive. He managed to stumble twenty-five miles to Marlborough, his fate forgotten in the humiliating accounts that spread throughout the countryside of the discomfited and proud Mathilda being compelled to ride astride like a man.

The fighting that had engulfed Wiltshire and its neighbouring counties died down after Winchester; John Marshal reached his accommodation with Patrick of Salisbury as he and the Earl sank their differences in a common desire to cling onto their lands and influence amid the catastrophic power-struggle between Stephen and 'The Empress'. He was a grandson of William the Conqueror who had seized the throne in defiance of his oath to support the claim of Mathilda who, born the daughter of Henry I, was known as 'the Empress' from her marriage to Henri, the Holy Roman Emperor. He, however, had died and while Mathilda and her second husband, Count Geoffrey of Anjou, disputed Stephen's claim to the Dukedom of Normandy by force of arms, Stephen busied himself consolidating his hold on England. It was a troublesome time for the Anglo-Norman nobles whose complex allegiances swayed like cornstalks in the wind. Matters had seemed settled when, in February 1141, Stephen had been captured at Lincoln, but Stephen's Queen rallied his forces and captured Mathilda's brother. An exchange of high-born prisoners liberated

Stephen, but in the mean-time Geoffrey of Anjou had completed his conquest Normandy, further blighting the questionable loyalty of those Anglo-Norman lords with lands in both Normandy and England and war flared-up again.

Such confusions had allowed the ambitious John, the King's Marshal of Horse, to gain lands and power incrementally so that his marriage to Sybil of Salisbury found him, as he was fond of saying himself, 'the cockerel atop the shit-heap,' at least as far as Wiltshire and its surroundings were concerned.

John the Marshal was nothing if not a man on the make; he had taken his survival after the burning of Wherwell, in the wake of saving Mathilda, as a mark of God's approval, rather than the all but incredible luck of a man of formidable physique. God's approval was important to him, for he had played a dangerous game in transferring his allegiance from Stephen to Mathilda. Thus his marriage to Salisbury's sister was a political alliance between himself and his more powerful local opponent, placing the two loudest cockerels triumphantly a-top the midden. And so he lay awake that night of his son William's birth in the year of our Lord 1147, aware that God had sent him a second boy by Sybil, and one whom, it was quite likely, he could indeed make good use of.

The child seemed lusty enough and in that first exchange of glances the father had gulled himself, perceiving something of the future. Prescience or not, the Marshal believed something of the sort, if only to drive away the contagious idea that possessed the boy's mother. John the Marshal had long lain under threat of excommunication for abjuring his oath to Stephen and preferred to think of his son's naevus as he did of his own disfiguring in the fire at Wherwell, as the touch of God's mystery rather than Satan's mischief. The child had not been conceived in sin because his divorce from Adelina had been sanctioned by Holy law on the grounds of consanguinity. The priests he paid assured him so; as for the wrong wrought upon Adelina, he had expiated that long since and the lady bore him no ill-will.

The woman Angharad was right, he convinced himself, and Sybil – God forgive her in the aftermath of long labour – was mistaken. John the Marshal, inebriated and content, finally slept upon such a comfortable conclusion.

*

As if the happy thought flew from his sleeping brow like a dark shadow, it settled upon the head of his wife and she woke in the false dawn, alive to the tragedy that had overwhelmed her. She had few feelings for her husband beyond that of dynastic duty, aware that their union was one of policy and that her consent to the match brought peace to the neighbourhood of Marlborough town, to Cherhill and Wexcombe, the lordship of which brought under her husband's hand the Courts of the Hundreds of Bedwyn and Kinwardstone. The Marshal's writ now ran along the Vale of the Kennet to the head-waters of the Avon. There were other lands elsewhere, plus the fiefs and fees from three bishoprics: Exeter, Winchester and Worcester, to which those of the Abbot of Abingdon had to be added. But the price of such favour was no imp of Satan; the kicking boy she had born in her womb had mightier powers than those of a mere wight. She did not need to look into his knowing eyes, only to see their reflection in that single orb that shone in the ghastly face of his father. Something of greater portent, she thought, lurked there.

It had not been easy for Sybil of Salisbury to lie with such a man as John the Marshal. And yet…and yet… She could not deny that in John the Marshal a woman of her sensibilities did not perceive something fantastic, something powerful that went beyond mere ambition. And had not her handmaid Angharad told her something

24

of the vision she had had when the Lady Sybil had discovered that she was again pregnant? Angharad's visions were few and far between, but they were wrought out of a powerful magic. And while the Lady Sybil protested her repugnance for the Old Ways, there was no denying the uncanny accuracy of Angharad's occasional predictions. She had foretold an outbreak of the plague in Marlborough, and that the Lady Sybil's first-born would satisfy her Lord by being a boy. As for her second, the Welsh-woman had said that she had seen a dark figure, set upon a horse, who raised three crowns upon his sword-point as his charger trampled a score of corpses into the bloody mire beneath its hooves.

Angharad had not wanted to reveal all this, but the Lady Sybil insisted that if she had foreseen anything, she must reveal it. The gravid woman had chiefly in mind the child's gender and her own survival, and what the handmaid told her had proved so much more detailed than the revelations about her first-born. Although Angharad argued that the meaning of such things was rarely clear or simple, the fore-telling seemed terrifying to the over-wrought mother. In the last weeks of her pregnancy the Lady Sybil's mind had been plagued by anxious dreams, feelings of foreboding and unrest. Thus, in the exhaustion of post-natal reaction, she had seen in the birth-mark a confirmation of her worst apprehensions: her new-born boy bore the brand of the Devil. Now, as the daylight grew, she lay gently weeping while her snoring and hideously disfigured husband slept off his wine.

Below them the priest who had baptised the baby rose to the first office of the day. After his devotions, Nicholas de Sarum, as he styled himself, heard for the first time the tittle-tattle as the servants woke and spoke of the child with the birth-mark, the infant whose wrinkled brow he had the previous evening anointed with oil, baptised in the name of the Holy Trinity. Had he not noticed anything odd? he was asked by the girl who brought warm milk from the byre. Surely, she asked again, seeking guidance in her perplexity, one who bore Satan's image could not be christened like any normal child?

And seeing in the faint mist that rose from the pannikins of milk that chilly morning the finger of Almighty God pointing the way and simultaneously wagging at him for his lack of faith, Nicholas de Sarum asserted that, yes indeed, the infant's brow had been hot to his touch, that the water *had* sizzled upon the pink skin which had – despite appearances – the feel of old leather beneath his fingers…

Old leather was what came most to mind among the denizens of the castle of Hamstead Marshal when confronted by their Lord's dreadful visage. There was indeed something diabolical about John the Marshal.

And had there been a smell? As of something…

Like brimstone? Oh, yes, yes, most emphatically there had been a smell…

And a steaming, like that from a hot iron plunged into water…?

And during the hours that followed Nicholas de Sarum, God forgive him in his enthusiasm for the Truth, imagined no end of subtle hints that the spirit of Lucifer lay within the boy-child. Consequently, by sunset, all wondered at the priest's devotion in being able to hold so hot a thing and douse the dreadful spirit with the quenching of Holy Water. And all were profoundly grateful to him for warding off the evil that had threatened them. For that, at least according to Nicholas de Sarum, was what the sacrament of baptism had effected.

And when a sceptical Angharad pooh-poohed the story, saying the baby was no hotter than any other, the servants crossed themselves and muttered against her and her ancient and depraved notions. Of course to *her* pagan touch there was nothing noticeable, but such things were made manifest to a man of the piety of Nicholas de Sarum and had the Welsh handmaid not stood high in the favour of her Ladyship, they would have combined to denounce her as a witch.

And so William, son of John the Marshal and Sybil of Salisbury, entered a world that would ever and anon wonder if he were touched by God or the Devil.

Or even, being human, by both.

CHAPTER TWO: THE ANARCHY 1147 - 1153

Though few forgot it entirely, as the boy William grew and became a familiar sight running with his elder brother about the castle and the woods that lay beyond, his quiet disposition and good looks eroded the fear that his birth had engendered. He had his mother's brown hair and eyes and, gradually, when the naevus *was* exposed to view, observers were inclined to give the boy the benefit of the doubt, saying that perhaps, after all, it did indeed look more like a lion than Satan.

Fleet of mind, Nicholas de Sarum bent this perception to his will and the reinforcement of the True Faith: of course it did; it had been transformed by miraculous and Divine intervention at the instant of that hot baptismal moment. Truly the priest was a curer of souls!

Only William's mother persisted in her rejection of her offspring and his existence continued to trouble her. Instead, she lavished her attention upon her other children: John, her first-born and the Marshal's heir, and – in due course - two further sons, Anselm and Henry, along with three daughters. William was allowed to run wild; he seemed impervious to his mother's neglect and revelled in his freedom, the apple of Angharad's eye. An active, physical boy, as soon as he could toddle he showed interest in his older brother's wooden sword and buckler, his bow and arrows. Once able to walk properly he would be found in the stables, or with the Marshal's falconer, tending his father's two fine peregrines and his mother's little merlin tiercel, the first bird he took out hawking, the Lady Sybil affecting little interest in the sport. Such outings usually took place during the intermittent visits the Lady Sybil paid to Marlborough when William was left behind. On these occasions, though no more than four, he also did the rounds of the snares and traps set by his father's retainers, with whom he became a favourite. They encouraged him, made him things, like a small bow with which, upon one oft talked-of occasion, he shot a dog fox through the neck.

Enjoying such liberty the growing William came reluctantly to the schooling the ardent Nicholas pressed upon him. That he was compelled to by the explicit order of the Lady Sybil was the extent to which his mother took an interest in William's growing. As a consequence the priest had made William his life's work, watching him for any sign of peccant behaviour, of tale-telling, or bullying the castle's other children, of the slightest indication of cruelty towards any beast, of back-sliding or any manifestation of diabolical influence. At the slightest sign of demonic possession, the child was heavily lectured on the matter of honourable conduct and the Way of Christ. Seeing the boy's active nature and knowing his probable future success would rely upon William's martial abilities, Nicholas was worldly enough to encourage in the lad a sense of prowess, that fusion of skill and strength in the bearing of arms, to which he sought to add a strong moral sense grounded in duty, the only virtue consistent in a priest's mind with the wielding of a sword. In the perfervid imagination of Nicholas de Sarum, young William FitzMarshal, bereft of any other career, might make a creditable crusader.

During these early formative years, Nicholas de Sarum's sense of achievement would have been complete, had it not been for the influence of the Lady Sybil's maid, Angharad. Nicholas was at a loss to understand why the Lady Sybil tolerated the Welsh woman's presence. As far as Nicholas was concerned the bitch was too close to the Old Ways and it seemed to him that she had bewitched the Lady Sybil so that her Ladyship refused to accept the miracle of the boy's baptism, persisting in her superstition that the child was cursed. He did not understand that in allowing the boy a close familiarity with Angharad, she reposed her own maternal duty, writing it off in delegation.

By this argument Nicholas de Sarum saw in the boy a battlefield in which he, as God's anointed, fought for the soul of William against the Devil's agent, Angharad ap Gwyn. He would prevail, of course, but it was God's will that he must fight for the boy's soul and be ever vigilant when – which was rare, for the Lady Sybil kept her handmaid hard by herself – he saw the boy in the company of her Ladyship's confidential body-servant.

As for Angharad, she was aware of, but impervious to, the priest's hostility which grew with the passing of time. She was safe enough from any accusations he might level at her, partly from her blameless life and the hours of devotion she gave to the Lady Sybil, which earned her also the high regard of her Lord, but because she had grown up in the Salisbury household and, despite their difference in rank, had always been close to her mistress. This too had earned her the approbation of her Master.

Angharad ap Gwyn endured the Lady Sybil's sharp tongue in the knowledge that her Ladyship was not autonomous, but a creature at Fate's disposal. And such was the quality of their intimacy that the boundaries of birth both dividing and tying them, allowed Angharad to watch over the strange child to which her Mistress had given birth with the Lady Sybil's entire approval. If William's mother could turn her face away from her second son, it was knowing that Angharad would not; that between the surrogacy of Angharad and the devotion of the priest Nicholas, lay a means of offering the boy the opportunity her absent Lord would require of her. Contrary to the teachings of the Church, the Lady Sybil nursed a half-acknowledged faith that there existed in the Old Ways some palliation of the world's miseries. It was the only way she felt able to mitigate her own sin in finding her husband revolting. God had been good to John the Marshal, raising him up, and therefore He must approve of him. It was not for the Lady Sybil to imperil her own soul by an excess of doubt, or her husband's by a want of loyalty.

Loyalty was what bound them; it was not unconditional like love. One could not love upon another's bidding, but loyalty could be forged by sense and policy; it could – and should – be embedded in family for the general good. And in the absence of her husband, mindful of the vision of Angharad ap Gwyn, the Lady Sybil extended opportunity to her second son William, that he might indeed prove useful to her absent Lord.

That the Marshal was rarely at home was in part a consequence of his restlessness and his desire to watch over his newly acquired lands and tenures. But it was also due to the burning of his face and the revulsion he read in his wife's eyes when they were intimate. A once handsome man he found the whispering of sweet nothings to gain a woman's acquiescence as repulsive as he knew any woman found his uttering of them from his twisted mouth.

'Make my two boys worthy of my legacy,' he had commanded the Lady Sybil on his first departure after the troubled birth of his second son, and both husband and wife had understood the meaning of the agreement this sealed between them. In due course they would lie together and more children would be born, but it was no more than dutiful, a manifestation of their dynastic loyalties. Such intimacies were intermittent. In the years of William's infancy, the Marshal's absences grew longer as the extended period of quiescence following the siege of Winchester and escape of Mathilda came to an end. Alas, the simmering uncertainties of a divided England again broke out in civil war.

It became known as 'The Anarchy'.

31

*

Soon after William's fifth birthday, the Marshal rode out of Hamstead Marshal at the head of a body of men-at-arms and headed east, intent upon making his presence felt along the whole rich valley of the Kennet. He halted at Newbury where, summoning his tenants, he had his men throw up a palisade, selecting, as he had at Hamstead Marshal, an ancient barrow to use as the foundation of the stronghold. Here he installed his steward, Geoffrey, as constable, with orders to improve the fortifications and make of the place a proper motte and bailey castle, a crude version of Hamstead Marshal. This, the Marshal knew, would command the road between Oxford and Winchester where it met the track from Reading.

Geoffrey, who called himself FitzJohn, had hardly completed the bidding of John the Marshal when he found Newbury under siege by King Stephen; a short truce had been negotiated of one day's duration, after which the King demanded the surrender of the fortification. The bargaining permitted Geoffrey FitzJohn to send word to his Master and that evening a messenger, riding a mount lathered in sweat, rode into Hamstead Marshal. The horseman passed on the demands of Stephen and the circumstances in which Geoffrey shortly afterwards found himself. John was summoned by Stephen, first for erecting a fort without royal permission, and second for defecting to Mathilda. Geoffrey begged for relief of Newbury.

John the Marshal strode up and down the hall muttering, while the messenger took meat and wine.

'He who holds oaths cheap ought not to quibble when others follow his example,' he growled to no-one in particular, referring to the King's breaking of his own pledge of allegiance to Mathilda.

'Had he done so he might never have brought this present pass upon the country or his own head.'

At the far end of the hall the boy William, aware that something was up, stood amid his father's hounds, watching. The Marshal paused in his pacing and called the messenger to him. Bending his head, the Marshal spoke in a low voice, the messenger nodded and made to leave as his Master called for a fresh horse. After the man had gone, the Marshal began giving orders and soon the castle was astir. It was clear the surrender of Newbury was not imminent, but what was afoot defied prediction.

It was the following day that matters became clearer when the messenger returned. A few moments later William, chasing his older brother John and other boys round the bailey in a game of tig, was summoned to his father's presence. The Marshal sat at the head of the table in the hall from where, when not eating, he dispensed the business of his fiefdom. Seeing the boy blinking in the gloom of the hall after the bright sunlight of the yard he beckoned him and William came towards his father. John looked at his wayward second son with something like approval. He tousled his hair and asked, a lop-sided smile upon his disfigured face, whether he was ready to do a knight's service for his Lord.

Studying his father's seamed and rucked face with a seriousness that belied his years, and aware from his tutoring by Nicholas de Sarum that the question was important and bore upon his honour, the sturdy boy responded with a nod.

'Give me your word, and willingly,' his father responded.

'Aye, father, I am ready to render you knight's service if you ask it of me.' The boy's answer did not strike the Marshal as precocious. It was what was expected of him and the Marshal, smiling inwardly, made a mental note that Nicholas's mentoring reflected his Master's rise in the world. He looked up to fasten his one eye on the priest as he hovered, striving to determine what was happening.

'You have schooled him well, Father Nicholas,' the Marshal smiled.

'I have but wrought your Lordship's will, it being coincident with that of God, sir.'

'Indeed, but 'tis well done.' And again William had his hair tousled. 'Well, Will, you must assemble your traps, I am sending you a hostage to King Stephen and a horse shall be prepared for you within the half-hour. You shall have the beast as your first...let us say palfrey, eh? If thou does this thing well and to my liking, mayhap I shall give thee a destrier, eh?' The Marshal laughed, which made of his face a tortured grimace, and produced a noise of extraordinary quality that sounded very much like pain. The boy stood fascinated. Transfixed. 'Go!' his father prompted. 'Go, say your farewells, and be quick about it.' The Marshal rose to his feet and addressed the messenger, calling for four men-at-arms to escort him and the boy back to Newbury. Then he turned to the priest.

'You shall convey him hence and see that the King receives him well.'

Nicholas de Sarum bowed his head in acquiescence. 'As your Lordship commands.'

'You may return straightway. The boy must take his chance and you are needed here.'

The boy in question was bemused by what exactly it was that was expected of him. William went directly to Angharad who soon learned that her darling was to leave the shelter of Hamstead Marshal.

'I am to pack my traps,' the boy repeated dutifully as his mother's handmaid kneeled weeping before him. 'What is the matter?' he asked, his voice level, his demeanour undiscomfited by the outpouring of Angharad's love and anxiety. It was far less interesting than his father's behaviour. 'I am to do my father knight's service,' he explained, as if it answered all. 'It is what is expected of me…'

Angharad shook her head and wiped the tears from her eyes. Into her mind's eye had flashed the memory of the vision of the man on the horse who lifted three crowns upon his sword. There *was* something special about the boy, she realised with an intuitive certainty, and this moment had been long ago written in the stars.

'Aye, 'tis indeed what is expected of you,' she said, drying her eyes. 'Bear yourself well.' She leaned forward, kissed him on the brow and, pushing herself up from the rushes, stood, dusting her hands on her apron. He nodded solemnly, then stepped forward arms open and hugged her, his face buried in the smell of her none-too-clean apron. She pressed his head into her belly, repeating her injunction: 'Bear yourself well, Will, and all will turn out well.'

When he had gone she knelt again, the palms of both hands pressed down hard upon the bare, trodden earth of the old barrow, whispering words of the old prayers her grandmother had taught her and that she had brought out of Wales as a young girl.

Half an hour later Master William rode out of Hamstead Marshal on his father's gift, a small grey palfrey. The horse bore not merely a hostage for King Stephen, but John the Marshal's conscience. Alongside William rode Nicholas de Sarum and the messenger, a man named Walter, accompanied by four men-at-arms in pot-helms and leather gambesons, each of whom bore sword and lance. Learning of William's departure, his mother came down from her chamber in time to watch him ride out through the wooden gate. With the boy gone, the Marshal turned towards her, accompanied by their heir, John, his hand upon the older lad's shoulder. The Marshal smiled his awful, drawn grin.

'You have done your part well, my Lady. I told you he would come in useful…'

'Whither does he go, My Lord?'

'To the King as hostage against my good and acquiescent conduct.' The Marshal chuckled.

'And shall you act as the King wishes?'

'The King shall not have Newbury…'

'And the boy?'

'We can make another, Sybil,' the Marshal said quietly, his one eye staring gravely at his wife, his hand pressing the shoulder of his heir.

*

The King's camp before Newbury was William's first sight of an armed force. In truth, the army King Stephen had brought in haste before Newbury was not large, but it impressed the boy. Moreover, it was beyond William's appreciation that it was largely composed of Flemish mercenaries under William of Ypres. The party from Hamstead Marshal had ridden in after dark and William's first impression had been of the flickering of camp-fire flames upon a myriad of hard-bitten faces. He had been taken before the King as Stephen sat with his senior councillors taking wine before retiring for the night. Afterwards William recalled very little of that first encounter with the man in whose hands his very life now lay. He recalled a long table above which a row of solemn men regarded him coldly, but he understood the enormity of his plight. Having surveyed his hostage the King dismissed him, He was separated from Nicholas de Sarum and quartered with the king's pages in a tent bearing the royal device and adjacent to Stephen's pavilion. It seemed, for a day or two at least, a pleasant enough thing to render knight's service. His fellows left him largely alone, though one appeared to have been charged with his welfare. William was well

36

fed, allowed more wine than at home, and permitted to join the younger squires in their practice with sword and buckler. This the boy vastly enjoyed; unlike the wooden weapons at Hamstead Marshal, the King's junior squires bore real swords, short-bladed and blunt weapons, to be sure, but swords whose heft and sweep spoke eloquently of power, if not just yet of death. Though it did not surprise William, his ability at five years of age to parry the thrusts of lads six or seven years his senior impressed his captors. Even at this young age his body had all but shed its puppy fat and he showed evidence of sinew and muscle in the making. In this respect he was his father's son.

Seeing this display of martial precocity, one observant noble mentioned to the King that: 'the Marshal's spawn was to be watched with care.'

'Aye, as is his spy,' added another, indicating Nicholas de Sarum whose presence had been forced upon Stephen and who was increasingly regarded with suspicion, the longer he stayed. 'How long shall we hold him, Sire? As long as the boy?'

The King nodded. 'Aye. John the Marshal does not yet need to know we yet lack siege-engines and I would not seek to give him either comfort or encouragement. With his boy in our tender care John Marshal will stay his own hand and not trouble to hold Newbury...'

*

Caught-up in his martial exercises, William did not appreciate that Stephen's sudden appearance before the hurriedly raised wooden ramparts of Newbury castle left the King at a disadvantage. To his untutored eye the thin siege lines behind their ditch and sharpened calthrops, the tents, the men-at-arms, knights, squires and horses – hardy roncins, palfreys and magnificent destriers – gave the boy the impression of a mighty war-host. In fact Stephen's force was but a small retinue. The speed with which he had reacted to the news that his former Marshal and confidant had thrown-up a fortification and thereby made a direct challenge to the King, had meant that Stephen had left his French siege-engines behind him. Relying on surprise and the consequent immediate surrender of the garrison, Stephen had led a mounted column at a canter, only to find that the new works at Newbury were more substantial than he had bargained for. Nor were the garrison eager to give-up their charge and their defiance had led to Stephen prevaricating, exchanging the messages with the Marshal that had resulted in young William appearing as a hostage, and summoning his siege-train hither. Such decisive action, swiftly followed by stalling at the first set-back to his plans, was characteristic of the King, both in politics and war.

War was not in those days *à outrance*. It was a matter of stratagems and sieges, marches and counter-marches, skirmishes and, if it came to pitched-battle – which it rarely did – of hostage-taking, negotiation and monetary ransom. Of course, the common soldiery could expect no mercy if they found themselves caught-up in an armed clash and on the losing side. If they survived the fight itself, or any wounds sustained therein, no-one had the inclination to care for prisoners unable to redeem their pathetic lives with pecuniary reward. Often they were simply 'put to the sword,' as the phrase had it. The high-born, on the other hand, unless they were extremely unfortunate, were relatively safe. In an encounter, an armed knight was to be surrounded, his retainers out-numbered and killed or captured. As for their chief, it was his personal capitulation that was to be secured. Both his person and his destrier had worth, the former for ransom, the latter as a prize for the victor. His other horses, the palfrey used for ordinary travel and the pack-animals called roncins, all added value to the triumph.

By this means half-hearted peace accommodations were reached as ransoms were demanded, negotiated and paid. In these parleys alliances might be broken and others forged, and all took time, for war was as much about enrichment as strategy. The practice ensured the survival of great families, simultaneously making war an economic activity whilst encouraging a fluid confusion among them. Such had led to the marriage of John the Marshal to the Lady Sybil.

As for the local peasantry, if they lay in the grain of the contending parties and owned their feudatory duties to the enemy, they found their crops trampled, stolen or burnt, their animals sequestered, their villages and hamlets looted or set on fire by a marauding enemy intent on pillage and forage. Worse still, if their overlord was taken, their taxes rose to fund his ransom and release. Before such ineluctable forces they cursed and wept, bowed their heads in submission and turned the other cheek in Christian humility. However, such enemy forces were never large and the extent of their destruction, though near-fatal for those implicated, was not widespread. Indeed, the greatest disruption to the majority was the overthrow of the balance of powers, those feudal impositions enforced upon the English people less than a century earlier by the Norman conquerors under William the Bastard.

This was 'the Anarchy' caused by the struggle between Stephen and Mathilda which, though for the throne of England, spilled blood and leached treasure across both England and Normandy. Stephen's action in suddenly repudiating his sworn oath to uphold Mathilda's claim was eloquent both of his swift opportunism and of his poor judgement, and this lack of wisdom was a constant threat to the prospering of his cause. It made itself manifest before the wooden palisade of Newbury when, two days after the arrival of William and Nicholas de Sarum, under the cover of a wet night

John the Marshal threw into Newbury both reinforcements and supplies.

In the damp dawn that followed, Stephen was made aware that his inadequate siege-lines had been breached in the sleeting darkness. He ordered the boy William to be brought before him and a halter put about his neck. He sat staring at the impressive lad, his nobles standing behind him in a half-circle of coloured surtouts that struck the uncomprehending child as impressive. He knew none of them and was therefore unafraid. Quite unabashed at the scrutiny of the King, the lad stared back, turning slightly from side to side, as children compelled to stand before their elders are wont to do.

'Stand still, boy!' The King commanded, nonplussed at William's apparent composure. 'Do you know what has been put about thy neck?'

'A rope sir,' the lad responded.

' 'Tis a halter, Will,' the King explained, his voice less harsh, even kind to the boy's ears. 'A halter by which we may have to hang you if your father jests with us.'

'Are you at war with my father sir?'

Stephen smiled and leaned back, throwing a glance over his shoulder as a ripple of soft laughter ran through the assembly of chivalry in his rear. 'That I am, Will. And I would have it otherwise. Did you know that some few years since, your father was among my council, witnessed my charters. Dost though know what that means?'

'Aye sir. A charter is a paper of importance, writ for a King whose seal and sign-manual must be seen by others and thereby witnessed.'

A murmur of appreciation met this new precocity.

'You have been schooled well, my boy. Who is your Domine?'

'The priest called Nicholas de Sarum in whose company I came hence, sir.'

The King turned aside and spoke behind his hand. 'Go, one of you and summon the priest,' he said, then fell to studying the boy again. William stared back, beginning again to sway slightly from side to side.

'Pray do not do that,' Stephen said irritably. 'It is distracting…'

A moment later the knight sent to find the priest returned with Nicholas de Sarum in tow. The priest made his obeisance to the King.

'Go thee before this castle, Nicholas, and summon them to surrender in thy Lord's name. Tell the chief of that place that I hold his Master's son William a hostage. Say thou hast seen the hangman's noose about his neck and if the castle is not give-up to me by sunset, I shall hang the boy in the first light of the morning following and they shall awake to the sight.'

Without a word, Nicholas de Sarum bowed, backed away then turned and walked towards the castle. He made directly for the gate until he was about fifty yards off it when an arrow struck the ground at his feet. He halted and looked up. Half a dozen heads could be seen above the wooden stakes of the palisade enclosing the enceinte.

'Halt Priest,' a voice called out. 'I know thee; upon what business are you intent?'

His heart thumping, Nicholas de Sarum stared up at the heads silhouetted against the grey clouds. He could not positively recognise anyone, but thought one among them was the Marshal's steward charged with the defence of Newbury castle, Geoffrey FitzJohn.

'I am Nicholas de Sarum,' he began, the words tumbling from him in his anxiety. 'I am sent by John the Marshal to the King's camp with his son William who is this moment held hostage by King Stephen. His Grace the King has himself charged me with the delivery of a message unto your Constable.'

'I am he.' Geoffrey FitzJohn stood clear against the sky. 'Speak, Nicholas. We shall not harm thee.'

'You must offer-up this place to King Stephen before sundown. If you do not the boy William will be hanged at dawn tomorrow.'

Nicholas de Sarum saw two or three of the heads move close together as though conferring. They remained thus for a moment or two then drew apart and Geoffrey replied: 'My Lord has sent me reinforcements and supplies. He sent no message of his son a hostage. Is this a ruse played upon me by the King and using our friendship to conceal its falsehood? To surrender at your demand would incur my Lord's wrath.'

' 'Tis true, FitzJohn. I play no game at the King's behest and have come directly from his tent wherein the boy stands with a halter about his neck.'

There was a moment's indecision, then Geoffrey called down: 'Do you request the King opens his lines and permits me to send word to the Marshal to determine his will.'

Nicholas turned on his heel and walked back to where the King remained seated among his knights, the boy William now also squatting, cross-legged on the ground at his feet, the end of the hemp noose coiled about him.

'Well?' demanded Stephen. Nicholas repeated the request, causing a stirring among the nobles and an irritated look to pass over the King's features. Casting his eyes down, the priest caught William's steady gaze.

There was a protracted silence which lasted until the King pronounced his decision. 'Very well. But I want an answer by dawn. A man may ride there and back over-night and you shall do

42

it,' the King commanded Nicholas as he got to his feet. He was clearly angry and a murmur arose among his entourage from which Nicholas deduced they were none too happy with Stephen's acquiescence. 'And the boy can sleep without supper but with that necklace about him,' the King added. 'Do you impress upon the Marshal that I intend the execution of his son if Newbury is not mine by right of his reply. Now get you gone!'

And so Nicholas de Sarum traipsed back to where the arrow still stuck in the ground and delivered the King's response while a horse was made ready for him. Ten minutes later he was on the road to the west. William watched him go and wished, with all his heart, that he might have ridden by the priest's side.

And then the squire charged with his care came and bent to take-up the end of the halter, jerking William unkindly to his feet with such force that the boy felt the noose draw tight round his neck.

'You little life depends upon the love of your father now, lad,' the young man said as William loosened the constriction round his wind-pipe.

*

By the first light of dawn William was awake and hungry. He had suffered hunger before, but only on such occasions as he had been late home from a hunting expedition, having wandered too far from his father's hearth. Such had been a boyish hunger of no great consequence. Now he was truly hungry, ravenously so, his frame, big for a lad of his age, demanding nourishment. He was thirsty too and he stood, stepping over the hound that was his only companion in the small tent to which he had been taken the night before under orders not to leave it. The great dog stirred, lifted its head and growled at William and the halter tugged at his neck, secured as it was to the single tent-post. He could quite easily have untied it, but he recognised his plight. If he had done so, the hound would arouse those responsible for his confinement. Instead, he did as Brother Nicholas instructed him to do, whether in trouble or not. He knelt and prayed.

That is how the King's men found him when they came for him. The sight of the boy on his knees, his hands palm-to-palm, the hangman's halter already about his neck, touched some of them with pity. He was nothing but a child. Nevertheless, they led him before Stephen like a dog on a leash. As for William, he heard Angharad's words in his ears and bore himself as well as he could.

The King sat, as before, in the outer part of his tent, some of his nobles gathered about him. Excepting Stephen who wore a circlet of gold, all were bare-headed and all wore mail, coloured surtouts and heavy studded belts from which their scabbarded swords hung. Some leaned on the blades and all were arrayed for war. A handful of squires were in quiet attendance, holding helms and mailed gauntlets. Kneeling at the King's feet was Nicholas de Sarum, his dark woollen habit mud-spattered, his hood pulled back on his shoulders, but his head downcast.

A strange, hollow feeling seemed to open up in William's belly and his legs felt suddenly unable to bear his weight. Instinctively he drew in a great breath while his thoughts tumbled about inside his head and Angharad's voice abjured him to hold up. He had been told, clearly enough, that he might die that morning, but until this moment the reality of death had seemed far-off, inconceivable to a boy of his tender age. During his hour of prayer he had prayed for deliverance, for forgiveness and to be able to return home to Hamstead Marshal and the embraces of Angharad, but not from deliverance from death. Never before in his short life had he been visited by this visceral upheaval, this inner turbulence and the threatened failure of his limbs to bear him. He thought for a moment that he might be sick, but he swallowed hard and stared at the King.

Now the deep breathing and the quickening of his heart steadied him and witnesses afterwards remarked that he had seemed to hold himself like a man as he came to a halt before the King. There was a moment of silence during which no-one moved, then Stephen spoke.

'I asked the priest who calls himself Nicholas de Sarum to hold his tongue until you could hear what your father has to say regarding the surrender of this place.' Stephen jerked his head to indicate the rebel structure that defied his command to surrender.

William looked from the King to Nicholas and back again but said not a word. His fear seemed to have receded and he sensed somehow that the King would not kill him even though many of his nobles might. Intuitively he felt a powerful urge to cling to Stephen and held his gaze on him. The King, meanwhile, regarded the kneeling priest. 'Well?' he demanded.

Nicholas looked up, then down again. Then he turned his head to look at William, bewildered at the boy's composure, before swiftly lowering his eyes and staring again at the churned grass at the mailed feet of the King.

'Speak, priest, or by Heaven your own head will pay for your disrespect!'

'My Lord, I…' Nicholas hesitated then, suddenly emboldened, raised his eyes to the expectant King's. 'My Lord King, my Master, William the Marshal, replies to Your Highness with these words…'

'Go on, priest! Go on, for the love of God!'

'That he has both the hammer and the anvil to forge another son and that Newbury is not for the giving up!'

Although Nicholas de Sarum had uttered the sentence at the run, the second clause was lost in the rumble of horror that greeted the first. The King's eyes narrowed and he lowered his voice. 'He would sacrifice his son to hold this work of timber that I shall shatter before the sennight is out? Is that what you have returned to tell me, O Nicholas of Sarum?' The King's tone was sarcastic.

'That is what my Lord charged me with, Your Highness, and upon my honour.'

'Better he had laid the matter upon your soul,' Stephen muttered, before raising his hand for silence and staring at the young prisoner. 'Take him back to his tent,' the King ordered and as William was led out, he heard the King address Nicholas de Sarum. 'Get you back to your Master at once. Tell him I shall take him at his word and deal with his son accordingly. Now get out!'

As a weary, anxious and humiliated Nicholas mounted up and tugged his horse's head round to the west he noticed the arrival of siege-engines. He turned his head to seek out the little boy that he was abandoning to the vengeance of his master's enemy. Nicholas knew well that, until recently John the Marshal had stood high in Stephen's favour, that he had been a close counsellor of the King, had often been the sole witness to Stephen's signature and a boon companion of his table. It was not difficult to perceive how the King would take revenge upon him for his treacherous desertion to the Empress Mathilda's cause; what to the exhausted Nicholas was inexplicable was how the Marshal could so casually abandon his son. Was his own life's work to be given-over so easily?

There was now no sign of the boy, only the movement of the heavy tent-flap as the King and his nobles withdrew within. Nicholas shuddered and crossed himself, kicking his mount forward. And then, as he cleared the King's army's lines and dug his heels into his horse's flanks, he remembered the mark on the boy's shoulder.

*

46

William stood before the King who had with him only two knights, his cup-bearer and his hounds. The lad looked from one face to another, then at the churned grass that was covered with the remains of flowers strewn in respect to the King's high dignity. He sensed the gravity of the occasion though not its possible outcome. Death does not haunt boys as it does older men; besides, William rather liked Stephen who seemed a kinder man than his own father. William could not imagine him ordering so callous a killing. He, William, was not a chicken to be strangled for the pot, or a rat to be executed as vermin. Only the evening before the two of them had played 'knights,' a game of chance using crudely fashioned straw horsemen, each of which represented a mounted knight. They 'fought' a tourney on the throw of two die and Stephen had let William win. He could still see the extemporised horsemen, thrown to one side of the large tent, both on their sides, defeated. He noticed that the King's now lay on top of his own, identifiable by the strips of red cloth tied about them. The King coughed, interrupting William's distraction. He looked at the King and then down at his own feet.

'Your father defies me, Will. Dost think that an honourable thing to do when but a few short years ago he would have been here, at my right hand?' Stephen gestured to William de Ypres, who stood in the appointed place of honour and, at the King's gesture, drew himself up to his full height. His steel mail rustled with the movement.

'What say you, Will? Eh?' the King prompted.

William did not know what to say, though clearly something was expected of him. He felt nothing towards his father, though he could see the treachery well enough. His sparring in the tilt-yard had taught him that one stuck to one's fighting friends.

'I come to do my father's bidding, Sire. He bad me do him knight's service.'

'Hmmph,' the King responded. He had heard the phrase trotted out before and eased himself into a seat, dismissing his attendant nobles. Calling for wine he beckoned the boy towards him and placed a hand upon the lad's shoulder.

'Will, your father has abandoned you; given you up to my mercy. He has, believe it or not, given me his permission to have you killed rather than surrender this castle about which we now lie in some force. The place *will* fall to us. There is no doubt of that, so your little life is of so small a consequence. Do you see that?'

William nodded and lifted his face towards the King. 'Would you have me killed, Sire? If so may I request it is done by a sword. I have no liking for the noose that you put about my neck. I do knight's service and ask to die like a knight.'

Stephen's look of astonishment suddenly turned to one of pure delight and he burst out laughing. Stephen was neither a harsh nor a politic man; his vacillating character saw to that, and whilst the prosecution of the siege of Newbury bore witness to his swift resolution, he was equally capable of running out of energy, of abandoning a thing before it was seen through. Perhaps John the Marshal gambled upon this, perhaps Stephen himself thought the execution of a traitor's son a mean and unkingly act, but it was this aspect of his character, charmed by William's childish simplicity, that removed the threat of death from the boy's head. Such an act of clemency would do him no good.

But Stephen was no fool; he would try one last time to compel the garrison of Newbury to capitulate by using William as a pawn. He called out for attendants and when the tent seemed full of them said, simultaneously ruffling William's hair, 'put the boy in a mangonel and run it up towards the bailey wall. We will summons

48

them once more and if that avails us nothing, then prepare for an assault.'

William would better remember the sequel than any other feature of his time as the King's prisoner. Against the later memories of the cruelty, the burnings and the sackings that followed the final taking of Newbury, a back-drop of smoke, fire and the sight of the dead, the sharp exposure to which he was now subject stuck – as it was bound to in a boy's mind – as the epitome of his being held hostage.

He was led outside and along the line of tents, past the camp-fires of the King's army where men, going about their various tasks, stopped to stare at him. Everyone knew who and what he was and he stirred in them differing emotions. Some felt cold fury at the stupidity of his father whose callous attitude compelled them to risk their lives in an assault; others felt for their own sons, far away.

Eventually William and his escort reached the parked siege-engines, brought-up to force the wooden ramparts of Newbury. Men in leather jerkins were busy about them, preparing them for action, men from Normandy by their accents. Having arrived in a transportable state, the Norman artillerists had assembled the windlasses and were even then fitting the ropes that transmitted their power. A knight whose name William did not know called out and they stopped their labours to see what was a-foot. The knight indicated a large catapult. The mangonel appeared to be ready for action and, following a rapid succession of orders, men assembled from their work in sufficient numbers to roll it forward over the grass slope.

'Remark it, lad,' one of the men-at-arms guarding him said.

'What is it? William asked.

'An engine which, when we have thrown you over the wall, we shall fill with stones, or burning fire and so bring down yonder castle.'

William looked up at the man. 'Throw me over? What return me to my own kind?'

'You think they will catch you?' the man laughed. 'Happen they will riddle you with arrows whilst you are still in mid-air for fear of any contagion you might bring into their fastness.' He ended with a chuckle, and shoved William forward. The mangonel was clearly in place and ready, as those superfluous to the next task returned to their work, or moved to bring other strange siege-engines up to play upon the castle, leaving a handful to strain at the windlass bars and draw down the great ash arm, at the extremity of which was fitted a stout basket.

Even as William was led forward the defenders of the castle loosed a flurry of arrows. Having watched until the catapult's location was certain, the garrison now belatedly sought to discommode their enemy. On either side of the mangonel other siege-engines were deployed, three were springalds, ballistas capable of firing heavy bolts charged with fire into the wooden ramparts. William also caught a glimpse of a huge catapult which, he would learn, they called a trebuchet.

William was aware that the low grumble of a congregation of many men now increased to roars as one side shouted insults at the other. The desultory siege was, with the arrival of the engines, now taking a more serious turn. An arrow struck the heavy timber gantry of the mangonel that loomed before him, glanced aside it hit the ground some three or four feet away from him. Another followed. Then he was at the side of the great engine, behind the rough protection of a wicker-work shield. The catapult seemed huge, swarming with men in steel helmets and leather hauberks; men with hard faces and harder hands who first lifted William then passed him on so that, in a seeming trice and with little dignity, he found himself thrown into the basket. He would always recall the bounce of the wicker-and-leather contraption which, at the end of the throwing arm, was half-cocked. Winding the arm down fully would have concealed the King's intention from the men whose dark silhouettes against the grey sky, topped the rude wooden palisade of the castle.

'Stand-up, boy!' a voice shouted, and William rose shakily to his feet, his hands gripping the rough rim of the basket, his brown hair lifting in the wind. Somewhere below him a trumpeter blew a parley and the half-hearted volleys of arrows ceased. The besieged were clearly not anxious to expend their limited stock too precipitately, saving the greater part of them for the assault that would follow the bombardment. William took his eyes from the castle as it stood against the sky, his attention diverted to the advance of a horseman who rode forward, half way between the King's lines, marked by their sharpened calthrops, and the bottom of the tall palisade. All along the lines silence had fallen and men ceased their labours and stood, watching.

'By order of my Lord the King, you are commanded to capitulate! Throw open your gates within the next hour and my Lord will grant thee honour and compassion, notwithstanding the defiance you have maintained this last sennight against the King's power! Fail to obey the King's command and an attack will commence which can only have one outcome: death and dishonour! And to seal my Lord the King's intention you shall first have the son of thy traitorous master thrown at you! On his innocent head fall all the consequences of thy wanton rebellion and the treasonable disloyalty of you all, men of John the Marshal!'

The final phrases of this lengthy oration were issued in tones of powerful contempt. The strange silence seemed to William to grow in intensity, the only sound that of the wind and the beating of his heart, for he was now conscious of the grave peril in which he stood and his breast was torn by conflicting emotions. The comforting presence of King Stephen was no longer with him. He looked about but could see no sign of the King, his friend. For the first time he felt his isolation keenly. He did not want to fly through the air and be dashed to the ground like an unwanted kitten hurled to death from the tower of Hamstead Marshal. But neither did he want his father's men to give-in, to dishonour the Marshal's name, though he could not divine why his father had thrown up his connection with King Stephen for so fickle an undertaking as espousing the cause of the Empress Mathilda. William had grown to like the King, the first man of rank to show him any kindness beyond mere duty. Why, the King had smiled when William beat him at the game of 'knights,' and told him that, if he lived, he might himself one day be a great soldier.

'But only of you live, Will, and live long enough,' the King had concluded quietly, his face twisted into a wry smile the meaning of which the boy could not interpret beyond the obvious necessity of survival. That he had discerned some other vague meaning that lay beyond his powers of comprehension marked the boy's natural intelligence. But now it looked as though his life-span was to be circumscribed precipitately; he felt a strong urge to cry out; but who to? His father had abandoned him; his mother made no secret of her dislike for her son, while Angharad...

The thought of Angharad stiffened him as it had before. He must bear himself well. Perhaps that was what his foul-featured father had meant when he demanded knight's service. But it was Angharad who came to his rescue now. 'You have a destiny, Will,' she had said to him once in her low Welsh voice. 'I 'ave see it, boy, so whatever your circumstances, take courage. You were not marked by the devil, but by grace, Will, whatever the priests say. Hold fast to that, Will, hold fast to that...' He had only half understood her. He had no knowledge of his mark, never having seen it. His mother's mirrors were forbidden him and locked away. All he knew of it was a faint wrinkling of his skin when he put his left hand over his right shoulder and touched the naevus with his extended finger-tips. Now he gripped the sides of the basket more firmly with those same fingers, and drew the air into his lungs as he had been taught before striking his first blows in the tilt-yard. And then the answer came from the wooden ramparts of Newbury castle.

There had been some movement of the dark heads; they appeared to give way to one who was slightly elevated, as though standing upon a box, or log. All along the King's lines, silence reigned as they awaited the response.

'Throw the boy hence and we shall catch him! He is our own!' William recognised the voice of his father's steward, Geoffrey FitzJohn, and his heart leapt with hope. Could they possibly catch him? Suppose he fell short? Or sailed above them? There was no word about surrender, just that defiant challenge. Suddenly, as a murmur rose from the King's ranks, the basket shuddered. William was aware that the catapult arm was dropping lower as the men on the windlass turned the barrel and the twisted ropes drew the basket lower and lower. He lost his footing under the vibration and sat on his buttocks with a heavy thump. The basket continued to descend and suddenly he was level with men's heads; they stared at him, their faces blank, indifferent now.

In the distance William heard a command and the murmuring fell away, then a barked order. For a dreadful second, he thought he was about to be launched into the future where he would learn what it felt like to be a bird before being dashed to pieces – or caught by some miraculous intervention of God, or Geoffrey FitzJohn. Did not such things occur in the Bible? Had not the walls of Jericho…

The mangonel shuddered and instead of the release of tension flinging William high into the air, a dark cloud lifted off the ground, arched upwards against the sky with a soughing like a gust of wind. For a distracted instant William though himself already dead, dead of shock and elevated, half-way to heaven as he watched his poor abandoned body flung towards his father's men. But there followed a rattling as some arrows struck the palisade, a few hit home, and men cried out as others sailed over the top.

Then things happened very quickly. William recalled seeing the other siege-engines being loaded, four or five of them. From somewhere men were running up with large, heavy stones and filling the baskets. First to be fired were the springalds, their bolts bearing smoky, burning pitch; then a helmed figure wearing a red, gold-emblazoned surtout rode up, behind him another knight bore a standard of like colours. The first man reached a mailed hand into the basket.

'Give me your hand Will, quickly now…' In a trice the boy was over the rim of the basket and settled upon the saddle bow of the King himself. As Stephen jerked the head of his destrier round he bellowed, 'Fill it with fire and stones! Newbury will be mine ere nighfall!'

An instant later William found himself standing somewhat shakily next to the knight who had led him forth, what seemed like a lifetime ago.

'See the boy is safe, Hubert, or answer for it to me.'

'Aye, my Lord King.' William felt a mailed fist on his shoulder. He was bodily turned to stare at the catapult from which he had just escaped. 'See, lad, what thou hast just escaped...'

The artillerists had already filled the basket with stones and a flaming ball of pitch. Almost as he blinked, William saw the pawl knocked out and the catapult arm released from its confinement. The arm flew up and over in an arc of such speed that it seemed marvellous, ejecting the stones and the smoking and flaring ball of pitch on a trajectory aimed to pass over the rampart. He saw, quite clearly, the group of rocks, black against the sky, diverge in their flight, spreading, some to strike the rampart, some to skim its top, or to pass over it to drop into the enceinte below. The fire-ball flew higher, dropping out of sight.

In the hours that followed, until nightfall, Newbury castle was subjected to an assailing of stones, rocks and combustibles. It was noticeable that the flights of arrows, so vigorously fired by FitzJohn's men that morning, had by the evening, fallen away to nothing.

*

'Well?' John the Marshal looked up from the small table at which he sat in the small chamber out of which rose the ladder to his wife's chamber above. It was his private quarters where he slept when not sharing the Lady Sybil's bed and where he conducted his private business.

'The boy is well, my Lord. The King keeps him close, but will not harm him,' reassured Angharad ap Gwyn.

'So you told me before, but I am not fool enough to see that a shadow lies upon your divinations. I do not recollect it there before...'

'I...' began Angharad, faltering before gathering her thoughts. She was about to speak when John the Marshal asked:

'Tell me, to assuage my own curiosity, from where do you conjure your divinations? I see no device, no mirror or silver surface, no smoke, nor any ash twig…'

Angharad looked at the mask of the Marshal's face and felt that sharp twinge of revulsion and fascination. It was easy to conceive him an agent of Satan, as some said he was, recalling the rumour that he had sired his second son for the Devil's service and threw him up to King Stephen's mercy in firm conviction that Satan tended his own. But Angharad was a woman and not immune to the other qualities of her Master whose physique would turn any woman's head; moreover, she was flattered to be his confidante.

'In the silence, my Lord, when we have it here, such as at this late hour.'

'Whence cometh what you listen for?'

Angharad smiled, pointing downwards at the ground. 'You built upon sacred ground, my Lord. The spirits lurk beneath your wooden dungeon and sometimes they vouchsafe what they would have their servants know'.

John the Marshal nodded. 'And they do not resent the presence of priests or Christian men and women?'

'They know they will have their hour; besides the absence of Nicholas de Sarum seems to have eased their torment.'

The Marshal chuckled. 'Well, so what of the shadow?'

'When first you asked me what would be your son's fate if you sent him hostage to King Stephen I could divine no more than that his life would not be forfeit for your…' she faltered again, not wishing to use the word and provoke her Master to rage.

The Marshal smiled. 'My *treachery*? Is that what you mean?'

'By what His Grace will see as treachery, my Lord.'

'God's bones, woman, thou shouldest be a man and a finagling priest for you would work wonders betwixt Courts in opposition!' John the Marshal's hideous face was split by a wide smile.

'My Lord...' Angharad responded noncommittally.

'Go, get some rest. Her Ladyship will want you soon enough.'

Angharad paused at the door into the hall and turned to address the Marshal. 'My Lord, the shadow comes from the silence. Your son is safe but he will not return home to your hearth for many months...perhaps years.'

The Marshal nodded. ' 'Twill be as God wills it, but I thank you.'

Two days later Geoffrey FitzJohn was led into Hamstead Marshal on an ass, a halter about his neck, his hands tied behind his back, his ankles fastened beneath the animal's belly. He was sat facing the beast's tail. It was clear to all who saw the pitiful sight that Newbury had fallen and most assumed – at that moment – that the Marshal's second son had gone the way of all flesh.

*

'During my sojourn as a prisoner of the Empress I was fettered,' King Stephen remarked conversationally, sipping from his goblet before he moved the straw figure representing himself on the imaginary field of battle. 'Now, Will, how shall though answer that, eh?'

Almost before the splayed 'legs' of the straw dolly had been settled on the crude chequerboard the boy had leapt to his feet to move his own figure. Stephen smote his thigh in mock exasperation. 'By the Blood of Christ, Will, I know not how you do it but your winning streak, or your devilish cunning persuades me that I should not indulge you in such games, but fetter you, if only to teach you the proper manners towards your King.

William looked up smartly, his features apprehensive. 'Sire, I...I only thought this a game...'

Stephen rubbed his chin, his hand rasping on his beard his face feigning a frown. 'True in part, but it is a military game, is it not? Eh?'

'Aye,' responded the boy puzzled.

'And you repeatedly beat your King. It would seem that all the terrors I have inflicted upon you have not cured you of your father's conceit to defy me. What say you to that?'

It was the boy's turn to frown and it was unfeigned, for the King presented him with a puzzle with which he felt he had been living for weeks now.

'Well?' the King persisted.

'How can my losing to you, Sire, change my father's mind?'

'Would you do it, if you thought it might?'

William considered the proposition for a moment, then asked. 'Would it end the enmity between my father and my Lord King?'

Stephen smiled. 'Then there is no doubt in your mind who is your King?'

William sensed he had been led into a trap and bit his lip, torn between his filial duty to his father and his liking for the man who indulged him in games of 'knights' and whose wine goblet he kept topped-up most evenings on campaign. 'You have been kind to me, Sire. I know no other King.'

'Think you your father might be mistaken in his allegiance?'

'Who am I to think for my father, Sire? In truth, I cannot tell…'

Stephen looked at the boy, again passing his fist across his lower face to conceal his smile. He had a nimble mind, to be sure. 'Come let us play another game before you sleep…'

When it was over and William's last straw horseman lay on its side he looked squarely at the King. 'You beat me, Sire,' he said.

'Yes, Will, I beat you.' The King paused, tossed off the contents of his goblet and let out a long sigh. 'Now, to bed lad. Send in my man.' Turning away the retreating boy heard him say, half to himself, 'tomorrow or the next day Wallingford will fall to my arms too and then perhaps I can get some rest...'

After the fall and razing of Newbury and the despatch of Geoffrey FitzJohn on the back of an ass, King Stephen had moved his forces off to besiege the more substantial castle at Wallingford on the Thames. William had found himself in a curious position, both page and prisoner, a mock-squire who trailed aimlessly about the camp for the most part ignored, *in* the King's army, yet not *of* it. He was treated kindly enough, but any attempt to wander off, even if as innocently intended as he might have done at Hamstead Marshal, was met with arrest, rebuke and chastisement, so that he soon learnt from his sore arse that nothing was expected of him so much that he must keep close to the camp of the King.

Indeed, he was not unwelcome in the squires' tents. Outside them he found ready employment polishing harness and belts, sanding and sharpening swords, axes and war-hammers, and buffing their chasings and bright-work. Occasionally they would use him for exercise and by this means he grew in toughness and physique, acquiring considerable skill with sword and buckler. In this he earned a measure of respect and there were those that said if he lived he might win some renown for his prowess. '*If...*' they emphasised, retiring laughing and casting nary a look over their shoulder as the lad gathered-up their cast down weapons, the blunt swords and wooden shields they used in their martial exercises.

Being intelligent he quickly came to understand that by remaining obedient, no-one would maltreat him, for all knew he was the King's toy, an amusement for their Royal master's private moments. There were those who said more, but no-one ever found a shred of evidence for it and William never made any complaint, nor suggested otherwise. He had just become another camp-follower during weary months of campaigning and, even when the King's army went into winter-quarters, William still found himself mostly ignored, like an old hound, fed and indulged by an occasional game of 'knights,' sleeping somewhere in whatever castle the King had chosen to lodge. Here he was subject to Stephen's occasional half soliloquies.

'You are my sounding-board,' Stephen once remarked. 'Like the body of a lute,' he explained, seeing the boy's stare. William began to perceive something enlightening in all of this, but of what, he was not yet at all certain.

*

The time that William spent in the train of King Stephen's army turned into months and while the physical exercises and attending the squires tired his body, even in winter quarters, his mind had other occupations. As the former grew beyond its years in strength and stature, so his mind expanded with a stranger education than that inculcated by Nicholas de Sarum; he became a great observer and a quiet listener, so much an accepted part of Stephen's retinue that few thought to curb their words in his hearing.

Stephen's half-drunk ramblings lifted a curtain on the King's thinking from which, entirely without knowing it, the respectful and attentive William drew lessons in political thought and strategic logic. He was often tolerated in council meetings, a cupbearer to the King upon whose discretion, being a half-prisoner, could be better relied upon than one of the sons of Stephen's fickle nobles. By this proximity to Stephen, William acquired a knowledge both of the geography of southern England and of the means by which it should be seized and governed.

Only once was this almost idyllic apprenticeship disturbed and this occurred in the opening of the final campaign that ended 'the Anarchy,' in the late summer of 1153. Stephen's retinue rode through an anonymous and burning village beside the upper reaches of the River of Thames not far from Wallingford. Bored with the slow business of besieging, short of provisions and troubled by rumours of a relieving force approaching the staunch Angevin stronghold, the King had been engaged in a sweep through the countryside to forage what he could and deter the approach of any of the Mathilda's forces. They found little of the former and nothing of the latter and, frustrated, the order had been given to burn the next village to persuade the peasants to yield up their hidden stores of grain. While this act of uncalled for brutality was in train, Stephen ordered a halt so that his horses and those who rode with him might drink from the village well.

Turning to William on his pony he said, 'go with the men, lad. Root around and see what you can find that might be of use. Try first the priest's house.'

William did as he was bid, taking himself off, his dagger loosened in its sheath for fear of ambush by the angered peasants. As he approached the priest's house beside the low church he wandered into a cottage. The crude door had been torn from its willow hinges, the thatched roof had been burnt, what remained of the blackened rafters had collapsed and the cob-walls were blackened by the ferocity of the fire. He had no idea what had drawn him first into the cottage rather than progressing directly to the priest's dwelling, other than the cottage seemed to offer him a short-cut, but once inside he heard the mewing of kittens and found a litter of them in the meagre fire-place. Five were already dead, but two remained, staring about them with sightless eyes. William bent towards them and put out his hand. The first he picked up, dark and ill-marked, with a pallid flash of white across its nose, was so thin that he was astonished it still lived. The other seemed more robust, struggling up onto uncertain legs, a tiny wobbling and

61

mewling body of orange-tawny fur that screamed at him, demanding that he succour it in its extremity.

Something about its aggressiveness startled William and he did not touch it but rose from his feet and hurried out of the cottage, leaving it crying indignantly after him as if aware that the passing boy was its last chance of life, its mother having abandoned her litter, disturbed by the horrors of military rapine. Ignoring the pleading screeches, William half-ran across the small plot of kitchen garden to the priest's house. He was already too late; the men-at-arms who rode in the King's escort had beaten him to it and the place was turned upside-down with that speed and efficiency than only troops could achieve when on the march. He was about to return to the King's side when he bethought himself of the ginger tom-kitten. It was almost, he recalled afterwards, as though the little beast had called him back; certainly he was drawn to return exactly the way he had come, through the soot-stained cottage.

The kitten stood where he had left it, mewling furiously, standing upon its wobbling legs, its small orange tail upright as a lance. Though still blind, it sensed William's presence, even his height and appeared to glare up at him. He stared down at the dead litter and noticed that the dark kitten with the white slash had joined its siblings, the trauma of being handled having been too much for it. The small ginger tom was, like William, alone in the world.

On an impulse he stooped, picked it up and tucked it inside his gambeson. He felt it wriggle and grow still, as though it too had given up the ghost until, a moment later, he felt the prickle of tiny claws and heard the contented thrum of a purr. He had no idea how he might feed the little animal but returned to his place in the King's train.

Stephen saw, but took no notice of the lad's return. It was entirely characteristic of him to initiate something and then abandon it to others and William felt no need to report his failure to find anything of worth in the priest's house. If the King wished to know he would ask, but in his own good time. Besides, it was obvious the boy had brought nothing back with him and the little cavalcade soon moved off, back towards the siege-lines of Wallingford.

In fact William found a ready supply of milk from the King's kitchen, feeding it to the animal dripping it from a straw into the hungry little maw. At first he did this secretly, but after a few days it became known that he was harbouring the kitten and there were those among the younger squires who came and briefly stroked the tiny mite, and those that smiled indulgently before throwing down a sword and demanding that he spent his time on a better occupation in sharpening their weapons.

As the kitten grew, William fed it scraps and, once it could see, it rapidly learned how to catch mice and roved further than William's bed-place. Even the King got to hear of it and it accompanied William to the King's tent for games of 'knights,' drinking from a bowl the king himself placed upon the ground for it.

But one evening a knight William knew only as Godfrey FitzHugh, a man supposedly known for his devotional character, came deliberately to the boy and demanded to see the animal. William innocently held the tom-kitten out to him and he took it, holding it as though in distaste, causing William a sudden pang of alarm.

'You are marked, are you not?' Godfrey FitzHugh asked, adding without awaiting a reply, 'disrobe and show me!'

The peremptory tone had William stripping off before he realised he was doing as he was commanded. He had no consciousness of the birth-mark other than that his fellows had remarked upon it from time-to-time. As he had grown he had revealed it less often, but it had never troubled him as it did now as FitzHugh moved behind him to inspect the naevus. William felt himself suddenly spun round by the shoulder, almost losing his balance.

'That is the mark of Satan,' hissed FitzHugh with awful vehemence, bending to the boy's face. 'And *this*,' he added, thrusting the ginger tom into William's face so that he could feel its breath and sense its terror as it struggled and mewed in FitzHugh's grip, 'is witch-craft. It is how you have beguiled the King and damned his cause you cursed imp…'

And with a flick of his other hand, he twisted the little mammal's neck so that William heard the snick of the snapping spine. FitzHugh flung the lifeless body at William's feet. At that moment William recovered himself. Although tears welled into his eyes, his sudden emotion turned into a cold fury. In an instant that surprised FitzHugh the lad's dagger was in his right hand and he lunged at the knight. FitzHugh dodged backwards, feeling a sharp prick on his exposed arm.

'Get ye gone from here this instant!' William said with a voice of such imperiousness that it astonished FitzHugh.

'Why you damned little…'

But he never finished his sentence for, in attempting both to avoid William's dagger and lug out his own, his heel caught and he fell backwards.

'Guard!' bawled William while FitzHugh lay a-sprawling. Even before the discomfited knight had struggled to his feet Stephen himself came into the hut where William was quartered.

'What the devil?' the King roared, seeing the armed boy standing over the embarrassed knight.

'Aye, Sire, 'tis devil's work, the boy is bewitched,' cried FitzHugh, regaining his feet. 'See, he attacks me...'

'Only after you killed my tom-cat,' retorted William unabashed in the King's presence, and indignant with fury.

'And why would you do that, FitzHugh?' Stephen asked.

'And you believe the boy, Sire? He was casting a spell over you, having killed the familiar for the purpose. See, see the mark of Satan on his shoulder...'

'That is a lie, Sire!' William cried, but Stephen ignored his outrage, continuing to confront FitzHugh.

'I have never had cause to doubt the boy told the truth at any moment of our acquaintance,' the King said quietly, stepping forward, his gloved forefinger turning William so that he might examine the boy's birth-mark. He made a scoffing sound and ruffled William's hair. 'If that is the Devil's work, FitzHugh, I am no judge of anything. It has more the appearance of a noble lion rampant. I am inclined to think it a mark of God's favour and I bid you ask the boy's pardon and admit to a mistake arising from your...' the King paused, as if unwilling to give FitzHugh credit for such a thing, but concluded his sentence: 'religious fervour.'

'Sire, I...'

'It is a simple command, FitzHugh, though I do not press it. You may leave my service on the morrow, or still the boy's fear, for while you have an animus against him, you also have it against me.'

The King, who had been passing the hut when he heard sounds of commotion, had been followed into it by others, many of whom were suppressing laughter. FitzHugh, it seemed, was not popular and was now humiliated by his peers in the King's retinue. For a moment William felt almost sorry for him as he looked first at the King and then his barons. He could not find it in himself to apologise to a mere boy and, in a flourish of wounded pride, drew himself up, bowed to the King and left, pushing through the nobles clustered in the door. Here he turned.

'God save you, Sire, for you will see soon enough that I have failed to do so.'

There was a silence after he had gone. William looked down at the dead kitten and bent to retrieve it. As he stood, holding the still warm body he felt the King's hand again upon his shoulder, and the King felt the deep sobs wracking the boy's body. They came without tears, but it was plain the lad was fond of the dead kitten. And why should he not be? Besides himself, the creature had been his only friend.

'Go bury it, Will, then come to my tent and play of knights. Thou hast made an enemy of FitzHugh, alas.'

'Sire,' William mumbled and Stephen saw that he remained dry-eyed, finding pleasure in the sight. There was steel in the lad, as well as feeling. Had God willed it, he would have wished for a son of such mettle.

'Come my lords,' he said, and swept from the hut, leaving William to his sad task.

By the following morning Godfrey FitzHugh had ridden out of the King's camp; though none knew whither he had gone, most supposed it was to join the Angevins.

*

The King did not refer to the incident when they played 'knights' that evening but he did some months later as the year rolled on. The marching and counter-marching had come to an end and there had of late been comings and goings of a different nature, strange noblemen under escort riding in and out of the King's quarters so that the army was full of rumours. Although nothing had been said, the wild speculation was that peace was at hand, that that very day the King had reached an accommodation with his enemies and there was upon the faces of his counsellors something that suggested all now awaited an outcome from elsewhere. That evening Stephen, who seemed suddenly old, was more than usually ruminative and more than usually drunk, letting William win two games of 'knights' and conceding victory of the second with a weary resignation.

'You have beaten me again, Will,' he said, his speech slurred, reseating himself beside his goblet.

'No, Sire, you let me win,' William responded simply.

Stephen leaned on his elbows and rubbed his beard as William made to stow away the now battered straw figures.

'Leave them, lad. Come, sit beside me.' William sat, cross-legged at the King's feet and looked up at Stephen. 'D'you recall the day I sent FitzHugh from the camp for killing your kitten?'

'Aye, Sire, I do.'

'And I said you will have made an enemy of him?'

'That too.'

'You must walk carefully in the world, Will. Your father, a brave and bold man did not. He betrayed me and I might have had you killed in vengeance.'

'But you did not, Sire.'

'No.' Stephen paused. 'Do you know why not?'

William shrugged. 'I hoped that it was because you took a liking to me,' he said candidly, 'and that you might let me render you the knight's service my father sent me to undertake?'

But the King's inebriated brain was running on its own track. 'Do you know why your father deserted me, Will?'

'No, Sire, but from what I have learned since I suppose that he considered you had broken your oath to serve the Empress Mathilda, if, indeed, you ever swore such an oath.'

Stephen stirred at the effrontery and then recognised the diplomatic tag at its end. He knew it was what his enemies and some of his friends said about him. 'I had hoped to bring England peace. England cannot be ruled by a woman, least of all by a woman of Mathilda's disobliging stamp. But I brought only ruin and this,' he paused and William recognised the symptoms of wine-bibbed regret, 'this anarchy…'

'Is it not to end, Sire?' William asked, 'for that is what all the men are talking about.'

Stephen nodded. 'Aye, so it would seem, and you shall be returned to your father as soon as matters are concluded to our satisfaction.'

'Then you will have brought peace, Sire,' William said simply, lightening the King's mood.

'Think you so, Will?' he asked cynically with a smile.

'Aye, Sire.'

Stephen reached out a hand and ruffled the boy's hair. 'When you are fully grown to manhood, Will, I would have you remember to treat such barons as Godfrey FitzHugh with some circumspection. It is they who cause anarchy by their self-interested schismatics. Cleave to the crown to avoid the troubles that have overtaken our Kingdom in these late years.'

William frowned. The king's logic seemed bibulous. Had not his father clung to the crown which he thought lay upon the rightful head of Mathilda? Or was he a schismatic? Then another thought supervened.

'Sire, I am only a second son. Wherein lies the opportunity for me to disdain men like FitzHugh?

Stephen seemed to pull himself together, stirring upon his seat and shoving his goblet from him. 'You are marked by more than some accident. FitzHugh sensed it, but wrongly interpreted it. It is in my mind that you may not always be the second son. Now,' Stephen straightened himself, 'the hour is late and much hangs upon the morrow. Do you bring me that sword and belt that lie upon my chest.'

William did as he was bid. The weapon, lying in its scabbard and wound about by a studded belt, lay upon one of the several chests in the King's quarters. It was not the King's, for it was short, fitter more for a lad. Handing it to the King he was bidden to stand still while Stephen girded him with the belt, scabbard and sword, the weight of which William felt suddenly like a burden of responsibility. Then Stephen clenched his right fist and gave him a gentle blow on each shoulder, thereby dubbing him.

'The sword is steely and sharp and made for you. You have done me knight's service, Will, and in your father's name. You will be with him in a sennight. Now rise, help me disrobe and then get you to your bed.'

It was in fact ten not seven days later that William rode out of the King's camp and turned his horse's head towards Hamstead Marshal. The gelding was a second present from the King, a handsome bay palfrey that marked Stephen's favour and an implied pardon to John the Marshal. With an escort of two mounted men-at-arms from the King's body-guard, William rode through the frost-hardened and bare November countryside, Stephen's gifted sword at his hip. He had no sensation of going home, for he had been away too long, cast off by both his parents and this sense increased with every mile he rode.

CHAPTER THREE: M'SIEUR GASTE-VIANDE 1154 - 1160

The King Stephen who had sent him back to Hamstead Marshal was a shadow of the vigorous man who had ordered a noose about his neck upon their first acquaintance. It was widely rumoured that a fatal sickness lay upon him, compelling him to acquiesce to the demands of the noble barons on both sides who in their own interests sought an accommodation between the two contending parties. Even the ecclesiastical rivals, Archbishop Theobald and Henry, Bishop of Winchester, had for some time been preaching peace. Having secured the estates of his second son, Earl William, Stephen had ended 'the Anarchy' by conceding to the combined wishes of most. The Treaty of Wallingford afterwards ratified at Westminster in the Abbey-church of Edward the Confessor, Stephen acknowledged as his hereditary heir the Angevin Duke Henry of Normandy, son of Mathilda and Geoffrey of Anjou. The matter of the succession being thus settled, all lands were returned to their seigneurs, all grudges were supposedly buried, and all was restored to its pre-war state. The 'adulterine,' or counter-castles, erected without regal authority were to be dismantled and, in due course, all signs of John the Marshal's wooden fortification at Newbury where young William had discovered his father's perfidy, were removed from the face of the earth.

Something of the oddness of William's period as a hostage bore down upon the boy, for he looked much older than his six or seven summers – he was not sure. On his departure from Stephen he had sat upon the palfrey upright, the sword at his hip and a cloak about him over a hauberk of light mail. One of the mounted men-at-arms bore a small portmanteau of his personal effects, which were meagre enough, but contained, coiled-up, the noose that had for many weeks been about his neck.

Neither of his parents was at Hamstead Marshal when he arrived and at first no-one recognised him, refusing him entry. Eventually Nicholas de Sarum was summoned and, throwing up his hands in wonder and delight, fell upon his knees to praise God for the deliverance for which he had daily prayed, he assured William. The Lady Sybil, he explained, had gone to Marlborough, his father was in the Angevin camp, attending the young Duke Henry.

'You must go to Marlborough Castle at once,' said Nicholas, rising to his feet.

'No,' said William sharply, taking the priest by surprise. 'We must see these men are fed and lodged for the night,' he commanded, indicating his escort who nodded their acknowledgement so that the sun sparkled on their helms and they dismounted. 'I shall remain here until one or other of my parents returns.'

'Then I shall send word…'

'No, Nicholas, there is no need. Thy concern does thee credit and I have no reason to doubt it, but I have scant reason to love my father or my mother, it would seem.'

'But it is your duty, boy, commanded by God…' Nicholas began.

'I am no longer a boy, Nicholas, but am girded knight…'

'But that is impossible. By whom? Not by King Stephen?'

'Aye, by King Stephen, and to pardon my Lord father as much as acknowledge the service I have rendered the King himself.'

'But…'

'Say no more, sir,' William said. He had slid to the ground now and stood beside the priest. Putting his hand upon Nicholas's shoulder, Nicholas realised that William was much grown, almost as tall as he was himself, the priest being increasingly stooped with age. He had, moreover, a commanding air that Nicholas found disturbingly full of sinful pride. As William smiled at him kindly, Nicholas de Sarum crossed himself. How old was he now? Seven? Or was it eight? Surely more than the six years that he counted upon his fingers. Yet this was no child. The boy seemed to have grown quickly to a premature manhood. In that instant his faith faltered; it seemed all his schooling had been undone by the time William had been away, and no man – least of all a priest – can countenance his life's work unravelled. Just as he recalled the old assertion that William had been born Satan's imp he saw kindness in the boy's eyes and felt the gentle, almost affectionate pressure of William's hand upon his own shoulder.

*

Word was carried to the Lady Sybil that her second son had returned to the place of his birth and she, mindful of his duty to her, responded by commanding he attend her. Confident of his obedience she and her daughters prepared for his arrival and wondered at his dilatoriness until it became clear he was not coming. Instead reports arrived that the boy had made himself master of the castle at Hamstead Marshal, that he was out hawking on a fine bay palfrey, defiant of his mother's order. Worse, it seemed he was lording it over those few servants left in the castle, though in fact few objected to making up fires and cooking for the 'little Lord' whose easy manner enchanted them and was at such variance with either the peremptory commands of his ill-visaged father or his waspish mother, both of whom they had been free of for some weeks.

Sybil sent a message to her husband who was at the time still with Duke Henry accompanied by John, her beloved first-born, and John the Marshal came first to Marlborough and then, collecting his wife, went on to Hamstead Marshal. A mile from the castle he

72

sent his heir on ahead, commanding William to appear submissively at the wooden gate in the company of Nicholas de Sarum. This proved to be a mistake, for brother John found William in the tilt-yard and scarcely recognised him. When John had delivered his father's order, William laughed in his face and continued to hack at the straw target he had had erected, chopping it to pieces in an impressive display of strength. Affronted and angry, John returned to the approaching cavalcade full of confirmation of his sibling's disobedience.

The instant he had gone William sheathed his small sword and raced to the hall where he threw the rope noose over a beam. Then he drew up his father's carved chair and sat in it until his father's shadow, thrown by the low winter sun of the late November afternoon, fell across the threshold.

'What is the meaning of this disobedience?' roared the outraged Marshal, the Lady Sybil and brother John now flanking him. Slowly and with a precociously theatrical deliberation, the lad rose, walked towards his father and went down upon one knee. It was a moment he had been savouring.

'I have rendered thee knight's service, father,' he said in a clear voice for all capable of doing so to hear, 'and am knighted for it by the King. The noose I return to you in token of my loyalty to you and of your fatherly love.'

The precocious irony was lost on a bewildered Marshal, whose one eye took some time to adjust to the dim hall after the autumnal sunshine outside. He looked up from his son's bowed head and made out the frayed rope dangling above his recently vacated chair. When he again looked at his son he seemed shaken, uncertain that this boy of his was not indeed the Devil's work, a thought that seemed to have simultaneously enlivened his equally shocked mother.

73

'The whip is too good…' she began, but William broke in, rising to his feet, so that the Lady Sybil realised how much he had grown.

'Aye, Madam, you are right. The whip is too good for the William you sent away to his death, but I am no longer he. I am King Stephen's man…'

'He cannot be knight, father!' expostulated brother John. 'I am not yet girded nor dubbed…'

John the Marshal held up his hand for silence. 'If what he says is true, you shall be, and soon enough,' he said aside. Then turning again to William he addressed him in such a manner as to betray his own discomfiture. 'Do you consider the insolence of your behaviour, sir. The disrespect to my Lady, your mother; to your elder brother…' and here the Marshal got into his stride, 'and to me boy!' he roared, lunging forwards as if to catch William by his lug, but William dodged away then stood, his hand on his sword hilt. Both father and son stood confronting one another.

'You would draw upon your father?' gasped John the Marshal.

'Touch me, my Lord, and I shall return to the King in whose company I have been these many months, aye, and intimate with him so that I do not fear what thou might do that I shall procure retribution. As it stands my return brings thee pardon…'

'*What?*' The Marshal was almost beside himself, but his wife laid a restraining hand upon his arm as he made again to seize his son.

'The terms of peace bring pardon on all,' she said icily. 'No special powers are vested in you, boy.'

'There is, besides pardon, favour, Madam,' William responded, seemingly old far beyond his years.

'By God's blood the Devil does have his tongue!' hissed the Marshal, but the person of Nicholas de Sarum insinuated himself and, hands raised, lulled them with the beatitude: 'Blessed are the Peace-makers, my Lord…my Lady. It is fitting that the boy returns to obedience, but also that the God-given settlement in the Kingdom is reflected in every home throughout the land.'

There was a moment's silence then the wind went out of the Marshal. 'Damn you, priest,' he growled. 'Some of this is your doing...' He looked again at his wayward son, drew in his breath and sought to regain his authority, saying severely: 'you shall not again sleep under my roof, boy.'

'I have not had that privilege these last many months, father, counting a stable comfortable enough...' upon which utterance he walked towards the door where, to the astonishment of all, his father and mother made way for him.

'God's blood,' hissed his father, astounded at the boy's impudence. 'What are we to do with him?'

*

That was the question that occupied the following months at Hamstead Marshal. The result of hours in the company of King Stephen, William's attitude of cool effrontery was no mere precocity. The degree to which he had become the King's intimate confidant, even though no more than a sounding board for the isolated and indecisive Stephen, was inconceivable to his parents, but it had sharpened the lad's intellect and lent skill to his way with words. In the immediate aftermath of his exit, a raging John the Marshal had gone after him with a whip but had stayed his hand when William had indeed drawn his sword and stood his ground inside the stable, telling his father that if the whip touched him, he would inform the King and ensure his father was excluded from the goodwill and amnesty that surrounded the ending of the Anarchy.

For a long moment his father had stood looking at his son and felt the uncertainty of his age. Then, roaring mightily, he thrashed a wooden pillar in the stable, emerging into the tilt-yard and casting the whip from him into the mud where, within an hour, a providential and torrential downfall of rain washed away any sign of blood that might have resulted from the flogging he was supposed to have administered. That he had not touched his son remained between the two of them and, since he sent William with his mother to Marlborough soon afterwards, no-one saw the boy's bare back was free of any bloody welts.

Of more immediate consequence was a revival of that old calumny that William enjoyed Satan's favour, a pervading slander that further isolated the boy. At his grand-parent's place he enjoyed only the company of Angharad, who naturally followed in the Lady Sybil's train, and one of the Marshal's men-at-arms set over him as a guard but with whom William exercised daily with sword and buckler. This individual, a man of middling years known only as Rolf, grew gradually to like the lad and, being skilled in his craft and nursing ambitions of his own, came to reject the accusations of Satanic possession through the intercession of Angharad, for whom he developed a greater attachment than to William.

'It is only that he is clever,' Lady Sybil's handmaid insisted, 'gifted even. In my own land such children are set aside as touched by the Old Ways. He will be great in his day, you mark my words.'

Rolf scoffed. 'If you are right, we shall be lucky to see it. He is over-young…'

'Yet you yourself say he is good with his sword, don't you, *fach*,' interrupted Angharad. 'Quick, you said, quicker than any…'

'Quicker than most, I said,' corrected Rolf rubbing his chin and wondering if he could bed the woman. Then, thinking he was more likely to win her favour with a compliment to her darling, he admitted: 'If he grows in stature as he seems to be doing, he will be formidable.'

76

Angharad stopped her darning and turned the word over. '*Formidable*,' she said, liking the ring of the Norman-French adjective. 'Aye, and mayhap *parfait*.'

*

After a month in his mother's 'care' during which she had hardly spoken to the boy and saw him only at meal times when both sat at table silent, the Marshal summoned William back to Hamstead Marshal. The Lady Sybil had undertaken the task of guarding her troublesome son on the strict understanding that her husband resolved the problem of his future. The Marshal, much wrapped in his own affairs and those of the nation, had only made tentative arrangements and these were swept aside first by the retirement of Henry – some said in fear of his life – to Normandy, and then, in October of 1154 the death of the now enfeebled King Stephen. This event, though it released the Marshal from any lingering fear of Stephen's retribution, introduced a new uncertainty as the young Duke Henry of Normandy returned from his self-imposed exile to be anointed and crowned King Henry II of England and married Eleanor of Aquitaine.

In an attempt to right his own affairs during this period of uncertainty the Marshal had sold one of his properties, Nettlecombe, in Somerset. The new owner, Hugh de Ralegh, insisted that the deeds of sale include the consent of the Marshal's sons, John, William and their half-brothers Walter and Gilbert. To all except William, the youngest, came gifts of horses and gold marks; from henceforth the Marshal had decided that William should have nothing of the family's lands, neither before nor after his death.

As if this displeased the Devil – it could not possibly have been God, the Marshal believed – it was from this moment that the Marshal's fortunes declined. After a brief period at Henry's Court

77

and a tour of the Kingdom in the young monarch's train, John the Marshal retired from the King's presence, losing Marlborough Castle as a result of Henry's repudiation of the older nobility. Aware of a growing interest in the prophecies of the Arthurian wizard Merlin at Court, a craze that verged on the foolish, the Marshal had sought to ingratiate himself with the King. Having in his household Angharad, whose infuriating Welsh habits of story-telling and divination he only half believed in, he nevertheless thought this might be turned to good account in the privacy of Hamstead Marshal, enabling him to stem the loss of influence. Had he not defended the Empress Mathilda and lost his looks and one eye in her service? That the King should cast him off seemed an insufferable injustice.

From what he took to be Angharad's garbled nonsense, the Marshal was led to believe that Henry would again leave England to fight against Toulouse. From this campaign, the prophecies of Merlin said, he would never afterwards return to England. Armed with this 'truth' John the Marshal was rash enough to return to Court and bruit it abroad. As was intended, it eventually reached Henry's ear, whereupon, far from pleasing the King, he flew into one of his famous rages, accusing the Marshal of treason. Happily for John the Marshal, a greater irritant supervened. Early in June 1162 Henry's able Chancellor, Thomas Becket, had, upon the death of Archbishop Theobald of Canterbury, been ordained priest and then immediately afterwards Archbishop in Theobald's place. Upon his assumption of the Holy Office, Becket began to defy the man he had up to then so faithfully served, opposing Henry's policies so that the King instituted a campaign of counter opposition in which he found a ready ally in John the Marshal. Eager to restore his tattered reputation, the Marshal engaged in litigation against the Archbishop which was ultimately in the

King's interest. The upshot of this was a partial rehabilitation of the Marshal and the exile of Becket to France.

That same year the Marshal finally settled the fate of his second son by the Lady Sybil. For several years William had been kept at under the watchful and despairing eye of Nicholas de Sarum. For William these years held all the consolation of freedom, for the ageing priest could now do little with him and the head-strong boy insisted upon sleeping in the hayloft above his palfrey. The horse gave him licence to roam about the countryside, to hunt and hawk, the latter with a young peregrine of his own training in which he took much delight. In the tilt-yard he daily exercised against Rolf. Occasionally, when they visited Hamstead Marshal, he took-on his elder brother John, or his half-brothers, but William's superior prowess with his weapons quickly dissuaded them from such regular humiliation.

Only once did John the Marshal speak to William and in such a way as suggested he had found a means by which to discomfit the boy's declaration made that November afternoon of his return to Hamstead Marshal. Summoned into the castle's hall, William found his father sat under the beam over which William had long ago so provocatively thrown the rope noose.

'You once spoke of you being made knight by King Stephen,' William's father said matter-of-factly.

'Aye, my Lord. For rendering service…'

'The thing was an artifice, a flummery. The King was in his cups, no doubt.'

'The King seemed sincere, my Lord.'

'But you have not been in combat,' his father said. 'Such a dubbing, if there was any, is of no consequence.'

William considered his father's argument a moment and then responded. 'I was at the great tourney held during the parleying at

Winchester, my Lord, besides being placed in a mangonel before my Lord's castle at Newbury. I do not know how better to be in combat than to be used as a projectile.'

John the Marshal had stared at his son with incredulity and supressed anger. Christ in His mercy, was he so old that he might not best the boy? Where in the name of Heaven did a lad of such tender years learn to bandy words so cleverly but at the Devil's teat? All he could do was stand and, in turning to the door to his quarters in the tower, throw over his shoulder the declamation that: 'such a dubbing was meaningless. Thou art no knight for my service.'

In the aftermath of Becket's exile, as John the Marshal lived in hope of a restoration of the young King's favour, he found an answer to his wife's long nurtured desire to be rid of the lad, a desire which the Marshal now shared. Having concluded arrangements, he instructed Nicholas de Sarum to ready the boy for departure.

'Whither dost thou send him, my Lord?' the priest enquired.

'To Tancarville where he may learn his manners or have sense knocked into his head... or his head knocked off,' he added, as if this might prove the best outcome. 'The Lord of Tancarville is cousin-german to my Lady,' he explained before anticipating the priest's next question. John the Marshal relieved Nicholas de Sarum of his burden. 'You shall tarry here Nicholas. Your duty regarding the imp is done. No-one could have done it better and your patience and persistence is eternally to the credit of your immortal soul.'

'My Lord is gracious.'

John the Marshal grunted in response. Why in God's name had Stephen not avenged himself on the Marshal's treachery by throwing the boy into Newbury Castle? Well, with Stephen dead, the priest ageing and his own limbs stiffening, it was all too late now. Whether or not the Devil was in young William, he could at least dispose of him at last. The boy was too quick witted and to full of pride to last long amid De Tancarville's quarrelsome household. Someone would cut him down to size, one way or another. Men died in tournaments; not often, it was true, but the lowlier they were the more likely it was and, in the meanwhile, the boy's obvious prowess might add a shred of lustre to John the Marshal's fast fading laurels. Whatever happened, it ought not to be too difficult to dispose of an insolent boy.

And so William was sent to France, not into exile but into the service of Guillaume, the Lord of Tancarville, a man whose distant connections with the Lady Sybil's family offered the best prospect of bringing up the errant and rebellious boy.

William left Hamstead Marshall riding on the palfrey Stephen had given him; with him went Rolf and a servant. The Lady Sybil was said to have wept at his departure, some saying these were tears of joy. Certainly William's sisters shed tears, for they had found in William's stubborn character something oddly admirable, but Rolf knew that the woman Angharad wept the most, both for him and the young man who sat his horse in the sunshine, his brown hair flopping about his handsome features and who never looked back as they descended the long hill and disappeared into the woods beyond.

William had sat-up half the previous night talking to Angharad, leaving Rolf only a few hours to take his own leave of the woman.

*

De Tancarville was Chamberlain of Normandy and his stronghold was a great castle of stone that commanded a bend of the Seine within the walls of which Guillaume's household knights – his mesnie - lodged in great numbers and whose readiness for war was kept upon a permanent footing by their employment in sundry tournaments.

Man-hood came to William quickly at Tancarville and he was far better prepared for his new life than his father could ever have imagined. From Angharad he had learned patience and, after he had returned from Stephen's entourage, the art not of insolence, but of holding his tongue. From her too he had learned that mysterious sense of self denied him by his parents. Nicholas de Sarum had taught him to love God, obey his commandments, and cleave loyally to the right. King Stephen, in whose train he had for so long occupied his ambivalent position, had sharpened his wits, given him a ready word but tempered it further with diplomatic reflection. Such skill had been necessary even then, for a hostage must needs watch himself in his isolation among the squires in whose company he spent most of his time. They had largely quietly shunned him, knowing he was the King's favourite, jealous of him, but giving him no cause for complaint and including him in their exercises and using him as their servant, just he was the King's. Being so young and coming from such parental indifference, William had slipped as easily into being King Stephen's toy as accepting his odd position amid his fellows, but he had learned to be wary of entrapment and was, by default, a fair way to becoming a good judge of character.

Thus prepared and after making his initial obeisance to the Lord of Tancarville and receiving a warm welcome from Guillaume, he eased comfortably into life at Tancarville, as did Rolf, who had been charged with the lad's care. For William it was not unlike being part of Stephen's entourage, though much more congenial. Here, however, his growing body demanded more than a modest sustenance and he was quickly noted as much for his preternatural talents with his weapons as for his gargantuan appetite. '*Gaste-*

viande!' his peers called him, 'Greedy-guts!' And even the faithful Rolf was bound to agree with them. William developed a love of roast crane, a meat entirely new to him, circumstances that drew further mockery from the other lads, chief among them a young Norman named Adam d'Yquebeuf.

When he was not at table, exercising, cleaning weapons or attending one or other of the knights attached to the man all called 'the Good Master,' William slept as young men of his age do. But he did it prodigiously, growing by inches, they said, every week. His voice broke early and he learned to sing with a fine voice of which Angharad would have been proud, singing then being considered an accomplishment of a gentle-man. And if he failed to read Latin and missed Angharad's Welsh legends, such intellectual diversions found ready substitutes in the epics of Roland and Oliver and their Twelve Peers. While the Welsh mists swirled round the Arthurian myths and he associated them with childhood, the sound of Roland's horn blown at the moment of death in the Pass of Roncesvalles could still be heard in the echoing chambers of the mighty square stone dongeon of Tancarville and imbued him and his fellows with the singular nature of their military craft.

Here too there was a greater and more magnificent celebration of the Mass and the other Christian Mysteries than he had ever yet been exposed to, and they made a profound impression on William. That he had been close to an anointed King in his boyhood – for he now thought of himself as a man – seemed a great privilege which, far from inducing pride, engendered a profound, almost mystical sense of awe. He forgot that Stephen had often drunk more than was good for him, or that he too often vacillated, but he remembered something of the King standing apart from his nobles, all of whom seemed in retrospect ambitious and greedy men, just like his father.

83

But not even Stephen, King of England, in all his splendour could command a retinue as magnificent as Guillaume de Tancarville. Or so it seemed to William, who kept Stephen's girding of himself a knight, a secret to nurture his soul. Yet this secret knowledge proved the foundation of his prowess in practice, his ability to sit his palfrey upright and to bear a brightly be-pennoned lance, all of which assured him a place riding as shield-bearer to one or other of the lesser knights in Guillaume's mesnie, trailing amid the assorted squires as the Lord of Tancarville went out to tourney like a blazing comet.

*

Though William had witnessed a tournament in England it had been a poor show compared with the great events held in Northern France. Carried out over large tracts of where the lands of one magnate bordered his neighbour, tourneying was a tremendous enterprise involving the entire retinues of the contenders and many of their tenants and villeins. Besides the close agreements of the principals, news of the event was first broadcast by the heralds who rode about the countryside announcing the location of the encounter and the adjacent towns or villages which the challengers would make their head-quarters and take up their posts at the lists. Such advertisement drew every species of trader and opportunist, from those specialising in the martial arts to hawkers, vendors, money-lenders, pedlars, pick-pockets and common whores who swelled the populations of small towns for a few days of feasting and disorder until the famine of reaction set-in after the event.

Prior to such a tourney Tancarville was a hive of preparation and lads like William were to be found industriously preparing weapons, tending horses and their harness and running errands for their respective masters. A few were allowed to accompany the *hiraults*, or heralds, as horse-holders. On such an occasion William

84

rode with one of Guillaume's heralds whom he knew only as Gerard, a stunted and ill-favoured man of some thirty summers and few words who led the younger horseman in a wild dash across miles of countryside only to pull-up sharply and sit his horse for perhaps a quarter of an hour. At first William thought this was to give his mount time to get its breath until he realised Gerard was engaged in something else.

'Here, hold him,' Gerard commanded, slipping from the saddle some yards short of the summit of a low rise and walking forward with, William thought, a sort of furtiveness. William could not be sure, for Gerard's gait was hampered by being a cripple, his left leg being shorter than its fellow and twisted it was said from birth. He was thus ill-suited to advancement, being easily bested on foot, though he defended himself manfully enough in the yard at Tancarville. But what Gerard lacked in stature and comeliness he more than made-up for as a horseman. It was said he could make a horse do anything and that he knew their language and could talk to them, healing them when they were sick or injured and cozening them in such a way that, had he not lived under the protection of my Lord of Tancarville and proved himself most useful, would have attracted the notice of the Church.

His mare snickered anxiously as her master hobbled with obvious difficulty up to the ridge, stooping so as not to break the skyline. William watched with a mixture of pity and interest. Gerard's obvious caution was unnecessary, for they were not at war. Then the lad caught Gerard's intention: he was teaching William some sort of lesson, a realisation that so focussed William's attention so that he forgot his pity.

Having satisfied himself Gerard returned to the horses and William caught his eye. The inquisitiveness must have been obvious to Gerard who, in mounting and recovering his own reins from the youth asked: 'You are wondering what it is I am doing, eh?'

'Indeed sir.'

'Can you not guess,' Gerard said, kicking his horse into an uncharacteristic walk.

'I cannot, sir, unless you were espying…'

'Good. Good. I am seeking the lie of the land, William, learning it for our master and his mesnie so that full advantage may be taken of the countryside in the coming encounter. See,' he said as they all too obviously crested the rise and began a descent which Gerard halted again soon after they had dropped below the skyline, 'how this ridge falls away into a long and shallow country of rolling hills.' He swept his right hand across the vista before them. 'You may see the woodland and mark the two villages from the rising smoke and, since it is a clear day, see the distant town. But see also the patch of green pasture being grazed and through it, like a line of a different green, the willows flanking a river. Look over there,' he pointed, a steeper eminence crowned with some rocky outcrop. 'Now, suppose upon the day of our encounter the weather is not so fine as it is today; say there is mist, or rain. Our Lord will have pledged his word that we shall be in the field, yet we shall not have the advantage of such a view…'

'Unless of course you have made this reconnaissance,' William broke in with comprehending enthusiasm.

'Exactly my young friend. And where do you find our Lord's heralds riding when we go a-tourneying?'

William was less certain of this answer and responded hesitantly, 'close to his Lordship that you may acquaint him thereof?'

'You learn quickly,' Gerard replied with a grin and was about to dig his heels into his mare's flank when William asked:

'But Master Gerard, how do you recall it all?'

Gerard shrugged. 'One does, through practice, though 'tis a skill…' He kicked his horse into motion and, over his shoulder as William followed suit, shouted, 'but one easily learnt'.

After another fierce ride, by which time they had reached dense woodland and slowed their progress, Gerard allowed William up alongside him and asked, 'now, what lay to the right of that vista we surveyed from the ridge?'

'A rocky outcrop,' William responded promptly.

'And if you had been confronted by a thick mist and had headed directly down from the ridge, instead of obliquely as we in fact did, what would you have encountered?'

'A narrow river, sir, with trees – willows - running along it and which we should have come across suddenly after descending from open country?'

'And could we have ridden hard over that open country?'

William thought for a moment. It was not terrain they had actually traversed and he sensed Gerard's question was loaded. They had moved obliquely, following the track which had led them into the extensive woodland through which their horses now walked. 'I think not,' he said, making a leap of imagination, 'the ground was likely spoiled by rabbit warrens and for fear of the horses stumbling one would have to proceed with some caution.'

Gerard said nothing, but smiled and kicked his horse on ahead, leaving William to trail behind a little. 'Especially after rain,' he called, urging his own horse to catch-up with the herald.

That evening, when they had found lodgings in the town which that afternoon had been a smudge on the horizon and had finished their evening meat, Gerard leaned back on the wooden back-board against the inn-wall and asked, 'Now, before we sleep, tell me of the countryside through which we have ridden these last two days.'

'Was I right about the broken ground?' he asked first.

'You were. But now I require the whole of our traverse.'

William stared at him for a moment, then called into his mind's eye their departure from Tancarville and the ride up the northern bank of the Seine until they had branched off to the north-east. He began to describe it, as it unrolled before him, answering the occasional question with which Gerard interrupted him and concluding, somewhat sleepily, with the conclusion: 'and so we rode into this place, the name of which I am quite ignorant.'

Gerard leaned forward and ruffled William's hair. 'You must learn the names of such places but you have done very well for tonight. Do you not forget what you have learned this day but before you go there is one other thing to consider, lest your cleverness overwhelms you with conceit and it is this: once you have mastered the lie of the land to be a truly accomplished knight, you must know the more difficult art of *le coup d'oeil*.'

'And what is that, sir?'

'A trickier matter which raises your knowledge of the countryside to an art,' said Gerard, leaning forward, tapping the table with a crooked finger and speaking with greater intensity. He stared directly into William's tired eyes and held his attention despite the youth's weariness. 'It is the means by which you lead your men to great success through that very tourney-ground so that you turn a flank of your enemy unseen and take him unawares, or see an ideal place for an ambush, or even a hidden spot from where you can observe his motions unseen yourself. By such cunning and stratagems can you win and hold hostages and from them, of course,' Gerard concluded leaning backwards, 'you redeem them with ransoms enriching to yourself and your master.' He paused for a moment to see his words had sunk in and added: 'Now get you to bed!'

Gerard's lesson was well learned and everywhere he rode thereafter William laid down in his memory to the very best of his ability the lie of the land. When on tourney it was the last thing he thought about as he sought sleep and, during the winter months, after hours of exercise, he lay awaiting sleep, his mind ranging over the various landscapes across which they had roamed that summer past. That other, trickier matter – *le coup d'oeil* – he found more difficult until, unable to sleep one night for having partaken of excessive cheese at supper and with his gut twisting him so that he was obliged to rise and shit from the *garde de robe*, he realised that the knight banneret in whose service Lord Guillaume had enrolled him, a man of brutal strength and little wit called by his retinue Guilbert the Stupid but who possessed a grander name, had twice led them into ambushes from which they had only escaped by such hard fighting that several men had been injured and one, a poor squire, had afterwards died of his wounds. Since they fought with blunted weapons the poor man was unlucky but, as the squires murmured to each other, had Guilbert proved a proper knight he would have surrendered, as was expected of *un gentilhomme*, and paid his and all their ransoms. This, after all, was the point of the tournament, that the victor should make money and the vanquished, whilst resolving to fight and win another day, should willingly pay for his and his men's liberty. By such means were both prowess and knightly conduct encouraged, a code of conduct sanctioned by His Holiness the Pope and blessed by the Holy Church.

In considering this simultaneously with easing the trouble in his bowels, William realised that Guilbert could easily have taken a different line of march. The comprehending thought made him aware that it was just this very aspect of their tourneying that

Gerard had been encouraging in William, and that it was to be used all the time, in both defence and attack. And once that example had come to mind there were others; moments when in an excess of gallant zeal Guilbert had launched his small retinue at a well-placed enemy and been flung back for their pains; when they might have detached a part of their force, feinted to their front and allowed the detachment to move behind a low hill and catch their opponents in flank. Or when, in entering a thick wood, they had all been surprised when confronted by fallen trees and set-upon by the opposition. That Guilbert's retinue generally survived by hard fighting, earning itself a reputation among my Lord of Tancarville's mesnie for their endurance in the field – an attribute celebrated afterwards in copious quaffings of ale and wine - was one thing. But it often came at the cost of lost horses, bloodied bodies and broken bones. Whilst the last two were of little importance, the loss of an expensive horse was another matter. Unknown to William, after several remonstrations with Guilbert, Guillaume de Tancarville had refused to recompense him for his losses, giving Guilbert the alternative of doing so himself or leaving the mesnie and wandering, a knight errant. After three summers Guilbert was obliged to take the latter course but the young William Marshal had by this time long since imbibed the entirety of the lesson of Gerard the crippled herald.

CHAPTER FOUR: LE COUP D'OEIL 1160 - 1165

'My Lord desires that you wait upon him, Greedy-guts,' Guillaume de Tancarville's cup-bearer said genially, arousing the curiosity of the squires who dined below the salt.

'What new favour have you plucked from my Lord's arse, English William?' sneered Adam d'Yquebeuf with far less cordiality. 'Or has your big belly incurred my Lord's displeasure. You must be eating him out of his treasure.'

They made way for William on the bench as he lifted first one and then the other long leg over the wooden bench, kicked aside a hound and followed his summoner up towards the dais. He ignored D'Yquebeuf's jibe, having bested him that day in their exercises. William had been two years in De Tancarville's service and left behind him a now familiar muttering that this surely meant some new favour being granted the fifteen-year-old English lad. It was put about that, possibly through reasons of witch-craft, the interloper had beguiled their Lordship and addled his wits to their own detriment. Most of them had seen the Devil's mark upon his shoulder and some even went so far as to assert the existence of a tail, real enough, coiled within the compass of his breeches. William's great appetite had already confirmed one growing prejudice the Norman French increasingly believed of their uncouth, greedy English cousins, so it seemed likely enough that he had this other attribute.

Despite this personal bitterness amongst his peers, an air of expectation filled the great hall of the castle for it was late April and on the following day the entire household was to ride out to tourney, opening the season with a long awaited meeting with the Henneyers. As William approached the high table De Tancarville was deep in conversation with an elderly knight, into whose retinue there had been rumours that William was about to be appointed. That he had become the apple of his distant cousin's eye was all-too-obvious to the score or so of young men vying for advancement, but they would display more than the green-eye the following morning when they learned what Guillaume de Tancarville actually had in mind for his young relative.

William stood respectfully before the elevated table at which Guillaume and his chief followers ate until, in reaching for his wine-goblet, De Tancarville looked up and saw the waiting squire. He beckoned William round the other side of the table, making way for him and indicating a page should draw forth a stool for him to sit upon.

'We have had you close under our eye, William,' he began quietly, waving aside William's obligatory words of respect. 'Ever since Gerard spoke so highly of you, you have manifested promise, even perhaps prowess in your skill and conduct.'

William blushed to the roots of his brown hair. 'My Lord…'

Guillaume silenced him again. 'Now it is the time to see if all these compliments are justified. Tomorrow I am intending to place you at the head of half of the men-at-arms in the retinue of Roger de Vaux here,' Guillaume indicated the elderly knight on his right. The older man nodded and half smiled at the younger, but did not speak. William was astonished and it took some time for the import of De Tancarville's words to sink-in. 'Sir Roger will ride some little distance behind you with his knights, but you will lead and command his vanguard. He and I will give you your instructions tomorrow. Now go and pray and then sleep.'

Overwhelmed with this sudden responsibility, William quit the great hall, Rolf following him.

'What is amiss, master?'

'Nothing is amiss, Rolf,' William said, turning, his spirits alternating with a mixture of apprehension and a quickening eagerness, 'but much is afoot…'

*

William held up his hand, turned in his saddle and, once the column had halted, sent word for all lance heads to be lowered. Then, indicating that only the herald Gerard should ride forward with him, he kicked his horse forward, approaching the top of a hill near Gournay-en-Bray. Gerard had been especially assigned to William's entourage, a nursemaid-cum-assessor in the serious game of war in which to which the entire mesnie of Guillaume de Tancarville had been turned-out in all its panoplied magnificence six days earlier.

The track which William's column had been following had emerged from the woodland covering the Pays de Bray shortly before and his outriders had reported the low summit ahead of them without exposing themselves, falling back on the main body as William had ordered. Now he went forward with Gerard, stopping short of the skyline where he slid from his horse and handed the reins over to Gerard who took them with a rueful grin. 'The world, FitzMarshal, rolls on, eh?'

William was too consumed by anxiety to respond to Gerard's mock use of his inflated name and his reference to their reversed roles. He knew Gerard was sent as nursemaid, ready to prevent him getting into too serious a scrape and thereby both compromising and dishonouring De Tancarville's military household. Crouching, he loped forward, half hoping to see the spread of landscape that he and Gerard had witnessed two years earlier, which would have made of what was to come all the easier, but as his eye-line topped the low summit he saw no such well-defined features as the wood and river and rocky crag. The land descended, the track re-entering the dense woodland that covered a low, rolling country, the hill being an odd anomaly, a concealed hummock of barely covered rock nurturing some scrubby grass, but little else. Aware that he was not merely on his mettle but that some form of success was expected of him, if he was to advance his status among the squires, he was seized with a sudden dread. This seemingly benign landscape might prove the ruin of his ambitions for it occurred to him that he had just escaped ambush, that in his cautious approach – the lance-lowering and moving forward with Gerard – he had prevented them falling into the enemy's hands. It had not been the reason for so doing; on the contrary, being young and inexperienced he had assumed that it was he who was laying an ambush for others whilst in fact, had he crossed the crest he would have exposed the size of his force to anyone watching in the dense woodland below.

And the thought provoked a conviction that that was exactly what *was* happening. A sixth-sense told him that there was indeed an ambush awaiting him and that he was confronted with his first real decision in the tournament. Lying full-length upon the damp grass he studied the woods into which the track descended. Used for running livestock to market in the distant town, it lost its definition going over the hill, where the cattle wandered onto a wide front, but narrowed again as it entered the close-packed trees lower down. There was dense undergrowth there, especially under the edge of the wood's mantle, before the canopy of spring leaves kept the ground clear, so...

Then he saw something move. He could not be sure but he watched closely. The sun was half-way up the sky: mid-morning. No cooking fires would betray an enemy party at such an hour but he was almost certain he had seen movement, unnatural movement, just within the line of trees. He felt a strong compulsion to return to Gerard for advice and opinion, but a stubborn pride held him to the ground and he thought of a piece of advice a huntsman had once given him when flushing prey: do not stare at where you think something is, but lift you eye a little above it; any movement will the more readily catch your attention.

William did this for some moments without result. Then another disturbing thought came to him. Supposing the enemy was lying in wait; what then? There was, as far as he could see, no obvious way of out-flanking an opponent just at the point where the track led into the trees. Besides, fighting in the woods would be a desperate business, a matter of every man for himself. He ran his eye to left and right. What in the name of Christ was he to do?

In his final instructions from De Tancarville he had been sworn to consult Gerard if

he encountered any difficulty, but was this a real difficulty? He was unwilling to wriggle back like a child and seek the herald's advice.

And then he *did* see movement. Two movements in fact, the first a fluttering of lance pennon just beyond the first of the trees, with just enough breeze blowing through them to reveal them as green, the same colour as the spring leaves; then a man came forward, breaking cover a little, looking up the hill as though he could see William's head. William froze, knowing that with the wind ruffling hair to have moved might have betrayed his presence. Instead he kept still, like a grass tussock, watching and waiting. Half a mile away the scout, in a plain leather hauberk, emerged from the cover of the wood and appeared to scan the hillside. For what seemed an age he raked the crest and then, with an almost eloquent gesture of disappointment, he turned about and disappeared. In that instant, William knew what to do.

Very slowly he wormed his way below the skyline then he half-stood and bent as an old man shuffled back to where Gerard patiently held the horses. 'Take your post on the crest. They lie in wait where the track enters the wood and are impatient. They know we are coming; I don't know how, but they do. We will lure them but I need half an hour to make preparations. Do you keep watch. If they move out of the wood let me know.'

'Are you certain you know what to do?' Gerard asked.

'Aye. Give me both horses' reins and watch out front. The enemy is there.'

Gerard nodded and William led the two animals back to where his column of armed men waited. Some had dismounted and they spoke in the low tones of seasoned campaigners. At William's approach they looked up and he motioned them to gather round.

'The enemy lie in ambush on the edge of a wood about half a mile beyond the ridge. They are expecting us, of that I am sure, so I have a mind to draw them out, but it will need clear heads and fine judgement. I want four men to join me and move up towards the ridge. We will then raise lances and wave pennons. A small fire may convince them we are careless, that we have stopped for some reason; we shall light a fire and strike a stone as if attending a horse after a shoe has been shed. We shall make a noise but I will watch the ridge. The instant they are seen I will send up an alarum, shout and we shall mount up and ride back into the woods behind us. That is where we shall ambush them; that is where the rest of you shall be, half on either side of the track.'

William looked back at the ridge where Gerard lay, his heels towards them. 'D'you understand?' Murmurs of assent came from his men. 'Now who will stand with me?'

Almost the entire party held up their hands and William picked the first four with a wide grin on his face, his heart thundering in his chest with the excitement. They began to move closer to the ridge, lance pennons aloft, one of them singing as though the beauty of the morning was all that mattered. William watched them and then looked back towards Gerard, still at his post. The others mounted and began to trot their horses back to the woodland they had left earlier, all except Rolf, whose eye William caught.

'Ride back to Sir Roger, explain what is happening and urge him forward but not too fast. We shall be making a noise by way of lure and I do not wish him to think us troubled until it is the clash of arms.'

'Yes, yes, I understand, master,' Rolf responded impatiently, pointing over William's shoulder so that William spun round to see Gerard, bent double hurrying towards him.

William walked swiftly towards him and handed him his horse's bridle. 'They're on the move…the moment they saw that lot,' he nodded at the decoys who were already alerted by Gerard's hasty retreat as they waved their red and white pennons aloft.

'Do you get back into the wood with the others. I shall remain here.'

Gerard regarded William for a moment. 'Is that wise?'

'Go!' William said swiftly moving towards the waiting men. 'Make ready,' he said unnecessarily, for each man was poised to mount and the singer had fallen silent. William, his heart pounding, drew in a breath and began to sing himself, an air he had first heard sung by a troubadour said to have learned it at the Court of Her Grace of Aquitaine: 'My heart is laid low as the grey-goose at sundown…' His fine voice rang out and he no longer minded that it had irritated his fellow squires at Tancarville. He gave little thought to that now and he glanced back down the hill as Gerard followed the last of the column into the wood and vanished. 'My lady bestows smiles on all…' and here he trilled nobly, 'but me…'

He got no further. One of the decoys threw up a warning shout and the horses were all too truly startled so that the mounting up of the quintet had every appearance of surprise and disorder as twenty lances bearing green pennons broke the line of the hill against the sky. They were coming up at the gallop only yards away. 'Ride!' William shouted, throwing aside his lance. Catching his intention, two others did the same. Now all was breathless terror. William was seized with a strong urge to laugh maniacally even as he all but felt the breath of his pursuers' horses upon the back of his neck. He looked back once, then lowered his head as his palfrey lifted his hooves to the drum-beat of a gallop matching, then out-running, horses that had already covered half a mile uphill.

William was no longer laughing but urging his horse on with unintelligible words that Gerard had taught him, words that sounded very like those used in private by Angharad ap Gwyn. And he was lugging his sword from its scabbard, a surer weapon to use among the fast approaching trees than a lance

Then they were into the woods, lashed by branches, slowed by the constraints of the narrow track and the horses slowing to avoid the tree-roots so that it seemed an age before, to William's intense relief, shouts from behind him told where the rest of his men sprang into action. Reining in he shouted to his companions who joined him in drawing-up their horses, turning about and joining the mêlée. Immediately behind them their pursuers were in confusion as William and his party drove amongst them. Lances pierced the shoulders of the leading enemy horses and as they stumbled and fell, all behind them blundered into the falling beasts.

The remainder of William's men, having hitched their own mounts among the trees, were now running among the tangle of men and horses slashing at saddle girths or pulling the riders down and kneeling on their chests with daggers and swords at their throats, knocking off helms. If submission was not instant they struck the pommels of their swords to lay out their victims, leaving them unconscious so that they could the better dispose of the remainder.

In dragging his horse's head round William had got his sword clear of its scabbard. One man, the last of the enemy to ride into the wood, had hauled about too and set his heels to his mount, eager to escape the fate of his comrades. William made after him with a loud whoop, driving his horse through the chaos of men fighting on the ground and amid the undergrowth on either side of the track. The animal never lost its footing and horse and rider were suddenly clear of the wood again. But the other's mount was blown and William caught its rider's helm a tremendous blow with the flat of his sword. Senseless, the fellow toppled and sagged sideways, so that his horse, unbalanced, eased its stride until William grabbed the bridle and pulled it to a standstill with his own. Fortunately it was no highly strung destrier and submitted as William gathered up its reins and led it back into the wood where his men sat upon their prisoners and from the depths of the trees beyond Rolf, Sir Roger de Vaux and his retinue emerged. De Vaux took in the scene in an instant and sent a man up the hill to ensure no-one followed the assault. Reassured that they had taken the entire party, it was time to take the tally.

'You have done well, FitzMarshal,' the old man said. 'But next time I suggest you wear your helm.'

In the haste and excitement William had left his helmet at his saddle-bow. He grinned and nodded, wiping the sweat from his forehead. 'Aye, Sir Roger. Next time I shall do as you say.'

CHAPTER FIVE: THE HOUSEHOLD KNIGHT 1165 - 1167

William was eighteen when, in the autumn of 1165, word reached him of the death of his father. The news did not tempt him to return to England, for he felt nothing for the loss of an old man for whom he had had no affection and who had left him nothing by way of patrimony. Nor did the death of his brother Gilbert shortly afterwards prompt him to go home, even though this made him heir to his elder brother John. John, he had heard by way of a missive from Nicholas de Sarum, being short of his majority, was in any case in royal wardship, King Henry having assigned Alan de Neuville, a man noted for his greed, to manage the young Marshal's affairs. The almost illiterate William required assistance to get the sense of Nicholas's letter, but the priest made it clear enough that he at least found this situation unsatisfactory, a further marking of the fading fortunes of the family.

The truth was that ever since his *coup d'oeil* his star in the mesnie of Guillaume de Tancarville had been rising. Technically his first small triumph had been under the banner of Roger de Vaux to whom went the greater glory, but the affair yielded several fine horses, among which was a destrier which was given to William as a reward for his part in the affair, whilst he received a share in the ransom of three minor knights from Hainault. While success raised his status in De Tancarville's household it furthered jealousy among his fellow squires, chief among them Adam d'Yquebeuf. Still the honour of knighthood as recognised by the House of Tancarville eluded William, the wily Guillaume using William's growing prowess to his own ends. Retaining William in a subordinate position cost him less, but it also increased the young

100

man's desire for recognition, obvious to Guillaume as William strove ever more and more to add to his achievements.

In this Guillaume De Tancarville misjudged his man. William's striving was not to attract his master's approbation; it was simply a product of his natural ambition as he improved at what he was expected to do: fight in his Lord's service. As for the honour of knighthood, he knew that as a distant relation of Guillaume it must come one day, accepting that all the influence he wielded lay in his cousin-german's power. Although ambitious, he was not as greedy a young man as De Tancarville supposed and the steady augmentation of his possessions was satisfaction enough. Moreover, he nurtured the private conviction that he had already been girded and dubbed in secret by King Stephen. There may have been something of mockery or indulgence in Stephen's act, but the contempt with which John the Marshal had dismissed his son's claim to have been thus dubbed only increased the act's validity in William's eyes now that the old man was dead. William kept these things in his heart, along with the quiet advices of Angharad ap Gwyn and the exhortations of Nicholas de Sarum, all of which were a sure armour against the envy of his peers at Tancarville. Most of all, they were enough to prevent him from returning home to beg a living of his elder brother or even to position himself as John's heir. This William might have done in 1167 when, still bereft of the status of one of De Tancarville's household knights, John reached his majority. Early that year Nicholas de Sarum again wrote to him again, advising him that the effect of De Neuville's guardianship had been deleterious, that his own presence in Wiltshire might restore prestige to his brother. William pondered both the personal advantage to be gained by assisting his brother, and the satisfaction that might bring him after the schism driven between them by their father and his cutting of William from his will, but the notion

101

palled. He did not care to be beholden to John and, in any case, John was sure to wed and father a son of his own body, if he had not already done so. The mesnie of De Tancarville offered brighter prospects which held a greater and more immediate an allure, factors more certain to attract a young man's fancy. There was besides, a young woman named Anne in the household with whom William had become intimate. He was fool enough to think he was her only lover, but his lust for her was an added factor in him ignoring Nicholas de Sarum's plea long enough for matters to be taken out of his hands.

Beyond the small world of the tilt-yard of Tancarville and the tourneying grounds on the borders of Normandy, Flanders and the Vexin, greater affairs were in train. The same year that brother John came into his own, King Henry II and King Louis VII fell out. Among other rumbling disagreements, Henry resented Louis' protection in the Abbey of Pontigny of the exiled Thomas Becket. The disparate characters of the dogged and charming Louis and the ruthless, clever, cunning and intemperate Henry drew to each a degree of support among the great noblemen. Among those attracted to Louis' banner were Philippe, Count of Flanders, his brother Matthieu, Count of Boulogne, and the Count of Ponthieu, whose lands were contiguous to the eastern border of Normandy, all of which made war inevitable.

Despite being King in England, Henry was a subject of Louis, holding Normandy and his wife Eleanor of Aquitaine's extensive domains as French feudatories. However, as Philippe, Matthieu and Ponthieu mustered a large army on the Norman boundary with Flanders and Picardy, his marcher lord, the Count of Eu, joined by the Constable and Chamberlain of Normandy, namely De Tancarville and the Earl of Essex, poured garrisons into the castles of eastern Normandy. De Tancarville and Essex were charged with the defence of Neufchâtel-en-Bray, lying on the River Béthune, five leagues from the border.

It was here, on the eve of war, with little ceremony beyond a formal girding and the rough shoulder-punch of the dubbing, that De Tancarville made knights of William FitzMarshal, Adam d'Yquebeuf and several others among their fellow squires.

*

The position of Neufchâtel-en-Bray was supposed to permit its garrison to respond to any threat along a wide sector of the frontier. Notice, it was presumed, would be brought to Essex and De Tancarville in good time for them to ride out at the head of their combined retinues and throw back any invader. In the event the enemy crossed the Bresle between Eu and Blangy and laid waste the counties of Eu and Aumale, lying to the east of the stronghold, before those at Neufchâtel-en-Bray knew anything. Led by Matthieu of Boulogne, the main column of the Flemings appeared before the Norman fortress, taking Essex and De Tancarville completely by surprise.

So complete was this that D'Eu temporarily lost his wits, while the Earl of Essex, gathering a group of hot-heads, had the presence of mind to arm immediately, mount-up, and ride to the west gate of the little town that surrounded the ramparts and seize the bridge carrying the road that led to Eu.

De Tancarville stayed his own hand, roaring for his household knights to form up in good order to meet the enemy force that was better prepared than his own. With quickening heart, William, clad in mail and hauberk, steadied his now thoroughly restless destrier, leapt into the saddle and seized his helm and lance from the faithful Rolf. Rolf mounted beside him and both made ready to ride out to repel the invaders in the train of Guillaume de Tancarville.

As they approached the west gate they could see beyond the hard-pressed handful under Essex fighting for their lives on the Chausée d'Eu, the narrow road which lay between the houses of the faubourg that lay on the far side of the ditch. Here a large troop of knights leading mounted man-at-arms and foot-soldiers were pressing forward. It was clear that the defenders were insufficient in numbers to hold the bridge and, as De Tancarville rode up to the gate it was equally obvious that the town guard were eager to drop the portcullis and leave Essex to his fate in order to save the inner town.

Guillaume de Tancarville took-in the situation at a glance and drew-rein below the portcullis to prevent its being lowered and waved his knights forward. William kicked his heels into his charger's flanks but as he drew level with his master, Guillaume grabbed his bridle.

'Hold hard, FitzMarshal! Get back! Be not hasty, we are the reserve.'

William drew-up sharply and Guillaume let go, only to find the young knight took scant notice and, an instant later, drove his destrier forward, lowering his lance. There was a brief thunder of hooves crossing the wooden bridge and then he pitched into the mêlée as one of the leading knights coming to Essex's aid.

So savage was his short charge that William's lance shivered at the first impact. He pulled the destrier up short so that the beast sat back on its haunches, caracoling and kicking out its fore-hooves as it had been taught, giving William time to draw sword from scabbard. He laid about him indiscriminately, aware only of the pressure of many men and horses in the narrow street as the Normans felt the pressure of the assaulting Flemings. Suddenly William felt himself caught by the shoulder. A hook used to drag thatch from the houses in case of fire had been seized by a Flemish foot-soldier keen on ransom and William found himself toppling sideways. Almost at the same moment he sensed his charger founder under him. Another Fleming had run in and with a belly-knife eviscerated the destrier so that William fell to the ground among the steaming entrails of his horse.

He fought unsuccessfully for a footing, slithering in the mess of guts and stink of shit, losing hold of his sword; but he recovered sufficiently on one knee to whip out his dagger and drive it into the nearer of his assailants. The man's entrails joined those of William's horse, giving him time to stagger to his feet with the help of the wall of an adjacent dwelling. He picked-up his sword only to find that the crisis of the vicious skirmish had passed; Count Matthieu had called off his people and, for the moment, Neufchâtel-en-Bray was saved for King Henry.

'Cut it up for supper, have you?' asked Adam d'Yquebeuf superciliously, sitting his destrier in high good humour at William's discomfiture and indicating the remains of William's war-horse.

'Go fuck yourself,' William responded, turning and walking back towards the town gate with D'Yquebeuf's sarcastic laughter ringing in his ears.

That evening at table as the Normans, secure behind the barred gate of Neufchâtel-en-Bray, ate and drank to celebrate their triumphant defence of the castle, Essex also ribbed the young knight. 'Hey, FitzMarshal, make me a gift for your love and honour in the name of God.'

William swallowed his pride, eager perhaps to salvage something from the day. 'Willingly, my Lord. What service can I render?'

'Oh, some piece of harness that you took this day; a crupper, perhaps, or an old collar,' replied Essex with a grin, raising expectations of general amusement in the great hall of the castle.

105

'My Lord Earl, I have none, since I lost my horse. What I have left belongs to my Lord de Tancarville,' responded William gauchely, only vaguely aware of having become the butt of Essex's crude humour. What he might have expected from D'Yquebeuf, he had not anticipated from a great Lord.

'What?' Essex mocked him. 'In the name of Christ, I could have sworn you had, oh, forty or sixty at your disposal this forenoon. How can you claim to have nothing now and use me so ill as to refuse me such a small thing!'

A roar of laughter met this guying. Most had heard of William's precipitate rush forward and while they conceded his gallantry, his arrival back in the castle covered in slime and shit had provoked the ridicule readily released in the aftermath of struggle.

William rose, red-faced at the loud guffaws, aware that Essex was sharply reminding him that he had lost a destrier and failed to take any prisoner in recompense, not even an item of horse-harness. The taunting of D'Yquebeuf still rang in his ears and the rush of blood was accompanied by a flush of anger which he instantly supressed, going down onto one knee, an unexpected action that quickly compelled silence.

'My Lord Earl, what need of harness have you when you command my life!'

There was a moment of complete quiet then Essex raised his goblet to De Tancarville. 'My Lord Chamberlain, you have raised the eyass well. He has the keen eye and the quick stoop. Perhaps he will yet strike his prey for your enrichment.'

More loud laughter rang round the hall. Essex was not merely needling William, but making an oblique thrust at De Tancarville's lost opportunity.

Slow to comprehend at first, William quickly grasped the Earl's jibe, and looked sharply at his master. De Tancarville lolled back on his chair and, without looking at William, coolly responded.

'The eyass slipped his jesses, my Lord of Essex. I shall either bind them tighter or abandon him to the crows.'

More laughter ensued and William, redder than ever, returned to his place at table to finish his meal in silence. He was ignored by most of those about him, except, of course, Adam d'Yquebeuf and those others who wished to make him the butt of their jokes.

*

The peace agreed between Henry and Louis in November of 1167 had a profound effect upon young William. He might have expected Guillaume de Tancarville to make good the loss of William's destrier at Neufchâtel-en-Bray, but this the Lord of Tancarville seemed disinclined to do. Whispers circulated the mesnie that their Lord was out of funds following the campaign and the Chamberlain of Normandy made no secret of the fact that those among his retinue who wished to leave and seek employment for their lances elsewhere were at liberty to do so. If William was meant to count himself among this number he was too naïve or trusting to act. Rather, relying upon his distant kinship with Guillaume, he assumed that both this and his youth bound him to De Tancarville's household, so he remained, on sufferance, awaiting a turn of events in his favour.

Like De Tancarville, William found his purse as pinched as his master's. He was obliged to sell the cloak he had purchased for the bare ceremony of his dubbing to purchase a squire's roncin to act both as pack-horse and – when required – destrier. This left him his palfrey to ride, a situation which William bore with some fortitude amid an unprecedented restlessness among the mesnie of the Chamberlain of Normandy. And then came news of a great

107

tournament to be held in Maine, across miles of land between St Jaume and Valenne. The household of Tancarville, including William, was ordered to make preparations. Money was suddenly forthcoming for new equipages; saddles, harness, bright lance-pennons and even war-horses. These were dispensed among the younger members of the mesnie, all excepting William. In vain did he approach De Tancarville's Steward for a destrier, pleading the service he had given at Neufchâtel-en-Bray, only to be told that: 'His Highness is not inclined to include FitzMarshal since, having granted him the honour of knighthood, he had failed to return the complement with hostages or ransom therefrom.'

This cold refusal angered William and he went directly to Guillaume to confront him. Seeing the lad in a half-supressed rage, D Tancarville laughed. 'Oh, have one if you must,' he replied off-handedly, 'But do not forget that I held you back at Neufchâtel-en-Bray, you were disobedient and paid the price in losing one of my horses. Well, no matter.' Guillaume summoned his Steward and whispered into his ear. This made the latter smile and William found himself the master of a fractious beast whose spirit had not been broken. Amid more laughter from his fellows as they gathered at the news, William took possession of the horse which tossed its head and struck sparks from the cobbles as the young man clung to its bridle and attempted to mount.

Drawing back his clenched fist he struck the horse hard upon its nose and, in its suddenly quiescent state, led it out through the gate. That evening he entered the castle upon its back, returning it to the stables where he rubbed the animal down, all the while talking to it in a lcw voice. The incident did not go unremarked and at table that evening De Tancarville caught William's eye and silently raised his goblet in salute.

That same night he spent in the dismal chapel of Tancarville. Prior to his dubbing he had had no vigil, as the sons of Norman noblemen were wont to do, the expedience of the moment had eliminated that from the hurried ceremony prior to the defence of Neufchâtel-en-Bray. But now, driven by some imperative to seek guidance from Almighty God consistent with the principles inculcated into him by Nicholas de Sarum, he sought a spiritual strength. Full of promise, the years at Tancarville had worn him down with the constant need to keep his end up against the unholy jesting and victimisation of his fellows. That he had stood the test with little outward appearance of hurt was a measure of his inward steel; but it had not left him unaffected. The small triumph of besting a difficult horse that was clearly given to him as a further humiliation had failed to raise his spirits; rather it emphasised his isolation, forcing him to come hither and pray.

Now fully aware that he too should have left De Tancarville's service when the hint had been dropped, he went down upon his knees to seek God's purpose for him, just as Nicholas de Sarum had taught him. In truth the experience yielded him little beyond an excruciating pain in his knees and back and, in the cold light of dawn, he emerged tired and discontented. The castle was already a-stir, for the mesnie was to ride out that day for Maine and, on his way to the stables to tend his horses, he ran into the girl Anne.

'You leave today,' she said simply.

'Aye.'

'Then you must kiss me,' she laughed, drawing him off into the stable and pushing him against one of the wooden pillars as his three horses snickered their welcome and the destrier pawed his stall and rolled his eyes.

*

William rode off in the rear of De Tancarville's entourage. Twice he looked back to see Anne waving, but at the second glance she had gone, swallowed by the massive curtain wall and her duties within the bailiwick. Their encounter had been brief, intense and exciting and it left William's tired mind troubled. Part of her attraction had been a certain likeness to Angharad; a similar cast to the way she carried her head, the colour of her hair and something about the lilting way she spoke Norman-French, for she came from the far western county of Brittany. If God had not touched him, he had the weird sensation that Angharad had conjured-up Anne to restore his faith in himself and his star. In his sleepless state it seemed a natural enough thing and, as he half dozed in the saddle of his palfrey, he forgot the carnal encounter and thought of the Old Ways of his childhood-nurse. Until, that is, his new destrier, still fractious and trailing on its lead, demanded his full attention. He administered a sharp embrillade, which so jerked the animal's head that it moved forward obediently.

*

Whether it was God's good grace, Celtic magic, or the acquisition of the destrier, in the ensuing tournament William added to his reputation for prowess. Such was his quite extraordinary run of success, all of which added to the lustre of De Tancarville, that it was quietly put about that it was no longer acceptable to speak pejoratively of the young man. In a series of brilliant encounters he unseated three distinguished knights, one a courtier of the King of Scotland. In the parley which followed the discomfiture of their opponents by William's martial proficiency, he set aside the heralds' services and proved a suddenly and surprisingly canny negotiator. In this way he raised a considerable sum in ransoms, besides horses, harness and saddles.

That his companions-in-arms were now full of praise for him was only to be expected. Even Adam d'Yquebeuf was less of a thorn in his side, but they were no longer lads, William being close to his coming-of-age when it was natural enough that men would cease to torment him. Although he had not forgotten the taunting and the jibes, these were of little consequence, to be thrown aside with contempt, for he had gained a sudden maturity during the events of the last year, taking matters more-and-more into his own hands. Such an assertion of independence, crowned as it was with martial success, transformed his situation. He found the fact that Anne had, in his absence, taken-up with another less easy to bear. Indeed, he learned that she was not averse to stringing along several of the young men of the mesnie. His new triumph made her reassess her relationship with William, but she was too late.

In repudiating Anne it occurred to him that he had no need to remain in thrall to the whim of Guillaume de Tancarville either, that he might now – if belatedly – take the hint and leave the service of the Chamberlain of Normandy. Not that it would do him any good to do so peevishly, so he sought formal permission to return to his family, which De Tancarville granted with a show of equally formal reluctance.

'I trust in God that we shall see thee in Normandy again,' he had said, pleasantly enough, displaying that courteous manner that was becoming a fashionable trait, disguising inner feelings. And William had responded, bowing and going down upon one knee to kiss his master's ring. 'King Henry does not permit tourneying any longer in England,' Guillaume remarked, as though reminding William that he was venturing to the uncivilised wilds of Ultima Thule.

'I hope, my Lord, that I shall swiftly return to this country. I thank you for your kindness to me, but my neglect of my family demands I seek thy goodwill and settle my affairs in England, tourneying or no.'

In such a courtly speech William dissembled. He had little interest in continuing to add to Guillaume's achievements, nor, for that matter of attending to any family demands beyond what might be expected of him. He had set his heart upon seeking service under the device of another relative, for he had heard whispers of a campaign being prepared by King Henry against rebels in Poitou. And among those named in this connection was the Earl of Salisbury.

CHAPTER SIX: THE KNIGHT ERRANT 1168 - 1170

'William, Her Grace the Queen would speak with you.'

'My Lord?' William looked uncomprehendingly at his uncle, Earl Patrick of Salisbury, in whose train he now rode though the Poitevin countryside. Patrick jerked his head, indicating that William should answer the summons with promptness. 'You heard me. The Queen commands your presence by her side.'

William kicked his mount, broke out of the line of riders, both men and women, trotting forward, the Earl close behind him. The hawking party was in gay mood, the day having been successful and besides the Queen's courtiers and her retinue of knights, consisted of her servants and falconers, who walkcd with their circular perches slung upon their shoulders, encircled by the hooded raptors. William noted the Queen's magnificent white gyrfalcon on a perch of its own, carried by Her Grace's personal falconer. Not for Eleanor of Aquitaine any mere lady's merlin and the thought made him wonder at his summons.

On his return to England William had found his uncle at Salisbury itself. The young knight's reputation had preceded him and, and on Christmas Day, 1167, he had offered his services to Patrick. Appointed Constable of Poitou and ordered by King Henry II to cross the Channel, the Earl invited William, accompanied by the faithful Rolf, to join his mesnie. Henry had just subdued his rebellious vassals in his most troublesome possession, Aquitaine, and Earl Patrick had been attached to the Court of Queen Eleanor, consort of Henry II but Duchess of Aquitaine in her own right. His duties were military protection and the policing of her restless duchy.

Before leaving Salisbury William had made enquiries as to the state of affairs at Hamstead Marshal and learned that both Nicholas de Sarum and Angharad ap Gwyn were dead. Some sort of fit had carried off Nicholas, but poor Angharad had died of a fever, contracted no-one seemed to know how. It had taken her a week to die and she had been heard to mutter words in her native tongue that some said spoke of a man with three crowns born on his sword. Though affected by this news, piously crossing himself and remembering both in his formal prayers at Mass, the chief consequence of the deaths was that he made no attempt to visit either his mother or his elder brother, for whom he felt no attachment whatsoever.

He would have disappointed Nicholas, for he was not learned, could neither read nor write competently, but he would have delighted Angharad, for besides possessing a magnificent physique, being both immensely tough and hardy, he was by now a tall and handsome young man whose brown hair, though cropped, framed a strongly featured yet kindly face, whose brown eyes possesses a seductive power which worked on both men and women. Besides his prowess, for which he was increasingly well-known, he made up for his lack of intellectual accomplishments with a sharp wit derived from his association with King Stephen, and an easy manner among men of all ranks.

At this time he dropped the patronymic form of his name, assuming in his elder brother's lifetime, his father's title: henceforth he called himself simply William Marshal, though others still called him FitzMarshal.

Thus it was that on an afternoon in late March, 1168, William Marshal found himself in Poitou, a county of the duchy of Aquitaine and riding up alongside the great lady in whose service he, along with his uncle, now found himself.

114

'Your servant, Your Grace,' he said as she turned her coifed head towards him and he lowered his head in deep respect of her exalted rank.

'Ah, FitzMarshal, you would do me honour for I would hear you sing.'

William looked at her in astonishment. She had never spoken to him before and the directness of her regard stripped him of his usually ready tongue. Her upright carriage on her magnificent white palfrey with its harness of red and gold leather was deeply impressive, as was her face with its handsome features, the straight nose, the flare of her nostrils above her well-formed mouth and the imperious regard of her grey eyes. Despite her seniority in years over her husband, William realised how she had commanded the young and wilful Henry's heart, for all that the King was an inveterate womaniser.

The Queen's love of song and poesy was well-known and while William had felt occasionally moved by an air or a ballade, he enjoyed no pretensions at either art.

'Madam, I…I cannot sing… Not as you are wont to hear with any liking or fondness…' he responded, confused and, at heart, troubled. He did not consider himself a courtier and was in the Queen's household as a knight, not a troubadour.

'But I have heard you, sir.'

'Madam..?'

'You were grooming your palfrey below my window in Argentan. If you can sing to your horse, you can sing to your Queen.'

Utterly discomfited, William cast a desperate look about him. Earl Patrick rode close-by, caught his eye and simultaneously both grinned and nodded his command to obey the Queen without delay.

'Come sir, I have seen you in tourney and remarked upon your prowess. It is inconceivable such an accomplished gentleman cannot sing.'

In a kind of suspended agony William swallowed and stared ahead. The green and rolling Poitevin countryside was marred by the wreckage of the castle of Lusignan on its hill away to their right. Almost destroyed by King Henry a matter of months earlier it stuck up like a ragged and broken fang. In those few moments thoughts tumbled unbidden into his baffled mind. Sing? What could he sing? He could think in that awful moment of no song whatsoever. What had he sung to his horse that had so beguiled Queen Eleanor that she asked for him by name?

The Queen appeared both impatient and amused at his callow faltering. 'A courtly modesty behoves one, FitzMarshal,' Eleanor remarked sharply, 'but…' She left the implication hanging as she leaned forward to pat the neck of her mount.

William swallowed hard and stared at the road ahead where it dipped into woodland only to emerge on the far side, curving towards Lusignan itself, whither the cavalcade was bound. His distraction irritated the Queen to a growing and contemptuous anger. The man was a fool.

'FitzMarshal,' the Queen said, her tone peremptory, intimidating. 'I would have you sing, sir!'

'Madam…' he began again, desperately temporising and acutely embarrassed. Then suddenly everything changed. There was something about the wood ahead that reminded William of poor lame Gerard and he felt a visceral twisting in his guts. Although the country had been subdued by King Henry, it remained a recent and imperfect victory and they were in Lusignan country, a fiefdom notorious for the disloyalty, disobedience and independence of its barons who were now dispossessed and desperate men. William

116

was privately critical of his uncle in that Earl Patrick had not sent out an advanced guard and, beyond a brace of out-riders, had let Her Grace head the column. Now his worst fears were confirmed for he already saw what he had feared in that prescient moment: the first movement of men and horses. 'Madam! my Lord!' he exclaimed sharply, pointing, 'we are ambushed!'

He already had their attention but now he diverted it to their front where, from the woods, a column of mounted and armed men emerged at the gallop.

The Queen was first to recognise the device flying from their pennons, reining-in her horse. 'Lusignans!' she cried, 'Treachery!'

'Christ's blood!' blasphemed Earl Patrick looking back along the column from whence he hoped for help from the knights riding in casual conversation. He addressed the Queen. 'Madam to the castle! William, call up the escort! Squire, hither, my hauberk!'

William wheeled aside as the Queen dug her heel into her palfrey and, with her ladies and close householders spurred away towards the ruined keep. With a great shout and a wave of his arm, William summoned up the knights and handful of men-at-arms they had taken out on a day's pleasuring. Then William hauled his horse's head back round to confront the rapidly approaching enemy. Though wearing sword and dagger, none of the party was armed properly for combat and as Earl Patrick called for his leather hauberk, William took the initiative.

'Cover the Queen my Lord! I'll hold off these bastards!' he cried to his uncle and the minute he had been joined by five or six of the knights in whose company he had, but ten minutes earlier, been chatting, he led them off directly towards the Lusignans.

Behind him the Earl, still bereft of his hauberk, gathered up a few more and made after the Queen and her mounted courtiers, leaving the remainder of the escort to split themselves between his own close escort of Queen Eleanor or pound after William FitzMarshal.

Seeing the column divide with the conspicuous figure of their quarry on her white horse at the head of one party, the Lusignans swung to their left. The Queen was their objective, to be captured and ransomed. Veering off the rough road to the right to hit the Lusignans in their flank, William led his small detachment to the attack.

He felt a terrible elevation of spirit. The nervous reaction consequent upon discerning the ambush combined with the pure sensation of relief of not having to sing, galvanised him. This somehow lent wings to his horse and an impetuosity to his charge. Alone, ahead of his fellows, he careered downhill into the enemy. Within a few seconds of crashing into them he had bowled one unsuspecting destrier over and tumbled its rider onto the ground before rapidly unhorsing four or five others, his sword slashing left and right. A great cry went up as those behind him rode up to his support. Unbeknownst to him he had already cut off Guy de Lusignan and the fury of William's attack entirely disrupted the clumsy ambush.

Thus it was now the turn of the Lusignans to divide their forces as one group wheeled about to contain William's attack on their rear and defend their liege-lord from capture while the rest, under Geoffrey de Lusignan, rode pell-mell after Earl Patrick and the Queen. The Earl, his hauberk still across his saddle-bow had yet to catch-up with the Queen who, a superb horse-woman, rode like the wind itself.

Seeing his charge well ahead of the pursuit Earl Patrick reined in, and was in the act of struggling into his hauberk with the assistance of his squire when the Lusignans over-took him. One knight, slashing at his attentive squire so that he fell, half severed, from his horse; another, ran his lance into the Earl's back so that he died upon the instant, emitting a great roar.

'By the bones of Saint Denis, the Queen escapes!' someone shouted.

'Look to my brother! And take those hawks!' commanded Geoffrey as he spurred after the Queen, leaving his retinue in some confusion as to whom to follow. Most turned and joined the mêlée some hundred yards away where it whirled about Guy de Lusignan, William and their respective followings. Others rode off in search of easier prey to where, in a bewildered huddle, the Queen's attendants who had been on foot, including her falconers, watched with horror as the afternoon of pleasure ended in disaster.

Meanwhile William continued to lay about him with a prodigious fury. He had briefly broken out of the mêlée and seen his uncle fall, heard the terrible death cry and a deeper fury had been aroused within him. He redoubled his effort, determined to die with honour, taking as many of the treacherous Lusignans with him. One man with the Lusignan device at his side caught his raging eye and William began to cut his way towards him, emanating a tremendous energy. Infuriated by the closing of ranks about the chief of these brigands, William's sword bit bone after bone, but the reinforcement of the men sent by Geoffrey de Lusignan ended William's bold intervention.

His horse, no destrier, crumpled underneath him and he flung himself clear, striking the man at arms who had hamstrung the animal and throwing him bleeding onto the trampled grass. William now found himself surrounded and fighting for his life. On foot, unarmoured and unhelmed he backed against a large gorse-bush and stood his ground. The faithful Rolf was at his side, blood pouring from a wound in his arm and another in his head, gasping with every heft of his sword until he sank exhausted to his knees and then forward onto his face. William himself was weakening now; a slash above his own eye all but blinding him as the blood ran down his face.

'Take him alive!' a voice roared.

William staggered, drawing breath in great rasping gasps, half leaning on his sword, an animal at bay staring through one eye at the half circle of armed men about him, most now on foot, but one or two beyond on horseback, their weapons glinting dully in the fading light of late afternoon. The hiatus was menacing, inexplicable. He awaited the death blow.

Then William felt the lance-point, thrust through the gorse-bush from behind. He realised for what his ring of opponents had been waiting and of which he had been quite unaware. The lance entered his thigh and ran him through. For a long moment he stared down at the point as his blood ran cold. Then came the agony of retraction. He tottered forward before sprawling on the greensward. An instant later a dull blow to the head knocked him unconscious.

*

When he regained his wits he found dusk had fallen. The low valley was filled with mist and the smoke of bivouac fires. His head and his bruised body ached abominably, both from the blows he had sustained and the exertions he had demanded of it. Fortunately his two wounds had clotted, though they throbbed, the one in his leg with a dreadful ominousness. He had a raging thirst and was chilled to the marrow lying on the damp sod. He raised his head. There was no sign of the Queen, nor much sense of triumph in the camp, but his stirring attracted the notice of an armed knight set to watch over him.

'So, we meet again.'

It took the battered William a few moments to identify the face bent over him in the twilight. 'FitzHugh, by the Devil...' he murmured.

'By the Grace of God, FitzMarshal, the Grace of God. And by that Grace you owe me your life, for there are those who would have you dead.' FitzHugh chuckled. 'You are accounted as nothing,' FitzHugh chuckled with a rueful amusement. 'Except, of course, to me. It was I who knocked you to the ground.' He paused and clicked his tongue. 'Tch, tch, but I do not do your obligations justice, Will; that is what King Stephen called you is it not? Will? You owe me more than your life, Will, you owe me my honour and whilst others do not know your value, I shall have it from you in ransom.' FitzHugh raised his head and his voice. 'Here!' he ordered, and two of his own men-at-arms approached. 'Bind him and guard him close!'

'Aye, my Lord.'

The two began to truss William as FitzHugh walked away but William called after him. 'FitzHugh! What of the Earl Patrick?'

FitzHugh stopped and turned. He appeared to be considering what, if anything, he should tell his prisoner. 'He was your kinsman, was he not?'

'Then he is dead?'

'Aye, as you would be but for my compassion,' FitzHugh reminded him sarcastically.

'And the Queen?'

'Do not trouble yourself about Eleanor of Aquitaine; she will not be troubling herself about you.'

It seemed that FitzHugh's remark about Eleanor's indifference was as accurate as his unguarded confirmation of the Queen's escape. For several months William was trailed about in the wake of the rebels, thrown across the back of a pack-ass when the

121

outlawed force was on the march, his wounds untreated, suppurating and growing septic. Only his own physique and FitzHugh's malice kept him alive. In this desperate time William fought for his life. While the cut upon his forehead slowly mended, that in his thigh threatened his very life and caused him to fall into an intermittent fever. In his lucid moments William tore his long shirt-tails into rags and managed to plug his leg wound using half the bread he was given by way of victuals as a poultice to draw the poison from his wound.

As for FitzHugh, he believed he did God's work in prolonging his prisoner's agonies, knowing him to bear Satan's mark and zealous in his self-appointed mission. However, FitzHugh's place among the desperate and dispossessed Lusignans was by no means secure, his own following being small. However, it had proved useful to men who yielded to no yoke, nor ever kept faith with any feudal overlord. That they had attacked the Queen placed the Lusignans in a worse position than that of mere rebels, but Eleanor's escape put them utterly beyond King Henry's clemency, for their bungled ambush had yielded nothing with which to bargain.

On realising that the Queen had eluded them, Geoffrey de Lusignan had ordered the seizure of her hawks and falcons but the falconers had let the birds fly free before they could be taken so that, while they had paid for this effrontery with their lives, they had deprived the Lusignans of the only coin with which they might have engineered some compromise. As for Earl Patrick, the Lusignans had left the body of Earl Patrick on the field of battle where it was later found, taken to the Abbey of Sainte Hilaire and laid to rest. Here Queen Eleanor provided the means for annual masses to be said for Earl Patrick's soul.

William's life was saved largely by the compassion of a chatelaine within whose bailiwick the Lusignans briefly took shelter. This lady had him sent a loaf of bread from which the inside had been removed. Into this she had inserted some linen bandages and an unguent concocted from herbs.

It was here too that the Lusignans learned that King Henry had set aside his pursuit of them in favour of a campaign in Brittany where Eudes de Porhoët had heard of the King's seduction of his daughter Alice, sent into Henry's household as a hostage against her family's loyalty, after which the King's shaky alliance with King Louis fell apart and he was kept campaigning near Argentan.

Granted this stay of execution, it was only now that it occurred to the Lusignan brothers that FitzHugh's prisoner might have some value. Disappointed of any avenue of seeking a ransom for William it had long been FitzHugh's aim to hope for a slow and agonising death of gangrene. To his chagrin William had survived his lance-thrust and he slowly slipped from FitzHugh's control, gaining a degree of freedom and protection from the Lusignans who admired his prowess. One evening, seeing a group of the Lusignans playing a game of stone-throwing, William begged a turn.

Permission was sought from Guy de Lusignan who came in person to watch the contest, followed by FitzHugh.

'Well, FitzHugh, will our prisoner throw further than our own men?' he asked.

'*My* prisoner,' growled FitzHugh pointedly.

'Oh, I think not, sir,' responded De Lusignan coolly, raising his voice and calling out to his retainers to allow William a turn. Reading the hatred in FitzHugh's eyes, and fiercely eager to test himself, William rose and hobbled forward to take the proffered stone. Feeling its weight and seeking the line scored in the mud from which he must hurl the missile, he sucked in his breath as his captors drew about him. It was already dark and the light of several fires flickered upon their faces while shadows from their tense bodies seemed to dance about William as he aspirated, gathering his strength. No-one in that bivouac among the woodland of Poitou was in any doubt of William's former powers, for all had seen them, while his recovery seemed to them near miraculous. Moreover, few much liked the English knight FitzHugh in their midst. Most understood he had been banished from England favoured by no-one, and that he nursed an unseemly animus against his prisoner, though such things were not unusual. Nor was it unusual that he had attached himself to the Brothers Lusignan in their rebellion against the arbitrary rule of King Henry of England and Anjou. But this strong young man in their midst *was* a curiosity, and curiosity enough to while away an evening of stone-throwing.

And then with a roar that reminded some with a shiver of the death cry of Earl Patrick of Salisbury, William hefted the stone and a cheer of unfeigned admiration went up from the rough crowd as the stone flew three yards beyond the best effort of their own champion.

'By the balls of Belial,' swore Guy de Lusignan admiringly, turning to FitzHugh, 'happen you are right and he *is* kindred to the Devil. I have seen a man throw…but he bleeds!'

The effort had reopened William's newly healed leg-wound and it haemorrhaged profusely, blood leaching through the rough hose which he now wore.

'There my Lord Guy, God will not be mocked,' snarled FitzHugh with satisfaction.

'Help him to his palliasse!' Guy de Lusignan ordered peremptorily, ignoring FitzHugh's contemptible outburst. 'By God, sir, he is our only chance of restoring us to our lands!'

124

'You cannot treat with the King without my consent,' expostulated FitzHugh. 'By all the laws of war he *is* my prisoner…'

'You over-reach yourself FitzHugh. You seized him when fighting within our mesnie. Now come, I would have conference with my brother.'

They found Geoffrey de Lusignan in his bivouac assessing the diminishing contents of the brothers' war-chest. Sitting beside him on a branch of the tree from which the rough shelter was contrived was a large falcon. The bird was haggard, and bating frantically. It bore tattered jesses and one remaining silver bell.

'What in the name of God…?' began Guy de Lusignan as Geoffrey looked up at the intrusion.

'I think, my brother,' Geoffrey said with a slow smile, that our fortunes have turned and this,' he indicated the unhappy raptor, 'may be worth more than what little gold and silver remains to us.'

'But from whence came it?

'One of the men found her mantling her catch not an hour ago. She suffered him to approach and he, having some knowledge of the lore, caught hold of her jesses, though they are near eaten through…

'Is that not a gyrfalcon?' FitzHugh interrupted, with a frown, for all three men were thinking the same thing.

' 'Tis a rare enough variant to be the she-devil's own.'

'Would FitzMarshal know?' Guy asked suddenly, turning upon FitzHugh, his mind bright with a possibility. FitzHugh shrugged. De Lusignan scoffed. 'Bring him here!'

'And raise him from his slumbers?' FitzHugh asked with heavy sarcasm.

'Aye, before I consign thee to thine.'

FitzHugh left the two brothers. 'You think it possible that it is hers?' Guy asked Geoffrey.

'It is inconceivable that a bird of such quality escaped its master…or mistress…unaided. Who else might have had such a creature? This white variant comes, I believe from the farthest north. Our native birds are altogether of a greyer, barred plumage; this is a rare thing…'

'And 'tis a rarer that it has fallen into our hands…'

'Aye, but it has become too dependent upon its handlers to fly far…' Geoffrey de Lusignan broke off as FitzHugh thrust William forward, under what passed for a tent flap.

'Have you seen this bird before, FitzMarshal?' Guy de Lusignan asked, noting the rough bandage that had been applied over a pledget and bound so that the prisoner's bleeding had been staunched.

Geoffrey held up a lantern so that William could better observe the falcon, which bated again before recovering itself and settling, its feathers hackled and quivering.

'I do not know,' William replied, peeing at the bird. 'Perhaps…'

'Perhaps what?' said FitzHugh.

'You would wish me to say it was Queen Eleanor's, would you not?' William looked round at the three men. The reopening of his wound had left him weary. 'That I cannot say for certain, but in truth it bears a strong resemblance to the bird.'

'You may return to your rest,' said Guy de Lusignan with a peremptory nod of satisfaction. 'See to it FitzHugh,' adding with heavy sarcasm, 'after all, he is *your* prisoner.' And once the two men had left he turned to regard the falcon. 'Have we no hood?'

'Aye, I have asked the man who found her to make one by morning.'

'Good, And then we may send someone to Poitiers to offer it up to the Queen and open a negotiation for FitzMarshal.'

'Think you she will take the bait, my brother?'

126

'One or other of them, mayhap,' responded Guy. 'And let us send FitzHugh, for he is all eagerness and a devoted servant of God.' And they chuckled over God's good grace to them, crossing themselves piously.

And so it fell out that Queen Eleanor learned that her prized gyrfalcon and one William FitzMarshall both still lived. The latter fact ultimately proved FitzHugh wrong; Queen Eleanor had not forgotten the handsome face, so discomfited by her request that he should sing, nor had she forgotten that some inherent warlike instinct in the young man had saved her from the humiliation of capture by the treacherous Lusignan brothers. Under an arranged pledge and after formal redemption, William was brought to the Queen's Court at Poitiers where, out of regard for the gallantry of FitzMarshal in her defence, Queen Eleanor provided for the proper treatment of William's wound. Thanks to the skill of the Queen's physician he slowly recovered, to join the Court of his benefactress.

*

'Are you are fully recovered from your wound, Sir William?' Estranged for the first time from her husband, the Queen was holding her Christmas Court at Fontevrault and although William had followed in her train and eaten at her board, this was the first time she had summoned him personally since the affair at Lusignan.

'Aye Madam, perfectly, thanks to your favour and kindness.' William made his obeisance as the Court dined on St Stephen's Day.

'Nay, sir, I am acquitted of a debt, though I mourn your kinsman's death and pray daily for his soul.' The Queen crossed herself.

'Madam, I thank you for your kindness, I understand the monks of St Hilaire say Mass for his soul.'

Modestly Eleanor brushed this aside. 'Didst see the manner of his end?'

'But briefly, Madam, nothing but a glance amid the flurry of the mêlée.' William did not mention the bull-roar of the Earl as he received his death-wound. 'He was taken in the back whilst donning his hauberk, I was told.'

'A most treacherous act.'

'Perhaps, Madam, but 'twas war not tourney, alas…'

For some moments Eleanor regarded the young man in silence. He was indeed remarkably handsome and she sensed he possessed some qualities that might be of use to the House of Anjou. She would wait and watch. Good looking young men, she well knew, could prove fickle. In the mean time she would bind him to her.

'I shall not ask you to sing again, Sir William,' she said with a wry smile at the appearance of which he had the sense to bow his head in appreciation, 'but I should welcome your sword at my command.' She held out her hand for his kiss of loyalty.

Straightening up he replied in a low voice, unheard by the surrounding courtiers, 'As are my body and soul, Madam.'

And as he retreated from the dais his eyes boldly held the Queen's until he lowered his head again in a courtly bow.

'A remarkable young man,' Eleanor said to herself as she rested her right elbow upon the arm of her throne and raised her right hand to her shapely chin. 'To be feared or trusted.'

But then, were they not all of that likeness?

*

William stood among the vast gathering in the Abbey Church of Edward the Confessor at Westminster, bearing the banner of Aquitaine and overwhelmed by the soaring music of the choir and the splendour of the occasion. Deeply respectful of his duty to God and his obligations as a Christian, he could not help himself in the

128

contemplation of his surroundings and the change in his fortunes wrought in two years of warfare and service to Queen Eleanor and her consort, King Henry II of England. Their vast and conjoined possessions in France made Henry Curtmantle one of the most powerful princes in Europe.

William's change of luck had begun as soon as he had recovered from his wound when Queen Eleanor had rewarded the timely service he had rendered her hard by Lusignan castle. She had seen him lavishly re-horsed and re-harnessed, elevated to ride among her household knights and, while she kept her promise not to insist on his singing, often retained him close to her side when she ventured abroad, saying that he was her 'talisman'.

After the death of Earl Patrick, King Henry ordered Guillaume de Tancarville to take his place and William thus found himself reunited and closer to his distant kinsman than formerly. For his part, De Tancarville took his own credit for the sudden change in the good fortune of his former protégé. The irony was not lost on William who was not suffered to kick his heels permanently at the Queen's Court, but frequently ventured on campaign in the turbulent months of apparently ceaseless uprisings and rebellions that characterised the times.

Despite their vast powers, both Henry's and Eleanor's writ ran thin across their ancestral lands in France. Henry's greed for an ever larger Angevin empire embroiled him in Brittany, whilst Aquitaine was a notoriously large and almost ungovernable province, divided as it was into numerous counties whose subsidiary feudal lords, such as the Lusignans of Poitou, strove to cut their obligations from their suzerains. Henry might subdue a county and extract renewed oaths of fealty from his vassals, only to have rebellion break out a few months later once he was engaged elsewhere. Such endless turmoil erupted in a seemingly interminable succession, helped by neither King Louis VII, nor the brood of wilful princely sons that Henry and Eleanor had produced.

As King of France, Louis' power was very largely illusory without the obedience of his vassals, resting chiefly upon his status as an anointed King who ruled under God and the Pope. While the overlords of swathes of eastern and southern France owed direct loyalty to the French King, the actual domain of the French crown itself was smaller than his chief rival, Henry Curtmantle, consisting of the 'Île de France,' that parcel of land that encircled Paris, and territories extending south to Orleans and beyond. The chief instruments of Louis' policy were therefore sworn alliances that reinforced feudal duty or foreign treaties, combined with an intricate web of marriages.

With Henry, Duke of Anjou, Aquitaine and Normandy, being his most wilfully difficult vassal, Louis played the growing feuds between Henry and his sons with some skill. Such machinations absorbed a great deal of the gossip that preoccupied the Court of Queen Eleanor, touching as it did the movements of their patroness and thus their own fortunes.

It was early in her service that William avoided any involvement in such debates. He saw them as fruitless, beyond his comprehension in their complexity and, essentially, none of his business. What he observed in two years in the Queen's mesnie was an endless series of bad faith and broken promises by powerful men who made solemn oaths and broke them as lightly as Godfrey FitzHugh had killed the kitten. Having no claim on land of his own he felt a growing compassion for those lesser men and women whose paltry dwellings and possessions these squabbles compelled him to burn or carry off. Such a state of mind was, of course, subordinate to his military duty, and he did not shrink from hurting those constant rebels, the Lusignan brothers, by ravaging their countryside. However, it gave him little pleasure and hardened his attitude to disloyalty whilst strengthening his own sense of power residing in the proper hands. And for William the proper hands were those whom God anointed.

For this reason he felt a strange sense of destiny that day, the 14th June in the Year of Our Lord 1170, to be bearing the banner of Aquitaine in Westminster Abbey on the occasion of the crowning of the Young King Henry. This elaborate ceremony was designed by the fifteen year old youth's father to ensure the succession to the English throne. Henry II earnestly wished to avoid the chaos of the Anarchy that had torn England apart before his own succession. He therefore followed the French practice of having his successor formally crowned amid the barony of England who, one-by-one, swore fealty to Prince Henry, henceforward to be known as 'the Young King'.

At the age of five, this princeling had been married to Louis' daughter Marguerite, issue from the French King's second marriage, following the annulment of his first to Eleanor of Aquitaine. Marguerite was not present at the coronation, her own being promised upon another occasion, but the great event was the culmination of a central plan of Henry II's own policy, mirroring that of Louis VII. For a few years of his boyhood the young Prince Henry had grown up in the household of his father's then Court-favourite, Thomas Becket, and at the age of eight had been party to a gathering of the realm of England's chief barons and senior churchmen to confirm the rights and privileges of the English Crown. Named the Constitutions of Clarendon after the location of this legislation, the contentious nature of its clauses became the primary cause of the rift between Henry and Becket once that statesman had been too swiftly elevated to Archbishop of Canterbury.

131

Indeed, the Young King's coronation had been delayed by the falling-out with and exile of Becket and the death of many of the King's courtiers lost at sea in a furious March gale as they crossed from Normandy. In the event Queen Eleanor and her retinue had embarked later in the year and the present ceremony was being conducted by Roger, Archbishop of York, assisted by six bishops, all of whom lay under the Pope's most extreme sanction. To circumvent any interference from Rome or Becket over the liturgical irregularity of employing the junior archbishop, or from Paris over the absence of the Princess Marguerite, the south-coast ports had been closed after Eleanor and her Court arrived on English soil.

The echoes of the *Kyrie* faded away and William was swept-up in the utter grandeur of what he was witnessing. He had only recently set eyes upon King Henry, a man he knew to be of almost boundless energy who in his private life set little store by the forms of kingship, though he ruthlessly held his subjects to obedience. The sight of the short, russet-haired man with his thick-set physique and the leopards of Normandy emblazoned across his breast, gold-upon-red, seemed to confirm his own growing belief in his sense that an ordered realm depended upon duty and obligation: King Henry was every inch a monarch.

Nor had William's many months in Queen Eleanor's service done anything other than to add to this, for despite her being eleven years her husband's senior, there was an ageless elegance in her and every aspect of her was regal when compared with every other woman William had ever known. This compelling nature of Eleanor's demeanour made of her Court a glittering scene of accomplishment, both martially and intellectually, and although William had little time for the latter, he acknowledged the

132

cleverness of those who gilded his great Lady's itinerant household.

But if King Henry led a peripatetic life devoid of ostentation and his estranged wife was held throughout Europe to be the arbiter of taste and the emerging fashion for chivalry, it was the panoply of the Church that most bore down upon William that warm June day. He was beguiled by the soaring tracery of the Abbey Church, not yet finished in its building, but magnificent nonetheless, bright with banners, pennons, heraldic devices and glittering with ducal circlets and the jewels bedecking the principal ladies of the realm. At the altar the Archbishop and his attendant bishops and priests, gorgeously coped and mitred according to rank and precedence, their vestments reflecting the flickering candles, outshone all the temporal attendees but one: the young man at the centre of the Holy rite.

Henry, the Young King, surpassed both his parents and – or so it seemed to William in that revelatory moment – the great Princes of the Church of Christ. Tall, his head with its red-gold hair set upon a long and elegant neck, Henry's skin was lightly freckled and he regarded the world with eyes of a striking and commanding blue. Transported by these splendours and touched to his soul by the significance of the sacraments of anointing and coronation, William was deeply moved as Roger of York raised the Young King and presented him to the Lords and Commons, joining with all his heart in the common oath of allegiance and fealty that followed the individual submission and kissing of hands of the great barons of England.

And while the day would remain long in his memory for the numinous moment of monarchy that it enshrined, it would grow in importance as its significance as a further turning point in his own life became clear.

*

That evening, as the Court feasted in Westminster Hall, William found himself among a group of knights and their ladies who discussed the day's events, their tongues loosened by wine. A knight known to William only as FitzHubert leaned over to him amid the hubbub and remarked with a tired smile:

'You are silent, FitzMarshal. Have the day's events stopped your tongue or merely given you pause for reflection?'

'Pause, I think for wonder,' William responded.

'Aye, 'twas a noble sight to be sure, but I wish I saw in it some peaceful outcome.'

'You don't?' quizzed William, mildly surprised at FitzHubert's candour and noting the man's Welsh accent. He recalled Angharad ap Gwyn who had the second sight and wondered if this ageing chevalier possessed a like gift.

FitzHubert shook his head. 'You were not at Montmirail, I think, eh?'

'No, I was on campaign in the Limousin.'

'Ah, yes.' FitzHubert put his goblet down on the board and turned to fully face William on the bench. 'Well as you know the conference with King Louis settled this Young King of ours in the succession of the dukedom of Normandy and the county of Anjou, besides that of this our kingdom of England.' FitzHubert made a small, slightly dismissive gesture with his hands then struck off remaining sons of Henry and Eleanor on his fingers one-by-one. 'He settled Aquitaine upon the Lord Richard after the Queen's death and to the Lord Geoffrey he gave over Brittany, securing these arrangements with Louis Capet on the assurance of true fealty and the promise of betrothal of the Lord Richard with the Lady Alice…'

'She that is daughter to King Louis?'

'Just so.'

'And what of John, the boy? Is he not destined for Holy Church?' William remarked with an effort of memory in an attempt to appear interested in the old man's discourse and those ramifications he seemed to divine in the day's doings.

FitzHubert nodded. 'He is an oblate, yes, but they call him Lackland since his father makes no provision for him…' William looked at FitzHubert sharply, wondering if this white-haired and elderly man knew anything about himself. 'It is not a happy situation, to be perceived as cast-off, methinks.'

William looked again at his interlocutor. 'You know me sir… Wait!' he commanded as FitzHubert smiled again and was about to speak. 'You were among those about King Stephen at Newbury camp. It was you who took me from King Stephen after he had ordered me lifted from the trebuchet!'

The older man nodded. 'It was,' FitzHubert nodded and smiled, pleased that he had been so remembered, 'and I marked you then as I have watched you since. Take heed of what I say for I have no sons of my own and but one daughter, so the fruit of my observations cannot avail anyone but you. The young lions and leopards constantly bite the hand that feeds them. They will bring the old lion to his knees, along with the offspring from Louis' loins, hard though that may be to imagine of that lack-lustre King, nor will they keep any kind of peace among themselves. Cleave to the Lady Eleanor as long as you are able, for there shines a star not merely of splendour but of a rare constancy and take care to do no-one dishonour, for all this…' FitzHubert made an encompassing gesture round about them, 'is but a sham, hiding great ambition.'

'Is ambition not to be expected of so mighty a prince as King Henry?'

135

'Alas, yes, and 'twould be unremarkable were it to run with good sense, but…' FitzHubert leaned forward and lowered his voice, 'it runs instead with ungovernable temper.'

'I had heard as much,' William responded quietly, embarrassed at the turn the conversation was taking.

'Good. Then you will beware the King in a rage. As for his young help-meet I sense trouble.'

'How so?'

'Because our Young King will be irked; his younger brothers Richard and Geoffrey will have work to do, Richard in particular, for he was ever his mother's favourite, while her first-born will trail in his father's wake waiting for death to make a real monarch of him and,' FitzHubert turned and looked at the high table on its dais, 'by the look of our Sovereign Lord, Henry by the Grace of God the second of that name to reign over England, he is likely to keep the Young King in expectation for some years yet.'

William's eyes had followed FitzHubert's. The King was serving his son a boar's head and although the noise in the hall grew less at this royal gesture, William and FitzHubert were too far away to hear what was said. They saw Archbishop Roger make a comment and the Young King respond. King Henry looked for a moment nonplussed, then angry and finally turned his grimace into public laughter. It was only later William learned of the Young King's impudence, impertinence that seemed to confirm the prescience of FitzHubert's remarks, though some said it was a mark of the younger man's charm and quick-wittedness. At the time William saw only that Queen Eleanor was looking directly at himself and a wave of guilty apprehension swept over him at listening to FitzHubert's tittle-tattle as the old knight's head, full of wine, nodded forward over the wreckage of his meal. Embarrassed,

William turned to his table companion on his other side, Robert de Salignac.

De Salignac had witnessed the little scene at the high table. 'Despite today's events,' he remarked drily, 'they do not get on, this father and his son'.

'No better than did I with mine,' William confessed, the wine making him bibulous.

'What a pity,' De Salignac said with his ready smile.

By the following morning the effrontery of the Young King to his father was common knowledge, eagerly seized upon by the gossips of the Court. The Archbishop had remarked it unusual that a King should wait at table, but the Young King had demurred. 'But it can be no condescension,' he had flashed back, 'he is the son of a Count, sir, whereas I am that of a King!'

*

Two weeks later the Queen's Court had moved to Windsor and Eleanor rode out to hawk along the banks of the River of Thames. William rode in her train, his newly acquired peregrine upon his gauntlet. He had no great love of the sport but the falcon had been among the gifts Queen Eleanor had bestowed upon him in the wake of his return to her household after the affair at Lusignan, in compliment to the fact that the Queen's own raptor had played a part in the matter.

As for Eleanor's white gyrfalcon, it had become intractable after its period of liberty and had been replaced by a bird of similar magnificence though darker plumage. As was her habit, when several birds were started up from cover, Eleanor loosed her falcon in competition with one or other of her lords or ladies and while her own raptor usually brought down its quarry first, she was always courteous when another's achieved the quicker successful stoop.

137

That afternoon, after a day of good sport, the little cavalcade was returning to the keep, she called William to her side.

'I hope you entertain no apprehensions as to the lie of the land ahead, Sir William,' she said in an ironic tone.

'None, Your Grace,' answered William with a smile.

'I did not match my falcon against your today, and for that I am sorry.'

'Why 'tis no matter, Madam,' William replied quickly. 'I had satisfaction of Ranulf FitzStephen's…'

'Not such as I hope put him much out of countenance.'

'He admitted it good sport. His tiercel stooped at a heron which it missed and took a handsome mallard…'

'Whereas your own…?'

'Took the heron's mate, Madam.'

'Bravo, sir,' said the Queen, laughing.

But William sensed that this pleasant exchange was not the matter in hand and he was not long in being proved right.

'On the night of the coronation banquet I observed you in conversation with FitzHubert of Guent.' Eleanor rode with her eyes ahead, not deigning to turn towards William.

'Aye, Madam.' William was instantly on his guard. Had his act of listening to the old knight been indiscreet? It behove him to tread warily.

'He is much given to offering good advice,' the Queen remarked matter-of-factly.

'Indeed, Madam, he was as full of advice as he was of wine,' William said light-heartedly.

'And what advice did he offer you? I'll warrant it had little to do with matters concerning horse or hound.' The question was direct, a shrewd riposte ignoring William's parry.

'That I should cleave to Your Grace's service…'

'That is all?'

'That was the substance of the matter, Madam.' William had no expectation of being rescued a second time by a timely intervention of fate and had no desire to lose the good opinion of the Queen. 'True, he took a time about it…'

'Mine and none other?' Eleanor interrupted.

'To serve you in whatever capacity, Your Grace, and howsoever you should direct me.'

Turning towards him the Queen caught the anxiety in the young man's eyes. She beguiled him with the charm of the smile that set alight the poetic fire in some of her hangers-on. 'Well said, William FitzMarshal.' She paused a moment and then went on: 'You have no lands of your own, I understand.'

William could only wonder how she knew and answered, 'No, Madam, none.'

'A knight errant to be sure,' she said laughing. 'Well, well… The King would have conference with you tomorrow before he departs for Normandy. He will ask you to join the mesnie of our son. It is my wish that you obey my Lord the King. FitzStephen will conduct you.'

And then she kicked her horse into a canter; the matter was closed and William's future was sealed - for better or for worse.

CHAPTER SEVEN: A KING'S MENTOR 1170 – 1173

Ranulf FitzStephen beckoned William forward to where King Henry sat at a table strewn with papers, a clerk at one end writing something recently dictated by His Grace. After a moment Henry looked up.

'This is the man, Sire.'

William found himself subject to a scrutiny that seemed almost painful, expecting his legs to be felt as Henry might have done a prospective charger. He lowered his eyes respectfully until the King commanded: 'Look at me FitzMarshal.'

William recalled the long evenings with Stephen playing at 'knights' and found no comfort in the memory. This man was a king of an altogether different stamp. He could not imagine Henry a-dithering over anything.

'Does he know what I require of him?' Henry asked FitzStephen, as if William had no tongue of his own.

'No, Sire.'

'Then tell him,' the King said peremptorily, looking again at the papers before him, adding without looking up: 'Now.'

'My Lord the King commands that you serve the Young King Henry as his military tutor, that he so far regards your prowess as qualifying you for this honour as to bestow both trust and…'

'Yes, yes,' broke in the King sharply, 'that is enough.' Then he looked up again, directly at William. 'I would have you take great care of your charge, Sir William,' he said in an altogether calmer tone of voice. 'Do you understand?'

William did not fully understand, for the King's words seemed loaded with responsibilities beyond his means, but it behove him not to cavil. Queen Eleanor had, in a manner of speaking, warned him of something of the sort.

'You will be provided with all the means necessary,' the King added with a smile of winning charm before resuming the conning of his correspondence.

'My Lord King does me great honour,' William said, making his bow and withdrawing with FitzStephen.

Outside the chamber FitzStephen turned to him and held out his hand. 'We are to be fellows, FitzMarshal, for I too am to be of the Young King's household. You came under the good name given you by the Lady Eleanor, but the King took a liking to you, 'tis not a thing lightly to be thrown away.' The note of caution in FitzStephen's tone was clear.

'I have no intention of so doing, sir,' William responded.

'Come then, I shall take you to your sacred charge but I should warn you, your new Master is every inch a King in his own right.'

'I understand, sir, and shall look to my own comportment.'

FitzStephen chuckled as he led out of the Conqueror's White Tower and into the adjacent tiltyard where a dozen knights were at their exercise. William instantly recognised the figure of Henry, the Young King, on horseback, as were several of his companions, taking their turns at the quintain. FitzStephen waited until the young man had finished his mounted exercise and stepping forward made his bow. William followed suit as the Young King threw a leg over his horse's neck and slid to the ground.

'Sir William,' he said, holding out his ringed finger for William's kiss, 'so you join my mesnie. You are most welcome. You reputation for prowess precedes you. I shall, I hope, benefit from your skill. What think you of my tilting?'

It was a direct question and William considered it demanded a direct answer. The Young King was, at fifteen, eight years his junior and William had it not in him to act the sycophant.

' 'Twas good enough, Your Grace, in that you were not struck by the weight; but if you were any other I should answer indifferently.'

There was a sudden silence among the young men who had gathered round and all watched the Young King to see how he reacted.

'Would you now,' Henry replied, his tone affronted, 'how so, sirrah?'

'You did not see how close the weight came to the back of your head, my Lord, assuming that you had succeeded from not feeling it strike you. You took the quintain for what it was, a machine, swinging at a rate you have often seen and therefore knew. Had it been a man, he might have accelerated the counter-swing of his blade. In fact my Lord, in your desire to strike the target with your lance-point, you checked your horse…' William broke off and shrugged, affecting indifference, then went on: 'In the tourney or on the field of battle, that might well prove fatal, my Lord. 'Tis a matter worth your consideration.'

Henry said nothing, though his face flushed and he looked down, his fists clenched, as though governing his temper. For a moment William thought he might be struck but, without looking up, Henry beckoned and one of his knights William later learned was Hugh de Gundeville came forward and bent to Henry's mouth. 'Two swords, Hugh…' William heard and watched as De Gundeville walked to where a brace of squires held blunt practice weapons ready. Taking two, he placed one in Henry's hands, the other in William's. The Young King straightened up, saying casually, 'shall we, Sir William?'

142

'*À outrance*, Your Grace?' William responded coolly as the knights moved back and formed a rough circle.

'*À outrance*...' replied Henry placing himself in a posture of defence.

William planted his legs wide and sank slightly upon them, his blade low, the blunt *pointe* touching the gravel of the yard. 'When you are ready, my Lord King. It would not be seemly for me to make the first move.'

Henry said nothing but swivelled forward, his sword, held with both hands, across his breast. He was breathing as someone had taught him, to strike on the exhalation, and William filled his own lungs with a slow indraught, measuring the ground between them.

He caught the thought of it before Henry made his move and, even as Henry swung, William leaned backwards in an arc, avoiding the swipe of Henry's blade and raising his own. Then, with a roar of effort, he twisted his muscular torso with a speed that caught the Young King napping. Before Henry could recover himself, the flat of William's sword smacked into his half-turned back, knocking him forward so that he lost his balance.

Henry staggered sideways, almost toppling over as William followed, raising his blade again. Recovering his balance, Henry boldly swung back in an attempt to catch William in flank, drawing in his breath to do so. But William was ready for him; having checked his own swing after hitting the Young King, he parried Henry's blade with a shock that rang across the yard but pressed his opponent with all the weight and impetus of his body. Henry was forced backwards, tottered for a moment and, as William, maintaining pressure, shuffled forward, fell backwards. The sight shocked those watching.

William dropped his own sword and stepped forward, offering Henry his hand and heaving him back on his feet. He was hardly out of breath while the Young King stood for a moment, astonished at his discomfiture, panting, the sweat pouring down his handsome face.

'You have somewhat to learn, my Lord King,' William said quietly, 'if you would prove a true adept yourself.'

Henry gasped for breath, staring at his opponent. William FitzMarshal was, Henry noted, besides being older, both taller and broader than himself. He was sensible enough to realise that whatever his house knights thought of the affair, it was no dishonour to lose in practice to such a man. He blew out his cheeks and stared about him.

'Well, my Lords and gentlemen…' he said at last. 'We have our match. It seems that we would do well to heed what FitzMarshal tells us or, by the Blood of Christ, we shall never beat him!' Turning to William he added with a smile: 'welcome to my mesnie, Sir William. Henceforth you shall be my Marshal.' This good natured response released the tension and Henry waved to the squires to stable the horse. 'Come,' he said, turning to William, 'you shall dine with me that we become better acquainted.'

For William, the dispossessed second son, the accolade that the Young King had laid upon him threw aside the shadow of his dead father. Henceforth he was generally known as William the Marshal in his own right and the only shadow on this new appointment was to find Adam d'Yquebeuf already in the Young King's mesnie.

In the following weeks Henry insisted on an intense period of exercise, proving a quick and eager learner, finessing his raw swordsmanship. Unlike all those with whom he had been previously matched, William conceded no quarter, nor submitted to the Young King's rank when in the tiltyard. '*Á outrance…*' became a jest between them as they measured swords or lances, but William was careful not to let this camaraderie spill over into any

144

presumptuous intimacy elsewhere. William became a stickler for the observation of protocols such that the other knights laughed as those had done by his exceptional conduct whilst at Tancarville, and William suspected a continuing hostility on the part of D'Yquebeuf. Such behaviour no longer troubled William; his time in the Court of the Queen had further taught him the wisdom of keeping his own counsel. He gradually became a man to be respected, if not yet feared, his prowess at arms remarkable and, as far as the Young King was concerned, to be kept as a great asset in Henry's mesnie.

Amid all this William considered FitzHubert's prophecy proved accurate: the Young King did indeed have little to do beyond his military exercises. For the moment this seemed not to trouble him for the admission into his household of a man of William Marshal's prowess diverted the young man's energies to an increasing desire to tourney. His revenues were meagre and he privately nursed an ambition to shine amid the noble game practised by the Franco-Norman knights across the Channel. For the time being, even as his younger brothers made names for themselves on campaign, he was confined to England by his father's orders.

For William these were months of both honing not only the Young King's skills, but those of his household knights. Henry's constant references to tourneying and the very obvious necessity of preparing the man destined to rule over the Angevin Empire drove William to seek ways of extending his charge's wider experience. When Henry suggested a hawking expedition, William agreed, but refused to take his falcon. When asked why, informed the Young King that he would presently reveal the reason. Such was the growing respect and even affection of Henry for the newcomer, that he took no umbrage. Upon reaching open country north of

London Henry and his entourage sought some sport but the instant Henry had loosed his bird, William drew him aside.

'You could have been ambushed here, Your Grace,' he said halting his horse alongside that of the Young King's. 'See how the woodland crowds the track as it comes down from Hampstead Hill yonder. Mark this as a lesson, no knight intent upon profit from the tournament, nor any King embattled, should misread the lie of the land. 'Tis as much a part of mock-war, or war itself, that you should see this and understand it.'

Henry looked at him with a dawning comprehension. 'As my falcon does?'

'As best you can, my Lord, as best you can.'

'But you well know we cannot prosecute the tourney here; my father has proscribed it in England and I am left here whilst he is in Normandy settling affairs with King Louis and Becket.'

'All the more reason to use such ventures as today's to learn the craft.'

Henry reached across and patted William's. 'You are a wise man, my Lord Marshal.' Henry grinned at William who smiled back.

'And now your falcon, my Lord King. See, she has not wasted the day...' William pointed upwards.

Henry looked up and watched with pleasure as his peregrine came stooping out of the grey sky like a thunderbolt, its wings half-closed. It struck the wood-pigeon in an explosion of down and feathers. With a shout of exaltation Henry set spurs to his gelding as the broken body of the bird, wings awry, fell to earth and the falcon, still plummeting in the stoop, dipped beneath, jigged, rolled on its back and caught it in a flash of yellow legs and steely talons.

*

'The news of the King is not good,' announced Ranulf FitzStephen, coming in from the outer bailey where the squires were clearing up after the morning's exercise. They had all seen the messenger ride into the Tower bailey, his horse in a lather and word quickly spread that he had come directly from Southampton. 'His Grace is brought to bed of a raging fever at Domfront...'

Later the senior knights of the Young King's mesnie learned more. Having made his peace both with King Louis and Archbishop Becket, King Henry was not expected to live. He had signed his will, confirming the succession provisions of Montmirail, and the priests now gathered about him, interceding for his soul. The loss of his physician Roger de Beaumont in the March gale in the Channel earlier that year was now widely held to be evidence of God's disapproval of King Henry's adulteries, his setting aside of Queen Eleanor in favour of Rosamund de Clifford, his disobedience to Pope Alexander and Archbishop Becket, and his bad faith with his sovercign overlord, Louis VII of France. It was, men whispered, the moment when God wrought his divine vengeance even upon a mighty Prince such as Henry, King of England and Lord of Normandy Aquitaine and Anjou.

This was confirmed when, at the beginning of September, it was learned from the master of a merchantman lately arrived from Havre de Grâce that King Henry II was dead. The Young King ordered a Mass to be sung for his father's soul and waited impatiently for the formal messengers to arrive, bearing the King's seal. He dare not move prematurely, though he feared the intervention of brother Richard in particular, and gave up his daily exercises as he considered himself no longer the 'Young' King but the actual monarch, Lord of the Angevin lands extending from the border with Scotland in the north, to that with Navarre and the Pyrenees in the south.

147

For several weeks, as the Channel was wracked by the Equinoctial gales of autumn, matters remained in a state of suspense. Once again William recalled the words of Fitzhubert of Guent. The old man's prophecies looked awry: Henry would come into his inheritance sooner that FitzHubert had suspected. But when, towards the end of September, the bad weather subsided and intelligence arrived from Domfront, it created mixed feelings.

King Henry II lived: shaken by his experience, he was on his way to Rocamadour, deep in southern Aquitaine on the border between the Limousin and the French county of Quercy, to prostrate himself before the Black Virgin in gratitude for his deliverance. The Young King ordered church bells to be rung and Masses said and Te Deums sung, privately grinding his teeth that he remained as far from ruling as before the crisis. FitzHubert's remarks now took on a different hue, William mused, as Henry went into a sulk, praising God one moment and cursing his ill fortune the next.

In private William, now high among his counsellors, cautioned patience and gratitude.

'The Lord King bears many burdens, Sire,' he said to the younger man. 'Do not wish yourself in his place before you have mastered the arts of war and policy.'

As always when he made some such statement, the Young Henry regarded William with an immature irritation before deflating. Somehow William's trustworthiness seemed the only rock to which he could cling in his uncertainty. Besides, Ranulf FitzStephen, Hugh de Gundeville and his confessor echoed his military mentor, adding that news had also arrived that Thomas Becket, the exiled Archbishop, was returning to the See of Canterbury.

'Little good will come of it,' FitzStephen pointed out, 'and Your Grace may have your hands full here in England…'

148

'Such matters may test your mettle, Sire,' De Gundeville added, 'for which we must be prepared.'

*

And little good did come of Becket's return. Converted from devoted servant and close advisor of King Henry II, to faithful servant of Almighty God by his elevation to his Archbishopric, Becket repudiated the Constitutions of Clarendon, took issue with the prelates that had officiated at the Young King's coronation and set himself against the Old King's will. At his Christmas Court in Normandy, the latter's injudicious and off-handed aside regarding his desire for someone to release him from so troublesome a priest was taken literally by four knights. Having crossed the Channel they confronted Becket in his cathedral at Canterbury at Vespers five days after Christmas 1170, demanding he lift the orders of excommunication. Becket piously refused, pleading he served God above all others, infuriating Reginald FitzUrse who was the first to strike at him before the altar. Defended by only one of his monks, Edward Grim, who received a severe wound for his pains, Becket was otherwise deserted. As Becket fell, the top of his skull struck off by FitzUrse's blow, Richard de Briton, William de Tracy and Hugh de Morville struck at the prostrate man in an orgy of bloodshed that left the Archbishop dead in his own gore.

The act outraged Europe, reducing Henry II's prestige at the first sword-stroke. Becket became an instant martyr and led to him being asked to intercede with God by the faithful, making him almost instantly a saint in the popular imagination. When, soon afterwards, miracles were attributed to him, Holy Church followed and canonised him. Mortified, taking to sack-cloth and falling into a profound depression, Henry confined himself, seeking expiation. For six long weeks he remained thus, shut away from the world, and when he did emerge he cried out for God to be his witness that he had not sought the death of a man who had once been his intimate friend and counsellor. He sent emissaries to Pope Alexander and although the Pontiff kept him on tenterhooks, in the end he accepted Henry's contrition and excommunicated only the four knights guilty of the bloody crime.

But the Old King made no attempt to eject the four murderers from their fastness within Knaresborough Castle in Yorkshire and, evoking the authority of the previous Pope, Adrian IV, ordered his war host to Ireland to conquer the island for Christ, closing the ports in his rear in case Alexander III changed his mind.

By his absence in Ireland, Henry temporarily conceded powers to the Young King to rule England in his stead, to Geoffrey and the fifteen year old Richard to hold sway in his ancestral lands in France, and to Eleanor in her own domain. But with rumours of miraculous cures emanating from the shrine raised over the tomb of Becket, all of which would lead to the dead Archbishop's rapid canonisation, the Old King strove to show an absolute humility from his Court at Dublin. This eased the tensions across Europe and it was clear that Henry's diplomacy was aimed at a return to Normandy as soon as the storm arising from Becket's martyrdom subsided.

Accordingly the Young Henry, enjoying the profligate pleasures of his illusory kingship, maintained himself and his Court in an increasingly lavish manner. Privately he resolved that when displaced by the inevitable return of his father, he would set himself the seductive task of becoming a champion at the tournament. If his father would snatch back the authority he had been obliged to grant his heir, such a policy would win him prestige and wealth, and set him in a fair way to out-shining his father and over-awing his ambitious younger brothers.

These events further transformed William's status for, while he remained a close companion-at-arms as the Young Henry continued his military exercises, these grew in scope and scale. Under his delegated powers and with his eye upon his future ambitions, the Young King now gathered about him as the closest members of his *mesnie privée*, a number of distinguished knights. Besides William Marshal and Adam d'Yquebeuf, from Tancarville, and FitzStephen and De Gundeville, these included Simon de Marisco, Gerard Talbot, Robert de Tresgoz, Hasculf St Hilaire, Judhael de Mayenne, Jean de Préaux, and Robert de Salignac. He was joined too by Robert, Count of Meulan, a great Norman vassal and cousin to King Louis, and Baldwin de Béthune who was destined to become Count of Aumale, along with literate scholars and clerks such as Robert, Advocate of Arras, Henry Norris, Richard Barre, the Young King's Chancellor and the Keeper of his Seal, and William Blund, his Steward.

All were ambitious men, eager for the favours expected of a feudal overlord and rumours of those among them inclined to plot and intrigue, encouraging the Young King to assume powers that his father was reluctant to delegate, eventually and inevitably reached the Old King's ear. To the Young King's fury, he had Hasculf St Hilaire dismissed, insisting upon an absolute loyalty from the Young Henry, simultaneously recovering powers from his other sons as he came out of his self-imposed isolation in Ireland.

'God's blood!' the Young Henry bawled, flying into a fury at his father's interference in his affairs when told to send Hasculf and others among his own knights away. 'Would he seek to keep a young hawk hungry?' he raged, pacing up and down his chamber and kicking over a chair that he had lately sat upon. Spittle flew from his lips and his face was empurpled. 'Would he snatch its meat to compel its obedience?' Those present drew back as Henry thrust these unanswerable questions in their faces.

'Calm yourself, my Lord,' said William sternly so that the Young King turned on him.

'Do not you brook me, Marshal,' Henry snarled, though it was clear that William's intervention had made him aware of the figure he was cutting. Nevertheless, he remained stationary before William, his eyes glaring. 'He forgets it might turn upon him for his pains.'

William stood his ground and a heavy silence fell so that all could hear the Young King's heavy breathing. For a long moment nobody moved and then, with one last savage kick at the upset chair, Henry withdrew and in the hiatus his courtiers turned away, avoiding each other's eyes. All except William, who exchanged glances with Robert de Salignac, both recalling the grand insolence of the Young King towards his father on the evening of his coronation. Slowly the chamber emptied and after Robert had ordered the attendant clerks out, the two men were left alone.

'Matters do not augur well, my Lord Marshal,' Robert remarked with that courtesy he afforded William out of a deep respect for the younger man's abilities.

'No, my Lord,' William replied, 'but can we expect better?'

'You are not used to intrigue, William,' Robert said with a wry smile, as though stating a fact.

'I always hope to avoid it.'

Robert blew out his cheeks with a hollow laugh. 'Would that one could. But I fear such intemperance can lead to only one conclusion.'

'Open rebellion…?' William hazarded.

'It is more than likely, I fear.'

'That will not play well.'

'I fear not.'

William looked at the older man. He was perhaps two or three summers his senior. 'My Lord,' he asked directly, 'was it not you who was behind the removal of Hasculf St Hilaire?'

'Me?' De Salignac's astonishment was unfeigned. 'Upon my oath, no!' he retorted, 'though I mislike the man and deplored St Hilaire's influence well enough.'

'Then where lies your own fealty?'

De Salignac might have taken affront but he coolly returned William's gaze, 'I have no love for Henry of Anjou,' he said, referring to the Old King, 'and he hath no love for me, for my father was suspected of treason and I doubt his death was the accident all present claimed it was. I am, like you, the Queen's man and, like you charged with our young Lord's welfare.'

'Then you are no agent of King Louis?'

'Your persistence would do you no favours elsewhere, sir,' De Salignac said, a hint of steel in his tone.

'I know,' William responded, 'but my bluntness arises from my own experience. I do you the honour of believing your word, should you confide in me.'

'Then you may take it that I am the Young Henry's man and not Louis'.'

'God's praise for that. At the Coronation feast in Westminster I took you for a man of French loyalties.

'Then you took me ill, FitzMarshal, and I am sorry for it. I thought you my friend.'

'Forgive me, Sir, I am perhaps a little too cautious.'

De Salignac smiled disarmingly. 'I understand, FitzMarshal, and caution is no bad thing. As for forgiveness, there is nothing to forgive.'

William smiled with relief.

*

On 27 August the Young King was united properly for the first time with Marguerite of France. Alongside his wife, he was crowned and anointed for a second time in Winchester Cathedral, the Bishop of Evreux travelling from Normandy to officiate, the See of Canterbury remaining vacant after Becket's martyrdom. Archbishop Roger of York and the Bishops of London and Salisbury had all been forbidden to attend. To William's eyes the ceremony lacked some of the splendour of Henry's first coronation but, he thought ruefully, much had changed since then. He was less of an ingénue and the gloss of the occasion was diminished by the emerging character of the chief participant, and the absence of his father.

Perhaps too, it was the person of the Queen that altered his perception, for Marguerite was lissom and composed, bore herself with the grace expected of the daughter of a regal house but seemed to William unsuited to a union with the Henry he now knew better than ever. He felt a pity for her, for she seemed to be no Eleanor.

The ceremony at Winchester had been at the insistence of King Louis and it was to Paris that the Young King, his newly crowned Queen, and his Court travelled next. For all his intemperate rages, Henry of Anjou was every inch a King compared with Louis VII of France. Though tall and not ill-favoured, if one set aside his prominent nose, Louis' long yellow hair had a lank and listless quality and he carried with him the mark of the cloister for which he had been intended had his older brother not been killed by falling from his horse. Notwithstanding this, the French King was courteous and capable of displaying considerable charm, but there was, withal, an almost infantile simplicity that he brought from his early years of devotion and this sat uneasily upon the shoulders of a King. Or so it seemed to William.

154

However, there was a vein of deep cunning in Louis and he had invited his daughter and son-in-law to visit him that November in pursuit of a devious policy ultimately aimed at increasing the bounds of the domain of the French crown and the dismembering of King Henry's. Thanks to Robert de Salignac, who had it from both Ranulf FitzStephen and Adam d'Yquebeuf, William soon learned that their host was lending a sympathetic ear to the Young King's petulant complaints about his increasing frustration, of his sense of being held impotent within a golden cage and his growing hatred of his father, not least for his interference in the removal of Hasculf St Hilaire.

'This is a most unsatisfactory situation, William,' deplored De Salignac confidentially. 'We cannot let this work upon our Lord King. Between ourselves Lord Richard, having the Queen for a friend, is likely to throw over his oaths of fealty and, should he do so, his jealous sibling will follow suit of only for fear of losing much to his brother. Such turmoil can only lead to rebellion...'

'I see your meaning if not your purpose, Robert,' agreed William anxiously, the spectre of open warfare with the Old King looming like a dark cloud.

'What might we do?'

William looked at De Salignac. 'Why ask me? I am only...'

'This is no time for modesty, William. You know you alone might persuade the Young King to temper his discourse. You have his heart more than I, who have only his ear and he is surrounded by hotheads like De Marisco, D'Yquebeuf and the others.'

'If it is as you say it is, then are we not too late?' William asked, his brow furrowing.

'If we are, we are compromised, you and I...'

'How then do we draw the poison? Might we not carry a message to the Old King? Your confidential clerk, is he man enough to ride a horse into Normandy?'

'Your man Norris would be the better…'

William considered the proposition a moment. 'He would be willing to ingratiate himself, to be sure, though I uncertain of his discretion…'

'What would you have such a letter say?'

'That it would be seemly for His Grace to spend Christmas with his own father rather than tarry longer in the Court of his father-in-law.'

It was De Salignac's turn to ponder and then he nodded. 'Would you agree that the letter should come from us both? It would make our own joint position clear.'

William felt uneasy about Norris and quickly changed his mind. 'Let us send Norris with a verbal message…'

'Easier to repudiate…'

'Aye, and have it passed him by your confessor, an act to find a place in both our hearts…'

Robert de Salignac smiled warmly. 'You learn to dissemble, William.'

'I thought it diplomacy, Robert, and learned much of it from yourself.' The two men chuckled, their eyes meeting.

'But I could not go with you.'

'Which would be to your benefit,' William said then, taking advantage of the accord between them and airing a matter that was increasingly preoccupying him. 'There is one other matter. Know you anything of this new-comer, Bertran de Born?'

'The troubadour? Only that he is madman of violent passions who writes poetry and enjoys slaughter. They say he dispossessed his elder brother of his lands in the Dordogne.'

156

'He has too quickly gained the ear of the Young King, I fear, through my Lady the Queen.'

'You would have a watch kept upon him?'

'Aye, Robert, if it pleases you to do so.'

Although by the end of November the Court of the Young King had been duly summoned to join King Henry at Chinon on the River Vienne in western Touraine, the Young King had no intention of obeying and told William so.

'Do not counsel me otherwise, Marshal, I will not go.'

'Sire, I would never advise you to act against your interests, but do you not see that you are falling victim to the policy of King Louis, who would exploit the estrangement between yourself and your father?'

'Since when did you have an opinion upon matters of policy?' the Young King asked sarcastically.

'Since Your Grace made it a necessity. By your own conduct you have been indiscreet and if Louis suborns you it will be for his own purposes…'

'What do *you* know of King Louis' purposes?' Henry flared. 'You forget yourself, Marshal…'

'Is that not why Bertran de Born is in My Lady the Queen's retinue? Surely,' William went on knowing that the only way to choke off the rage rising with the Young King's complexion was to persist with his argument, 'surely Your Grace can see that you will not lose your Kingdom by your father's malice, but you would certainly do so by Louis'. Come, Sire, if you would not join your father, to mark your independence you need only leave Paris and pass into Normandy where you would be less of a hostage to fortune.'

The compromise cooled the Young King and he fell into a musing, turning the idea over.

'Is that what I am, a hostage to fortune?'

'That is what you may become,' replied William, greatly relieved that he had mollified his master.

That evening at board the Young King drank a good deal of wine and, towards the end of the meal raised his glass and called out: 'Would that I was not called Henry after my father; would that I was Christened William after my friend. William, I take wine in your honour.'

'Sire, I…' William lowered his head with embarrassment as the Court raised their goblets to him. 'My Lord King…' he began but Henry had not finished, announcing that they would travel to Bonneville, not far from Bayeux in northern Normandy, and celebrate the great and Holy Feast of Christmas there. Glad at the prospect of leaving the stink of Paris there was a sudden revival of conversation in the hall.

'By God, what *is* it about FitzMarshal that he has the ear of the King our master?' De Salignac overheard Adam d'Yquebeuf remark to his neighbour. But there was more to aggravate the growing jealously of D'Yquebeuf. All of a sudden a voice rose above the others as a clever and quick-witted courtier named William St John shouted out than none but those named 'William' ought to dine with the King at Christmas. Even as the Young Henry assented, not ruling out others, William sought out Bertran de Born. The man looked up sharply at the Young King's decision, and although his face was a mask, William knew his own master, Louis, would be furious.

And thus it fell out: that Christmas King Louis fumed in Paris, and King Henry II did likewise at Chinon, keeping a wary eye on Queen Eleanor, Duke Geoffrey and Duke Richard. Meanwhile, far to the north, the Young King, having attended Mass, kept a merry board and on St Stephen's Day more than over one hundred gentlemen named William sat down at his table.

' 'Twas a near masterful compromise, my Lord Marshal,' Robert de Salignac said to William afterwards, referring to the holding of the revels at Bonneville, 'but I fear it will have consequences.'

William nodded gravely. 'Aye, I have little doubt but that it will.'

Neither man could, however, have guessed how quickly, nor in what dramatic manner the matter would culminate.

*

Marking the Young King's open defiance by his spending the Holy Festival at Bonneville, King Henry II issued a summons that his eldest son could not ignore, for it included other magnates and his absence would not merely be noted, but would act to his obvious disadvantage. The message came with the New Year and threw the Young Henry into a dark and suspicious mood. Nevertheless preparations were immediately put in train for the Court to ride south, beyond Chinon into the Limousin region where, at Limoges in late February 1173, King Henry II revealed his latest dynastic intentions in the presence of men whose writ ran from beyond the Pyrenees to beyond the Alps. They were King Alfonso II of Aragon, King Sancho VI of Navarre, Count Raymond V of Toulouse and Count Humbert of Maurienne, and all were inclined to ally themselves with the Old King. Robert de Salignac was not of the company, but had leave to ride with his retinue farther south to his lands on the Dordogne.

'Farewell, William. I know not where we shall meet again,' he had said on their parting. 'I fear little good will come of this assemblage.'

This meeting of such great lords was to affirm the situation pertaining across the Angevin Empire so assiduously constructed by Henry II, that they might bear witness to his diplomacy and calm

159

any remaining division among his sons by the intimidation of their collective presence.

The Old King optimistically opened the gathering with an announcement. The commitment of his youngest son John to Mother Church was to be revoked. Although only five, the princeling was promised in marriage to Alice, daughter of Count Humbert. Humbert had no sons, so such a union would, in due course, add the trans-Alpine provinces of Savoy and Piedmont to the Angevin Empire.

'And with my son's hand,' Henry went on, 'and upon my death, the Lord John shall have the castles of Chinon, Loudon and Mirebeau here, in my lands of Anjou and Touraine, and in England he shall inherit three English counties…'

He got no further. Unfazed by the presence of the Kings of Aragon and Navarre, the Counts of Toulouse and Maurienne, the Young King thrust himself to his feet in an explosion of wrath and high dudgeon.

'God's blood, father! All are promised to me!' roared the outraged Young King as the assembled kings, nobles and courtiers stirred at the unseemly outburst.

'Stay your temper, sir, until I die what I have I hold and is mine to do with as I please,' roared Henry, equally furious at the interruption of what, for him, was intended as a solemn moment.

'But your promise…at Montmirail…' spluttered the Young Henry.

'The workings of diplomacy must needs be flexible,' Henry retorted, embarrassed and reining-in his own temper with difficulty, 'as you shall learn in God's good time.'

'This means that Chinon remains yours until your death!' the Young Henry shouted back, forsaking all attempts at self-control. 'Shall I never come into mine own? Look at Richard! Look at

160

Geoffrey! They rule in their own right! I, *I* am the elder son! *I* am Count of Anjou, yet you would hold Chinon and Mirebeau until John comes of age!' The young man was beside himself with rage now such that William was truly alarmed.

'Hold hard, my Lord,' growled William, standing behind Young Henry who turned away to hide his face and his wounded pride, choleric and almost choking in his fury. 'In all faith,' he gasped, 'God's good time cannot come soon enough.'

'Come sir,' the Old King commanded, 'you shall set your hand regnant to this instrument of betrothal…'

Young Henry caught his breath and partially recovered himself. 'Would that my hand *was* regnant,' he snarled. 'You betray me, my Lord.'

William half expected the Old King to burst into one of his own famous rages but in front of others he continued to retain his temper. 'Your hand, Harry, I command it,' replied the Old King quietly, tapping the parchment on the table in front of them where a clerk in holy orders patiently held quill and ink-pot.

'I shall not!'

'By God you shall, sir! Or I shall have you arraigned for treason. You are still my sworn liegeman.'

The whole assembly waited in a silence so absolute that it was said afterwards they could all hear the agonised breathing of the Young King. Finally, however, with a shaking hand and cheeks the colour of a russet apple he scrawled his signature as a witness, disinheriting himself with each mark of the goose-feather which he flung from his hand the instant that he had finished, as though it were white with heat.

'That is well and nobly done,' the King remarked in a bland and conciliatory tone, pulling at his beard and smiling about him.

161

Lowering his voice he added for his son's benefit, 'you will attend me in my privy chamber presently.'

Later that evening, when the Young King returned to the company of his household he flung himself on a fur-covered settle with a high oath. 'He buys me off,' he said with a petulance that startled William.

'How so, my Lord King?' William enquired.

'Do not call me that! I am nothing, nothing until he is dead!'

'You must not speak so, my Lord,' snapped Richard Barre, the Chancellor, crossing himself, lest you imperil your own soul…'

But Henry was not listening. 'His Grace goes into Brittany, but I am to be given money with which to amuse myself…' Henry looked around him, trying to read the reactions of his closest associates. Were they his friends? Would they cleave to him or his father if he did what he was contemplating? 'Methinks,' he said in a low tone, 'that the hawk has grown too hungry to obey. What think you of this humiliation, my Lords?'

There was a non-committal mumble from those present. Young Henry sighed. 'You are all a-feared of Henry Curtmantle…' Damn it, he would put them on the spot: 'What say you, William Marshal?'

'My Lord, in jest I recommend wit; in tournament I advise boldness; in war I commend caution; in the Court of His Grace I counsel filial acquiescence.'

There was a surge of agreement among the company, an acknowledgement that the Marshal had rescued them all from a pit yawning before them. Emboldened, Richard Barre, added his own advice: 'My Lord you still have your own seal.'

'What difference does that make to a King without honour or place of government, eh?' It was clear the Young King was not to be mollified and scowled at them all, but most pointedly at William.

'Damn you, Marshal! You have become too much the courtier…'

'No Sire,' William responded, 'I can claim no aptitude for diplomacy, but I have ever striven to be a strategist.'

The Young King shook his head. 'In God's good time, eh?'

'Just so, my Lord King,' William answered with a bow.

*

The Young King sulked for several days and awaited the departure of the King of Aragon before he again raised the subject as the Court lolled at table and the Old King threw scraps to his hounds. The atmosphere of mistrust was palpable: Queen Eleanor remained regally non-committal though it was well-known that she favoured the company of her two sons Geoffrey and Richard to that of her husband. The two young princes likewise avoided their father and were barely civil to him. For himself, the Old King held his tongue and his temper, maintaining a cool front while visitors remained in his company and hoping that matters might blow over. Secretly he gnawed upon the humiliation that the Young Henry had meted out to him and he must needs keep his eye on Richard, Geoffrey and his wife.

There was little conversation and the awkward silences were eased by a more than usual quaffing of wine until, just as it seemed the Queen might rise, Young Henry spoke out clearly.

'You deprive me, my Lord King, of my lawful right as agreed. What use is a Treaty such as was made under your hand at Montmirail when you can repudiate it at will? Pray tell me if that is wise and prudent kingship? Surely, if a King cannot keep his word why dost thou chastise your vassal lords when they break theirs? What would you do if I were to swear I signed that instrument of disinheritance under duress?'

163

King Henry leaned forward, his brow furrowed, his expression intense as he again governed his temper.

'Are you questioning my fitness to rule?'

Eating a preserved orange brought by Alfonso, the Young Henry shrugged. 'It would seem so,' he remarked with casual insolence.

'Who has put you to this effrontery, eh? Which among the foolish hawks in your mesnie or the priests who minister…'

'Think you that I cannot make an argument for my own sake?' responded the younger man furiously. 'Am I not a son of Anjou myself, a leopard in my own right?'

'Is it Robert de Salignac, or William FitzMarshal? They are uncommonly close, I hear.'

'By the Holy Blood, Father, it is I, *I*, Henry, Count of Anjou that claim these things for myself!' The Young Henry was on his feet now, stabbing his index finger at his own breast. 'What interest have FitzMarshal or De Salignac in these matters?'

'Then learn obedience, boy!' Henry roared, rising to his own feet, watched by the assembled courtiers who were all obliged to stand.

'At my father's knee, Sire and by my noble Father's example,' responded his son, 'I have learned nothing else but obedience and in return you filch my Lordships and make me thus a creature of your own intention when I am but lately crowned your equal…'

'You are *NOT* crowned my equal! You are crowned my successor! Be careful that I do not further disinherit you…'

'Ah! Then you admit it!'

'Aye, I admit it, and I would further disinherit you if it is politic so to do, by the Holy Cross!'

'And give all to sweet brother Richard,' Young Henry sneered, 'or perhaps the boy John who will suck his thumb for years yet…'

'Aye, perhaps, if they show more kingly qualities than you display at this moment. Go, lie with your wife and vent your manhood within her, for you show no such talent here…'

'Ha!' raged the now incandescent Young King, 'I shall most certainly take the advice of one whose whores litter this place like hounds beneath the board…' The young Henry gestured below the table as his father flushed and all braced themselves for the coming outburst, for he seemed lost for words. But Young Henry had not yet finished. 'And whose household knights cut down a prelate in the House of Almighty God!'

King Henry staggered forwards, leaning on the table as his son stared about him. 'And ask how dost thou treat thine own Queen, my mother, Sire, that you should advise me therein? Go, Sire, and fall upon the tired paps of the Fair Rosamund!' And here the Young King turned his back on his sovereign lord, took Marguerite's hand and swept from the chamber.

There was a stunned silence as all watched aghast the Old King who let out a bull-roar of fury, closing his eyes and striking the table with both fists before sweeping it clear and over throwing the board itself. Those standing about it jumped clear, retreating from the insensate monarch. No-one could assuage his rage as he began stalking up and down the dais kicking aside the vacant stools, his fists beating his head and tearing at his own hair. Oaths and blasphemies poured from his mouth in a torrent of abuse that had the priests present clamping their hands over their ears.

In the end he fell upon his knees, his hands clasped as if in prayer, tears running down his face into his beard. But whether the tears were of anger or contrition, or whether he prayed to God or the Devil, none could say as they backed away and left him to Eleanor and his waning rage.

The following morning William received a summons from the Old King and appeared before him. Nothing about Henry's appearance gave any hint to his tempestuous outburst of the previous evening other than that he dismissed his attendant clerk and rose to stare out onto the bailey below where the Young King's retinue was preparing to leave.

Slowly King Henry turned towards William and in an instant he read the agony in the King's eyes. For a long moment Henry scrutinised him.

'Did you put him up to this, FitzMarshal?'

William was affronted. 'No, my Lord King, I did not,'

'You are his counsellor, are you not?'

'In military matters, yes. In matters of state, no.'

'Have you no opinion?'

'What opinion should I have, Sire? He is your son. Who am I to have…?'

'Oh, what *courtesy*, FitzMarshal,' Henry cut him off sarcastically. 'You have learned well in the Queen's Court, by God, but I did not appoint you to my son's household to encourage…'

'I have encouraged nothing, my Lord,' interrupted William with great temerity, 'beyond a skill at arms.'

The King regarded him sharply. 'By God, FitzMarshal, you o'er step the mark!'

'Then I crave your pardon, Sire.'

There was a prolonged silence and then the Old King said, almost conversationally. 'I am told you bear the mark of Satan.'

William expelled his breath, a vile spectre rising before him. He was aware that he had risen far and fast; he was aware too that he had his enemies; was it all to be torn down by this mischance of birth and the foul temper of two powerful men?

'I bear a blood-mark upon my back, my Lord King. I am told by some it has the appearance of Lucifer on the presumption that the appearance of Lucifer is known. Others tell me it resembles a lion. Not having a silvered mirror I am unable to tell you what I think of it myself.'

'What? You have never seen it?' There was a genuine astonishment and curiosity in the Old King's tone of voice.

'No, Sire, not properly.'

'Disrobe, sir.'

'Sire?'

'You cannot mistake my meaning. The opinion of a King has the rule of Law, does it not?'

'Aye, my Lord King.'

'And the command of a King should be obeyed, should it not? Or are you of the same opinion as my son that my rule is invalid?'

William suppressed a shudder, recalling that Godfery FitzHugh had subjected him to such a scrutiny. He loosed his belt, drew off his curtle and then his shirt and under garment. The King motioned for him to turn his back towards him. William's heart beat furiously, for this was like trial by fire, at the caprice of no just agent, but of corruptible opinion. Would this unpredictable King confirm the judgement of the weak and vacillating Stephen? There was a long silence then he heard Henry chuckle.

'Turn about, FitzMarshal and draw on your clothes.' As William did so the King went on: 'I would not say the credulous could not see something resembling what we are told might be a devil of sorts, but I incline to the view that a lion rampant is a more fitting description.'

William could scarcely disguise his relief. 'I am obliged to you, Sire.'

167

'Aye, FitzMarshal, you are,' the King said pointedly. 'Now go and tell my son that he shall not leave today, but that he shall ride north tomorrow in my company and we shall together go a-hawking on the way.'

'Whither are we bound, Sire?'

'Chinon,' said the Old King with a wicked gleam in his eye. 'Now you may go…'

William made his bow, gathered up his belt and made his way to the chamber door. He was lifting the latch when Henry called him back.

'You wear my son's device, do you not?'

'Aye, my Lord; as I am of his mesnie.'

'When it comes the time to adopt your own you should take the red lion, rampant; the ground to be of your own choosing.'

William's met the King's eyes as he was dismissed with a nod. When he reached the yard below be sought out the Young Henry's Steward, William Blund, and passed on the Old King's order. Blund said nothing but shook his head then nodded over William's shoulder. William turned to see the Young King entering the yard, leading the Queen Marguerite to a litter before leaping into the saddle with a show of bravado.

'My Lord King,' called William, 'I am directed to advise you that the King your father would accompany you northwards, that he would make of it a hawking party and that we should not leave until the morrow.'

'You had conference with my Father?' the Young King asked incredulously.

'Aye, my Lord King.' William lowered his voice. 'He summoned me and asked me if I had any part in fomenting a rupture between your Lordship and His Grace. I told him that I had not.'

'And that is all?'

'No, my Lord. I told him that you were of your own mind and that my only duty was to school you in military matters, that I had no knowledge of affairs of state. Yours or his.'

Henry grunted and looked sideways at William. 'And there was nothing else?'

'Nothing of moment.'

'What mean you by that?' Henry's tone was sharp.

'The King your father was curious to see the mark upon my back and ruled it resembled a lion. He ordered me that, when the time comes I should adopt a lion rampant as mine own device.'

'That time has not yet come, Marshal...'

'As you say, my Liege,' William responded.

'And you take orders from my father now, do you?'

'No, Sire, I merely tell you what His Grace told me to tell you...'

The Young Henry bit his lip so that the blood flowed and looked about him. 'I do not see him,' Henry said, blood flecking his spittle.

'But he no doubt watches you and expects you to obey.'

The Young Henry stared up at the surrounding walls again then turned and studied the Queen's litter. The curtains had just been dropped and he appeared to sink into a moment's deep thought.

'Hawking, d'you say?'

'Hawking, en route to Chinon.'

'By God, he would rub my face in the shit!' Henry snarled at the mention of the contentious castle.

'Sire...'

'Very well, give the order to dismount and postpone matters until tomorrow.' William did not like the tone of sudden acquiescence, nor did he catch Henry's remark that matters might wait until they arrived at Chinon as he turned away and rounded-to alongside the Queen's litter. A moment later he led Marguerite back into the castle leaving William to order Blund to unload the pack animals

169

and the rest of the mesnie to dismount and return their horses to the stables.

*

The large cavalcade rode north next morning with every appearance of forced amity. Hawks and falcons were flown at prey, but on the second day, as their route followed the Vienne, a more purposeful pace was set by the King's household with which the Young King's was obliged to keep up. Among the stages they made they stopped at Poitiers and Mirebeau before arriving at Chinon. Here, as if confirming the Young Henry's worst fears, the Old King announced they would rest and feast, but after retiring that night William was shaken awake by Adam d'Yquebeuf

'What the devil…?' In the light of the guttering candle D'Yquebeuf bore, William could see he wore mail beneath his surtout. Behind D'Yquebeuf, wiping the sleep out of his eyes stood William's body squire. The young man named Odo who had assumed the office after the death of Rolf, had been rudely awakened from his palliasse laid across the door to William's chamber.

'On what authority do you…?'

'Young Henry rides out from here this night,' D'Yquebeuf responded shortly. You, my Lord Marshal, are commanded to follow him, armed for war.'

'Since when did I take orders from you, D'Yquebeuf?'

'You know well that I command tonight's guard. The command is the Kings, not mine. Go now and ready horses for the mesnie privée.'

'No more?'

'No. Carry only what is necessary. FitzStephen wakes the rest of the mesnie privée. I go to order Blund to load up and to bestir Barre.'

170

'Is this rebellion?' William asked shortly. 'If so what part am I to play…?'

'Whatever part you choose…'

'You, it seems, have decided.'

D'Yquebeuf shrugged, staring at William through the gloom. 'The Old King was warned by the Count of Toulouse that Richard and Geoffrey intend it and Eleanor stands by… Now, for God's sake, I have no time to debate the issue.'

'God in Heaven! 'What you say implies treason D'Yquebeuf.' William was already out of bed and dressing quickly.

'You are with us?' D'Yquebeuf asked.

William said nothing but with a few words he directed Odo to do his bidding. Hearing this, the suddenly hesitant D'Yquebeuf left the chamber.

Half an hour later, at the head of no more than thirty lances and a small pack-train, and after a brief argument with the sergeant of the guard at the gate which was quickly quelled by the arrival of D'Yquebeuf, the heavily cloaked Young King and his closest followers had ridden out of Chinon and taken the road north.

It was far from an orderly escape. Once aware of the small size of the cavalcade Richard Barre rode alongside the Young King and demanded to know if he intended defying his father. When assured that he did, Barre turned back and disappeared into the night carrying the Young King's Seal and taking the King's baggage with him. Despite William's protest, Henry let them go. During the night others thought better of their precipitate action and turned aside. The Young King did nothing to stop them.

William would never forget that night. His feelings were deeply divided. He was well aware that Queen Eleanor's estrangement from her husband was as much about his politics as about his mistresses. Moreover, the flaunting insincerity of, in particular, the

171

Lord Richard, amply demonstrated the Old King's hold on his French lands was feebler than the Limoges conference might have persuaded him. Now William's protests of innocence to the Old King would ring hollow; his only defence was his sworn allegiance to the Young Henry, but the Old King could set that side at a stroke. Towards dawn, as the horses tired, Young Henry eased the pace and called William to ride with him.

'You think me a fool, Marshal,' he began.

'I think nothing, my Lord, beyond astonishment, not least that we have left Queen Marguerite behind.'

'That is a matter soon to be remedied. My father will not trouble himself over her. It is of the others that I would have conference with you.'

'The others, Sire?'

'You are too dull a fellow to notice and have not had Robert de Salignac at your elbow to apprise you, but my brother Richard is about to rise in open rebellion and will be followed by Geoffrey. Raymond of Toulouse paid homage to both my father and myself which ends one squabble but opens another with Richard who has my mother at his back. I had audience of Count Raymond; he will favour me against my father. Meanwhile my father cannot believe that my mother would stand against him with Richard and Geoffrey. They have worked too hard together for him to consider her capable of any perfidy that would weaken his realm. That is why he left her with them at Poitiers and hoped to confine me by the silken threads of filial obligation.' Henry chuckled. 'I slipped the leash, you know, even though the old fool insisted I slept in the same chamber.'

'How many of your mesnie knew of it?'

'All but you, and of the household, Barre and Blund.'

'Would that you had left me asleep…'

172

'Pah! You do not mean that.'

'Do I not? This is not your rightful claiming of your rights, Sire.'

'Is it not? Then pray, what is it?'

' 'Tis a conspiracy and you are not the fire of it, only the fuel.'

'Why say you that? You witnessed my defiance of the King…'

'Would that I had not that too. No, this is a plot laid by King Louis, ignited by Bertram de Born and Adam d'Yquebeuf. I had long marked the former and the presence of the latter in my chamber this night spoke all better than words.'

'Damn you, Marshal,' snarled the Young King, spurring his horse onwards and leaving an embittered and entrapped William in his wake.

*

Before daylight they had changed horses outside Fontevrault, clear evidence that the escape had been carefully planned. Although the Young King would not admit it, D'Yquebeuf confided that they rode for Paris but would not turn east towards Louis' domains until across the Norman border at Alençon. William now threw out pickets, both ahead and behind them, ordering the loose formation of the much reduced mesnie into a warlike formation in expectation of trouble.

In the event they avoided it. Although the Old King was after them before daylight, he was given the slip and on a windy March morning the Young King clattered into Paris and the open arms of Louis VII.

Here the mesnie kneeled to reaffirm their fealty to the Young King in the presence of King Louis and when the Old King, held at the French border, sent a deputation of hurriedly summoned bishops to demand the return of his son and heir, the wily Louis enquired who sent the message.

'Why the King of England, Your Grace,' was the response as the worthy prelates invoked the Old King's highest power.

'How can that be,' responded Louis, disingenuously inspecting his long fingers and their equally long nails, 'the King of England is here, under my roof.'

Louis rose and stepped down among the bishops who scattered, bending low as Louis added: 'All the world knows the man who *was* King of England relinquished his throne to his son. Tell that man that he is no more than one who owes me his fealty for Anjou and the rest, and that if he would defy me he should look to the defence of his castles and the security of his person.'

CHAPTER EIGHT: WAR 1173 - 1174

'By the Rood but Paris stinks!'

'Robert!' William rose to welcome Robert de Salignac as he strode into the chamber where William sat at his muster sheets with a clerk. 'I am glad to see you and, as regards Paris, hope we shall not tarry here long as the summer heats grow daily.'

'I should have been here some time since had I not been summoned by Queen Eleanor who charged me with a message to you.'

'To me?' William's astonishment was unfeigned, De Salignac noted.

'Aye, you have earned her goodwill by your loyalty to her son. She bad me give you every encouragement to stand by Young Henry and to inform you that both the Lord Richard and his brother Geoffrey will join you here shortly.'

'So the rumours are true, she would secure Aquitaine for Richard beyond peradventure.'

'And in her own behalf, of course. No-one trusts Henry Curtmantle now, not after so open a dispossession of his heir. The whole of his lands are inflamed with rebellion and seek to make a better accommodation with the Young King…'

'For the betterment of their own fiefdoms, I'll warrant,' laughed William, relief flooding through him.

'Yes, but few of them think of the consequences of the embroilment of Louis. If the Young King emerges uppermost in this summer's campaigning, the King of France will extract a payment for his assistance and reduce the King of England's French domain.'

175

William nodded. 'Louis has already called in Guillaume De Tancarville and the Counts of Flanders and Boulogne,' he remarked, mentioning his former opponents at Neufchâtel-en-Bray.

'The city is full of their devices,' De Salignac remarked easing himself onto a stool and accepting the goblet of wine brought him by a page.

'They do not come unencumbered. Phillipe of Flanders is to have the Earldom and revenues of Kent and the holding of Rochester and Dover castles. Matthieu of Boulogne will receive the county of Mortain...'

'But what of yourself, William, you cannot have found the matter easy to decide.'

'Upon my soul, I had little choice. I was awoken by D'Yquebeuf and told to mount. He either had the Young King in his pocket or the King had him...'

'Eleanor has them both,' interrupted De Salignac, 'it is she that lies behind all this, but pray continue.'

William frowned. So the rumours were correct; Eleanor had flouted church rule and every convention, turning her sons against their father. He looked at De Salignac.

'You are shocked?'

'I am stunned.'

De Salignac shrugged. 'But yourself?' he pressed.

'Oh, as to that, at Evreux Henry had us all renew our oaths of fealty. I was already Henry's liegeman and I have no lands, Robert,' William resumed, his tone rueful. 'What should I have done? Henry Curtmantle has been close to death once and it was my duty both to him and to his mother to attend the Young King. I am bound by loyalty.'

De Salignac nodded. 'Curtmantle is a strange man. I heard that though the Young King's baggage train turned back after the flight from Chinon, he yet turned it about and sent it after his son.'

'Indeed he did, and with it a message that Young Henry was yet a King and would require the trappings of kingship. What does one make of such conduct? But like father, like son; the Young Henry let William Blund return to Chinon on his refusal to swear fealty at Evreux! Now, with equal contrariness, he requires that I gird and dub him knight, ruling that the girding had by his father's hand is as meaningless as his first coronation!'

'Well, it could not come from a better man,' said Robert de Salignac rising and clapping William on the shoulder. 'I had better look to my people. Is it true he left his Queen behind too?' he asked with an inquisitive chuckle.

'Marguerite? Oh, yes. Henry has kept her under his own eye, to the fury of her husband!'

Both men were laughing, not at Marquerite's plight, but at the Young King's discomfiture.

'The old lion outwits him with ease. God knows, but he may even fuck her for his further revenge, it would not surprise me and she is comely enough,' Robert de Salignac remarked as he quitted William's lodgings.

William watched him go. He found the thought of the Old King seducing Queen Marguerite uncomfortably disturbing. It seemed a long time since he had enjoyed a woman. His distraction was broken by a cough. He looked up at the expectant clerk who sat with his wet quill poised above its pot of oak-gall. 'Ah, Master Thomas, where were we?'

'The pack animals, my Lord Marshal...'

'Ah, yes, the supply-train... Do you make a note as to bow-staves, I would consider those presently...'

'And there is the matter of my Lord Matthieu of Boulogne's siege train. There is no sign of it.'

And William sank again into the details of his duties of Marshal to the Young King Henry. He was almost grateful.

*

'I need none of your counsel here, Marshal!' cried the Young King gleefully as he wheeled his destrier and brought it alongside that of William's.

'I should think I had failed if you did, Sire,' William responded. 'No King goes to war with his tutor.'

'Ha!' The Young Henry appreciated the jest then turned and looked along the line of dancing pennons and shining mail, delighted where the June sunshine sparkled off helm and lance-point, picking out the coloured devices of those who had shown their faith in him as the future of the Angevin Empire.

'We shall drive him into England, shall we not, my Marshal,' he said, leaning across his saddle-bow and speaking in a low tone. 'And then cross the Channel and hammer him from the south whilst King William of Scotland crushes him from the north, eh?'

The young man was in high spirits, for he had taken Aumale on the Bresle, and crossed into Normandy at the head of a large army which, besides his own muster, comprised that of his brothers Richard and Geoffrey, the three Counts, De Meulan, Boulogne and Flanders and the Chamberlain De Tancarville, who alone brought one hundred lances to the war-host. Meanwhile, far to the south, King Louis rode at the head of a second army intent on battering its way into Normandy through the gates of Verneuil, midway between Evreux and Alençon.

'It is a grand strategy, Sire.' William said noncommittally.

That evening the army encamped on the road to Neufchâtel-en-Bray. William was attending to his duties, walking the horse-lines

178

and bivouacs of the men-at-arms and common soldiers, the bowmen and lesser retainers as was his wont. It was already growing dark, the early summer night hastened by an overcast sky, as he tramped among the smoke of the cooking fires where the smell and sizzle of meat turning on makeshift spits sharpened his own appetite.

He was surprised to see among the soldiery another knight in his surtout, a tall man of his own stature, which was over six feet, who seemed occupied in a similar task to William's though he just then bent over a camp fire, speaking to a flame-lit group of upturned faces who seemed to regard their interlocutor in awe.

It was unusual for William to encounter any nobleman so employed at this hour on such a task and curiosity drew him towards the bivouac. One of the men on the far side of the fire saw him and nudged his neighbour so that the nobleman turned at the distraction and straightened up. William knew him instantly. Though they had never had previous discourse the tall man revealed himself, the firelight flickering over the leopards of England and Normandy.

'My Lord Duke.' William inclined his head.

'Ah, William FitzMarshal' Duke Richard said.

Richard smiled and held out his hand. 'I have heard much of you and am glad to meet you…and aptly in the company of these good fellows.' Richard gestured at the men round him, some of whom seemed uncertain whether or not they should be on their feet in the presence of the Duke and King's Marshal. 'I told them not to rise for the day's march has been long and we shall require all their energies on the morrow.'

'Quite right, my Lord Duke. The horses have all been fed and there is no more to be done this day but rest.'

'God be praised,' said Richard crossing himself, as did the men about the fire. He smiled at them then turned to William. 'Will you walk with me, or have you yet to finish your rounds?'

'I have as good as finished, if you came from the Flemings, then between us we shall have settled all.'

Duke Richard was ten years William's junior but he had all the commanding presence of his mother. 'I have not seen you since you were in attendance upon the Queen, my mother,' he remarked conversationally. 'I understand you stand high in brother Henry's opinion.'

'I could not say, my Lord. I am, or was, His Grace's military tutor. I hope that the present campaign will prove the point.'

Richard chuckled. 'And how think you this campaign will go?'

'My Lord?'

'Come, you heard my question.'

'Matters hang in the balance. The King, your father, is in the south where, I understand, the country is unquiet…'

'And only awaits our incursion into Normandy to hasten north to strike at us,' Richard said in a tone of voice that suggested he relished the prospect of the coming fight. 'But you are anxious…'

'Aye, my Lord.' William was silent for a moment as if considering his words carefully. ' 'Tis a matter I have long pondered and arises from my experience in the tournament…'

'The tournament? How so?'

'In war we settle matters from the acquisition of castles, towns, places of strength. We burn and destroy as we have been doing on the road from Aumale and will do around Neufchâtel-en-Bray and, probably Driencourt. Such a mode of warfare is slow…'

'But it consolidates our position,' retorted Richard, 'every place taken is to be bargained with, and every village burned depletes our enemy's revenues.'

180

'In theory, yes; in practice it merely leads to greater extortion of the villeins. Were we to move faster, isolating places of strength and attacking our enemy directly, there would be less cost and quicker recovery.'

'Isolate places of strength? But their garrisons might ride out in our rear…'

'And accomplish what, my Lord Duke? No, most chatelains and constables will remain doggedly holding their posts. That they are sworn to. It is only necessary to encircle them and starve them of provision. What is the point of destroying a fortress that, once taken or exchanged, requires rebuilding at the expense of treasure. No; isolate them, they can then be dealt with later, or the matter settled at any negotiation held to restore peace.'

'But suppose a relieving force is sent…'

'You strike at the enemy's heart and give him no time to organise such a thing,' William said with a ruthless simplicity. 'I do not say a siege is bad policy, or never a necessity, but I do say when a great matter weighs upon the outcome, then the fast strike may have the better consequence.'

Richard was silent for a moment, stopping and turning towards William who also stood still. Night had now fallen and with it a heavy dew. They were approaching the large tents of the nobles and could smell roast boar and hear the merriment of the lords and magnates as they sat down to board.

The Duke stroked his young beard and nodded. 'You would prosecute war on the model of the tourney, then, the chevauchée being pre-eminent?'

'Aye.' William nodded, his faith in the hot pursuit, the riding down and destruction of the enemy being, in his eyes, far more effective than the slow, methodical but wearying investment of a castle. Even such a flimsy structure as his father's Steward had

181

thrown up at Newbury had delayed King Stephen for weeks and sucked the King's resolve; how much more the delay before the ramparts of a Tancarville or Henry's great fortress of Verneuil?

'And have you schooled my brother in this?'

'No. It is contrary to the methods of his present principal military advisers, My Lord of Boulogne and Flanders, and it would be foolish to interrupt a plan concerted with the King of France. We have a common objective. In this case it is only necessary for us to reach Rouen before the King your father, to cause him grievous harm. I speak of general principles, strategies in which I believe you have an interest.'

Richard nodded. 'You have given me food for thought, Marshal,' he said solemnly. 'And I am grateful to you. Much will hang on the outcome of the coming weeks but as for tonight,' Richard's voice changed in tone, 'tonight we must eat…'

*

To start with the campaign went well. The two columns advanced into the Vexin and Normandy, laying waste and investing the major strongholds and the Young King's army invested Neufchâtel-en-Bray. In the west Brittany was in open revolt and first invited the Old King's attention then, far to the south, rebellion broke out across Aquitaine and beyond. Among those again in the field against their feudal lord were the brothers Lusignan who, with other greater magnates, claimed Henry's treatment of their Duchess, Eleanor, gave them cause to overturn his own rule. She meanwhile, was sent by her husband into Normandy, shifted from one castle to another so that none might know where she was while he, at the head of an army of mercenaries from the Brabant, did to the counties of Poitou and Touraine what his enemies were doing to the Vexin and eastern Normandy.

Backed by a rich war-chest, keeping both England and Holy Church on his side, the Old King remained wary, sending his savage mercenaries to do his bidding. Personally avoiding a pitched battle, Henry's forces were ruthless and while he never properly pacified more than the few square miles his army occupied, the savagery of his methods drew the teeth of the rebels, leaving them supine. Eventually, picking his own moment, he stormed into Normandy to confront his main and most organised enemies, the forces of King Louis and his own son.

Meanwhile in their attempts to conquer Normandy the allies were confounded by division and bad luck. The Young King's attack had stalled as his army sat down and invested Neufchâtel-en-Bray. Matters went ill, although siege-engines battered the walls and sappers under-mined the bastions of the fortress. William mused on the vicissitudes of war; this place had given him his first real taste of battle when he had been fighting in its defence. Now he was involved in attempting to seize the fortress and town that huddled in its shelter and it was proving time-consuming and tedious, just as he had told Duke Richard such operations would. Then everything changed: Matthieu of Boulogne was struck and mortally wounded by a bolt from a cross-bow and when news of his brother's death reached Philippe of Flanders, the Count raised the siege of Verneuil, withdrawing into his domain and taking his war-host with him. King Louis took over the siege of Verneuil and had barely grasped the lines of saps and under-mining there, than he learned that King Henry was advancing to the relief of the great fortress. Louis took fright, called for his horse and, followed by his army, retired on Paris.

What had begun in high hopes, ended in disaster and the pell-mell retreat towards Louis's capital had the appearance of a rout.

Within a week King Louis' retreat had drawn after it the portion of the allied army encamped before Neufchâtel-en-Bray.

Side-lined during this siege, during which the Young King had stalked the lines, full of bravado in the company of Matthieu of Boulogne until the fatal cross-bow shot laid him low, William now found himself alongside Duke Richard in command of what amounted to a rear-guard as the army retreated over the border towards Paris.

'We shall soon be found by my father's heralds,' remarked Duke Richard conversationally as the two rode side-by-side, 'for Louis' will have reached him long since.'

William said nothing beyond agreeing that this was likely to be the case. Privately he thought that King Henry of England Aquitaine and Anjou should have fallen upon the rabble of Louis' army as it wandered through the Vexin, maintaining itself by the cruel and casual plundering of the peasantry.

*

The late September sun shone from a sky of peerless blue and surrounding the two separate encampments the pennons, banners and devices fluttered in the light autumnal breeze that carried the comfortingly domestic smell of wood-smoke from the town of Gisors, not a mile away. The glint of lance-points and silver helms, the twinkle of scoured mail and the gloss on the necks and haunches of scores of magnificent horses was backed by the striped and conical tents of the three Kings, their great lords and magnates, as they assembled for the parley.

On both sides the heralds had blown their trumpets, calling the two parties to conference beneath the boughs of the great elm tree that stood beside the road on the border between the Angevin and Capetian lands, a spot that had become the traditional meeting-point of the Kings of France and the Dukes of Normandy.

William stood among the magnificent gathering of the lords and nobles attending King Louis of France, his heir Philippe and the Young King Henry of England - with them but not of them. Beside him stood Robert de Salignac and both were aware that their futures depended upon the outcome of the parley and watched as the principals came from both camps to meet under the old tree as its leaves assumed the glorious golden colour of the season.

Of those coming from the far side he recognised with certainty only the Old King, the man so many called 'Curtmantle' for the brevity of his scarlet surcoat, its golden leopards across his breast seemingly alive in the sunshine as he walked towards the elm. Shorter than his sons, but powerful and still energetic, the recent campaign had astonished his enemies for it had seemed they fought a far younger man. Despite his recent illness, Henry had made a forced march from Dol in Brittany across the length of Normandy to Rouen on the Seine in little more than a day. The fact had not been lost on William.

Going out to meet them led by the slightly wistful, blue-clad, blond figure of King Louis, were three of the Old King's sons. The Young Henry whose handsome frame seemed to William's keen eye to move with a degree of discomfort in approaching the physical presence of his formidable father. He was flanked by the tall and impressive Duke Richard, his hair the same flaming red-gold as his father's had once been, Richard strode with no such diffidence as his elder sibling. On the Young King's other side walked Geoffrey, Count of Brittany, and the sight of him prompted comment from William's companion.

'They say *he* is the craftiest of the Angevin leopard cubs,' murmured Robert de Salignac confidentially. 'Methinks little good will come of all this,' he gestured round them and fixed William with a knowing look. William's shrug was almost imperceptible.

185

He would wait and see, but the conviction in De Salignac's voice disturbed his thoughts. Despite his years of service, or his presence on this field of chivalry, he was yet a no-body. The tournament field had yielded him some small riches and his place in the Young King's mesnie provided a degree of prestige, but little more. True he had acquired a small mesnie of his own, some four knights and half-a-dozen squires, including young Odo, a number of mounted men-at-arms that enabled William independent command of twenty-six lances, but they, like the three servants, his clerk an armourer and even a falconer, were all maintained at the expense of the Young King's Treasury. Without lands of his own, he could derive no income other than that earned by his lance, at war or at tourney, his father had seen to that. His was no independent status, not that of a knight banneret who funded his followers from his own, personal largesse. As for at least one of the knights, Jean de Laon was a Frenchman and a spy in the pay of Louis, though an agreeable enough companion in the tourney and at table, whose ways with his lute were pleasing, if one liked that sort of thing.

'See, they are arguing already,' commented Robert de Salignac dismally, drawing William's attention back from his self-contemplation to the parley beneath the old tree. He saw the Young King stamp his right foot and guessed his tempestuous spirit was being stirred-up.

De Salignac sighed. 'I hear Henry Curtmantle has transferred all his affections to his son John who must be, what, eight years of age?'

'Aye, I had heard the same. The lad is not yet old enough to make trouble.'

'If he follows his brothers it will not be long before he does. Methinks the devil's blood courses through these Angevins,' De Salignac remarked with a hint of bitterness and William recalled the reason for his dislike of Henry the Old King. He had not told De Salignac of his own birth-mark.

'I heard too,' William soothed, 'that Henry favours his bastard, the other Geoffrey who stands with his father.' William had worked out who at least one of the Old King's retinue was. He ordered his thoughts and was about to shy away from dwelling on a lack of paternal favour, having had so little of it himself, but he was not obliged to because the parley seemed suddenly to be at an end.

Duke Richard had turned and was walking away when Henry called him back; he hesitated and turned. They could hear raised voices, then Louis lifted his hands as if acting the peace-maker, whereupon Geoffrey of Brittany leaned forward and whispered something in the Young Henry's ear which led to another explosion of choler. But by now tempers were fraying on the other side. William heard the Old Henry's voice and watched as Richard resumed his retreat to his own lines, shaking his head.

'Richard!' called Henry Curtmantle, but the Duke ignored him and was soon back among the French-led party shaking his head, his expression angry and his jaw clamped tight shut. The Young King was the next to break away and for a few more moments Louis appeared to be temporising until Geoffrey swept him away with an exaggerated courtesy, whereupon the Old Henry could be seen flying into a rage, both fists clenched to his bare head as he too turned back to his own camp and the waiting men there.

'We are at war again,' said De Salignac with a sigh.

William considered the matter; it was better for him that the war continued. He was unmarried, unlanded and had yet to find himself some honour beyond mere words.

*

187

A second attempt was made that same day to bring the two parties together again but the sun set on mutual antagonism and half a dozen exhausted heralds. After the parley at Gisors both sides fell back on their own armies and prepared for a renewal of hostilities. In the hours that followed William gradually learned of the rejection of King Henry's terms. Aware that although he had the upper hand, it was never in the Old King's interests to punish his rebellious sons; to do so would undo his life's work and his empire would soon fall apart. He was all too well-aware that this was King Louis' sole intent in offering support to the young cubs in their rebellion.

In an attempt to woo them from Louis's side the Old King had made generous offers to Dukes Richard and Geoffrey, particularly the former, who was to enjoy half the revenues of Aquitaine but have no hand in its governance. Nor was the Young King to get a penny-weight of political power, his chief grievance; he must be content with everything as it was, including the loss of castles to his brother John. A handful of fortresses elsewhere were offered, but Louis counselled the inadequacy of such provisions and since Curtmantle would not contemplate the slightest relinquishing of the reins of power, the matter rested upon the Old King's treatment of Queen Eleanor. Their mother, Henry told his sons, was a she-devil who was chiefly responsible for the blasphemy of an anointed monarch's sons rising against him. Most shameful of all was that the Young King had been turned from the absolute loyalty that he owed his father by the blandishments of a scheming woman. His wife, Henry, told them, would remain confined at his pleasure and none of them should forget that the responsibility for this lay with them. It was at this point that Richard, Eleanor's avowed favourite, had abandoned the argument.

Following this grand diplomatic failure, the general mood in the camp of King Louis and the Young King was apprehensive. The Old King's forces had moved up to the borders of the French Vexin and much of the strategic advantage had been lost to him unless the Angevin provinces rose again in his rear.

Then news came that King William the Lion of Scotland had invaded Northumberland, a province taken from him a dozen years earlier by Henry Curtmantle. The Scots, it was widely rumoured, were acting like beasts, laying waste the land, seizing women and ripping the unborn from the wombs of their mothers. Soon too came further encouragement when it was bruited about that a large army of Flemings, commanded by the Earl of Leicester, had landed in Suffolk and was marching inland, laying waste the country. Old Hugh Bigod, the treacherous Duke of Norfolk, had joined Leicester and suddenly the fortunes of the Old King's sons seemed transformed.

Duke Richard was the first to take the field again. Mindful perhaps of his discussion with William Marshal, he rode off into the west at the head of a strong force to lay siege to the Biscay port of La Rochelle, in an attempt to cut off one source of his father's supplies. The Young King and his forces rode north-east, into Flanders where at considerable expense a fleet had been made ready on the River Schelde with the intention of embarking to Leicester's support.

'If I cannot find victory in Normandy, Aquitaine or Anjou,' Young Henry told his Council, 'I shall seek it in the country where I am anointed King!'

It was brave talk and hot air. Though William strove to move up the necessary men and supplies, they wasted away as the wind remained stubbornly foul for the crossing to the English coast and Orwell Haven.

Nor was it long before the fortunes of war showed their caprice. William the Lion was driven back into Scotland, his pursuers, led by the English barons, sparing nothing in their path and forcing the Scots to sue for a truce. Leicester's small force was checked near Bury St Edmunds and cut to pieces by a large muster of peasants carrying scythes and led by Humphrey de Bohun, Constable of England, forcing Hugh Bigod to sue for peace. Meanwhile Richard's attack on La Rochelle failed while the Old King took the castle of Faye-le-Vineuse. With that hostilities subsided with the onset of winter.

William spent a miserable Christmas in Paris in the train of his master. There was little joy in the Holy Days despite the piety of the French Court, to whom they were all beholden. William found himself oddly concerned about Queen Marquerite, and vaguely ashamed that he had found her separation by her father-in-law from her husband amusing, even though it had been the latter's situation that had chiefly amused him and Robert de Salignac. He felt the stain of dishonour, just as he questioned the ill-fortune that had led him into the service of the Young King which, he had come to learn, was all obligation and no reward. Not that he expected much, but it seemed to William in his bleakest moments that he was no longer tutor to Young Henry, but merely the means by which the Young King made war. The young man showed little real interest in the detail of campaigning, unlike his father, whose hand might be detected in every movement of his extensive forces.

Young Henry had fallen under King Louis' cloak and, finding it both warm and comfortable, saw no very good reason to alter matters. Meanwhile his faithful Marshal, with the assistance of his clerks and the members of the Young King's Council, saw to his horses and his mesnie, from their pay to their pennons. It was not long before William received orders to prepare for a renewed attempt to invade England.

With the onset of better weather in the spring of 1174 the campaigning season opened. All parties had taken stock and by mid-summer the Old King had first subdued trouble in Anjou and Poitou. In Poitiers he broke-up what remained of Queen Eleanor's Court, looted the ducal palace and took as hostage all the great ladies who had congregated there. These included the Young King's Queen Marguerite and Alice of Maurienne, the lady promised to young John. He then hastened north to Normandy where he learned that the Young King and Philippe of Flanders were about to embark and join a vanguard sent to join Hugh Bigod with such success that by mid-June Norwich was in his hands.

Open rebellion had flared up again across the English Midlands, Nottingham had fallen to the rebel barons and William the Lion had broken the truce, come south again and invested Carlisle. The Young King was jubilant and eager to take ship, suddenly transformed into an active participant in the preparations that would, at a stroke, deprive his father of his greatest asset: England. But, once again the wind blew day after day, and day after day they waited until one of Count Philippe's knights rode into Bruges with bad news. In defiance of the weather the Old King had embarked and sailed from Barfleur with a fleet of forty ships. He had carried with him his hostages, the young John and Queen Eleanor.

They continued to wait at Bruges for several weeks, hoping for a shift in the wind, or news from England that suggested that God favoured them. It was widely believed and even preached that Henry's atonement for Thomas Becket's murder had been insincere or inadequate, while his bad-faith in holding hostage so many ladies was the act of an unprincipled man. William spent these weeks in a state of weary resignation, longing for the freedom and opportunity of the tournament, worn-out by the changing demands of the Young King who vacillated between throwing up the notion of invading England in favour of moving on Normandy in his father's absence.

In the end he chose the latter. The Old King had mewed up Queen Eleanor, shifting her from one castle to another in southern England as he had in Normandy. Marguerite, Alice of Maurienne and several other ladies had been confined to Devizes Castle, Alice soon afterwards expiring. The Old King had then undertaken a full act of penance and contrition before the tomb of his former friend and counsellor, Thomas Becket, at Canterbury. Bare-foot, divested of his robes and flogged by seventy monks he had remained prone for many hours. Having then made a bequest to keep a perpetual light burning over the tomb, Henry was granted absolution and it was preached that he was in no way guilty of inciting the murder of Becket except by the malicious misunderstanding of the four mischievous knights.

As if God now smiled upon him, the news arrived at Canterbury that Ranulf Glanville, Sheriff of Yorkshire had defeated and captured the person of William the Lion. When the Young King learned of all this he flew into a rage which no-one seemed able to suppress. All attempts at conciliation failed and King Louis sent word that the matter of England was closed. Already the Old King was turning the rebels' coats: the Flemish advance guard was allowed to leave the country under terms of a truce, the fox Hugh Bigod had forsworn the Young King's cause and submitted to the Old King with a renewal of his oaths of fealty. Everywhere the Old King appeared triumphant as support for the rebels fell away.

All except the burning ambition of King Louis to destroy Angevin power seemed lost and it was this that now led to the final act. Rousing the Young King and Count Philippe, Louis ordered a muster prior to the invasion of Normandy from the French Vexin.

*

Rouen: William regarded the city as he had done every morning for weeks now, searching for any change in those sturdy walls and the bastions towards which the sappers and miners had been working in mud and filth behind their shields of gabions. Did any yet sag, showing the first signs of their falling to provide the breach through which the waiting allied army might pour? No. He watched as the siege-engines began their daily toil, their weary crews winding, loading and loosing their projectiles and thought, briefly as he did every morning, of sitting in the mangonel before the wooden walls of Newbury in boyish innocence. He heard the dull thud as an arm, released from its pawl, struck against its rest, saw the arc of the projectile as it hurtled its way through the sticky, warm summer air. Caen stone, brought from the northern quarry on William's orders which had been seized on William's initiative, ready ammunition anticipated for one of the Old King's castles, but now used to bring him down.

Another engine loosed its own missile; not a block of stone but a fire-ball, soused straw looted from the unfortunate peasantry now set to fire the houses huddling hugger-mugger behind those stubborn walls. But would it? Beyond the ramparts rose a myriad of thin coils of smoke from the citizens' cooking fires but as yet no conflagration. But why should there be? On the occasions when the besiegers had seen the sudden, gratifying leap of flames and smoke, the River Seine had provided the ready means with which to extinguish them. Ah, yes, the Seine, that great artery that ran from deep inland, through Paris and Rouen to the sea, a means of resupply from Havre de Grâce – and possibly the way by which Rouen might be relieved. He could trace its passage through the countryside by the low mist that lay along its course, already burning off as the fierce summer sun rose in the north-eastern sky.

William sighed, sure that in that miasma lay the hidden source of the sickness now infesting the lines of the allied army. The trench sickness was carrying off men far and away faster than any action of the near motionless enemy. Not for the first time he felt gripped by a sense of deep frustration, a now physical feeling that uncoiled in his belly like that moment of fear in the waiting before battle, when action made of it high exhilaration. Then it was just a passing phase, a moment in the process of transcendence, now it gnawed at him: time was running out. Time for success, time for the Young King's arms, time for King Louis' ambition and, God forgive him, time for his own.

They *had* to take Rouen, yet Rouen was impossible to besiege effectively. It was no castle and presented too large a sprawl for even the mighty war-host of the allies to encompass properly. But without Rouen, the heart of Henry Curtmantle's power, their chances of achieving anything against the Old King faded away. They simply had to take this city for in William's imagination Henry had become like the many-headed dragon in one of Angharad ap Gwyn's old tales. One hefted one's mightiest sword and cut off one head, only to be confronted with another and then one found the lost head had regrown and one had achieved nothing. They had tried taking England, but Henry had retaken England, they had fomented trouble in Aquitaine, but Henry had seized the suzeraine of Aquitaine and held her in an English fortress while Duke Richard had failed to take La Rochelle. But if only they could take Normandy and then, perhaps Brittany, they might divide Henry's realms and bring him to terms favourable to Louis who was sure to dispossess him of some of his continental domains.

194

William knew they had had a chance. Henry Curtmantle had been occupied all year in England where he had acted with his characteristic energetic ruthlessness. William had heard the tales of Henry's humble and public mortification of his body, of God's forgiveness, of the immediate and almost miraculous capture of William the Lion. Henry had then turned defeat into victory as they had found their own endeavours confounded at every turn. Where they had baulked at the contrary gales, Henry had seized them and made the perilous Channel crossing; if only with a small following it had been a remarkable act of faith. Was Henry Curtmantle's anointing pre-eminent in the eyes of God, William wondered? It certainly seemed so.

'FitzMarshal!' William's increasingly anxious reverie was interrupted. He turned to see the Young Henry striding towards him followed by a knot of armed knights.

'Good morrow, my Lord King,' William made his obeisance.

'I see the day's work has begun, and I crave God's blessing upon it.' All present crossed themselves as the Young King went on, a smile on his handsome face, evidence of high good humour. 'I should give you ten marks for your thoughts. What think you? Shall we shatter their curtain first, or bring down a bastion?'

'I see no sign of either, Sire…yet…'

'Then how long must we wait?'

'I wish I could say, Sire…'

Henry looked at the city's walls. 'I am growing tired of this,' he said, his tone suddenly petulant before he turned again to William. 'But is there nothing we can do to expedite this matter? I saw you musing and ventured to think you might have divined a solution. King Louis has ordered a Mass sung for our success…'

William had lost count of the Masses Louis had ordered sung or said to ensure the triumph of his cause. So many it was enough to shake one's faith, William thought privately.

'Well,' Young Henry persisted, 'what think you?'

'My Lord, it will not please you, but I was thinking of your father and that were I in his place I should send, or bring a force into Normandy before this place falls to us…'

It did not please the Young King at all, on grounds of lese-majestie as much as presumption of defeat or in prospect of disloyalty to himself, and William knew it. As he watched the Young King's brow cloud and darken he added soothingly.

' 'Tis as well to consider the mind of one's enemy, Sire, for we make little progress here and should your father come in force, we would do well to be prepared.'

The Young Henry was now trembling with rage, his face brick red. William was aware that the rapid change of mood had been noticed by his knights, several of whom moved a step closer, one with his right hand on his sword hilt in anticipation of drawing it against William in defence of the King.

'I do not say this lightly, my Lord King, but if this place be not impregnable, then we do not possess the arms to invest it properly and thus render it so.'

'What should we do then? Raise the siege? Admit defeat?'

'Sire, there is great sickness in the army…'

'Pah! 'Tis but river fever, nothing more. A man shits for a week then cleans himself and resumes his duty.'

'Or dies. I see the muster rolls daily…'

'But they will be dying in equal numbers within the city.'

'I doubt it, Sire. They are accustomed to the river's gleets and miasmas…'

Out of the corner of his eye William noted the King's retinue had relaxed with the mollifying of Henry's mood. When he spoke again after a moment's consideration, the King's voice was low, normal and confidential. 'Then what counsel have you for me, FitzMarshal?'

'That we leave a force necessary to protect the siege-engines and withdraw the bulk of the army to the north where we may recruit our health and strength and lay athwart the route of any relief your father might send.

'But suppose he sends it by way of the Seine?' the Young King queried with an air of the grand strategist out-witting his old mentor.

'Then we shall hear of it and may make our dispositions accordingly.'

Henry considered this for a few moments, his head bent, his hand on his beard, the very image of his father. Then he raised his eyes and regarded William. 'You may be right, FitzMarshal, but Louis will never hear of such a thing!' And with that Henry turned about and William watched him stride away, followed by his knights. One or two looked back and smirked, sensing William had been discomforted, D'Yquebeuf among them. It seemed like Tancarville all over again, but it troubled William less and less.

*

Whether or not the Young Henry suggested a withdrawal to either Count Philippe of Flanders or King Louis, William never knew, though he suspected not. It was curious, he afterwards mused, that men like them could contemplate the withering of their troops with complete indifference. Possessed of vast lands and command over many lives, the supply of men guaranteed to be available under arms never troubled them. As for himself, his small mesnie and its reliance upon the Young King's bounty, made him

197

careful, and this concern, by extension, made him uncommonly mindful of that greater charge, the supply of the army itself which, by default, had come down to him.

All through July they maintained the siege, and on into August, increasingly certain of the delusion of success promised them daily by the sappers. Until, that is, a courier rode into camp from the Channel and word ran through the allied lines like wind through dried grass: Henry the Old King had landed at Barfleur and was marching on Rouen. Others followed: he had passed St Vlaast; he was through Caen, cutting of their supply of stone missiles; he had left Lisieux; he was at Elbeuf, not a few miles beyond the far bank of the Seine!

'What manner of force does he lead?' Count Philippe asked of a party of knights William had led out to reconnoitre. 'Brabantine mercenaries, my Lord, many of them, and what I take to be Welsh men, many of them too...'

'Welshmen?' queried Philippe, 'I thought they were in rebellion...'

'Not since my father married Emma of Anjou to that brigand David...' what is his name, FitzMarshal?'

'Dafydd ap Owain, my Lord King, Prince of Gwynedd,' William responded, catching the lilt of his old nurse with a twinge of nostalgia.

'Quite so,' said Young Henry as the attendant nobles stared at William's familiarity with a foreign tongue. It reminded those about the Young King that the Marshal was an Englishman and one likely with a tail in his breeches.

It was enough. That day Louis gave orders to raise the siege and Count Philippe commanded that the siege-engines be burned, an irony not lost on William. The following morning, the 14th, the once mighty war-host of France, Flanders and the Angevin rebels,

198

turned tail for Paris. Not man among the throng doubted but that the war had been lost.

*

Once again it became a time of heralds. The war-host melted away under its many feudal lords and two of the Angevin leopard cubs, the Young Henry and Count Geoffrey of Brittany, met at Evreux to hear their father's will. They made a brave showing as their cavalcade moved south, through Maine and into Touraine to humble themselves before Henry Curtmantle at Tours on the Loire whither he had gone after securing Rouen. Only Duke Richard remained stubbornly at large.

The year had turned and once again the glories of autumn fell upon the countryside that the column rode through. Already the patient and long-suffering peasantry had striven to repair the ravages of insurrection, making the progress of the column smooth as it took what it required in the way of sustenance by off-hand rapine. Indeed, one might have taken the combined mesnies of Young Henry and Count Geoffrey for a victorious procession, so gay were they with the new-fangled creations of heraldry, so strong did they seem in the numbers of armed knights in its train, and so light-heartedly did they help themselves to whatever took their fancy. And if their principals were nervous they did not show it; there was much bravado in their carriage as they discussed their grievances and made their case for defiance.

William commanded the vanguard, armed with his well-known reputation for having an eye for ambush; but he knew - if the two brothers did not - that the Old King wanted nothing better than to lure his sons into his hands. And what of himself? Might not the Old King mete out the punishment deserved by the Young King to his closest warrior knight? Was William's fate to be the whipping boy for the Young King, just as he had once been for his own father? Only the need for vigilance on the route kept his mind from dwelling on this, but at night, when he could not sleep for fleas and anxiety, he felt his vulnerability. The Old King could not strip him of his lands, for he had none, not would the forfeit of horses pay for high treason as it might have ransomed him in a tournament. If the Old King wished it, he could only pay with his life.

At Montlouis near Tours, in late September, they were joined by Duke Richard who, weeping in contrition or rage – for none could tell – fell to his knees at his father's feet. King Henry, greeting his sons, raised Richard to his feet and kissed him as a sign of peace. Such an act of penitence from so proud a spirit compelled his siblings to follow and they were all led to a great feast. On the following day a magnanimous and munificent Henry, blaming their various defections upon their youth and the influence of others, most notably their mother and King Louis VII, forgave them their disloyalty and settled castles and revenues upon them.

Yet these generous provisions were not without encumbrances. The three were obliged to swear an oath that they would never henceforth demand anything further from their father, nor would they raise their swords against him, nor cavil against the present settlement. In return Henry would not revenge himself upon their followers beyond ordering the destruction of any unlicensed fortifications. For all his apparent bounty, not one morsel of power did Henry II relinquish; though enriched by increased revenues, the Young King was left to accept the loss of his castles to brother John, whose inheritance now included lands in Normandy, Touraine, Maine and Anjou, the obvious favourite of the Old King. And beside him in Henry Curtmantle's affections stood Geoffrey the Bastard, the man who had ravaged the north of England in the Old King's name, so that William, the threat of execution lifted from his shoulders, heard the tittle-tattle among the Old King's

200

household when, after the fight at Alnwick that had secured the person of the Lion of Scotland, Henry had said to his illegitimate son: 'You alone have proved yourself my true son, 'tis the others who are the bastards.'

As for her sons' concerns for their mother, they were set aside by the Treaty of Montlouis. Eleanor was to remain incarcerated; where, no-one but Henry and his confidants knew, as she continued to be moved about his fortresses in southern England. Nor, for the time being, was the Young King's wife restored to him.

CHAPTER NINE: A-TOURNEYING 1175 - 1178

'You shall not go to Compostella,' the Old King said dismissively, turning again to his clerks and the litter of papers spread about them.

'You did not deny yourself pilgrimage when you felt your soul imperilled,' Young Henry remarked insolently, colouring up, but he failed to rouse his father to anger. 'But your soul is not imperilled,' retorted the Old King coolly. 'You renewed your vows of allegiance at Bayeux but a year ago and I have kept you close since...'

'Oh, aye, you have done that,' snarled Young Henry, 'and I have traipsed in your train hither-and-yon, I have met Papal legates, Welsh chieftains, Irish savages, Scots lords and slept in more castles than even my little brother John possesses, but not one act of governance have I initiated for all that I am named to succeed you when the Devil comes for your soul...'

The Old King looked up as the clerks crossed themselves at the blasphemy. 'Guard your mouth Henry. You cannot be certain that he will not come for yours first. You are besmirched by treason and have that which you hold by my clemency and the holiness of your oaths. I have shriven my soul...'

'Not of my mother's foul imprisonment!'

'Do not bring that hoary chestnut to my fire, boy,' growled the Old King. 'You better know your mother's part in the troubles in my Kingdom – our Kingdom, had you the good sense to see it thus.'

'She is your wife...'

'Aye and I wish to God she was not...' The Old King ground his teeth in suppressed anger and grief. Rosamund de Clifford had died

202

and he felt bereft. For all his louche living Eleanor had been his dynastic companion and helpmeet and to have this insolent, disarmingly good-looking young product of their conjoined loins acting like Almighty God was more than he could bear.

'But you cannot annul your marriage on grounds of consanguinity for fear of making bastards of us and losing Aquitaine…'

'Get out of my sight, before I take the flat of my sword to your arse!' Henry Curtmantle governed himself with great but impressive difficulty. 'D'you think I do not divine your wish to,' and here the Old King assumed a sarcastic tone, '*go on a pilgrimage?* Eh? It is but a ploy to slip across the Channel and make mischief, or go a-tourneying for your amusement. Who put you up to this, eh? That upstart and landless Devil's spawn William Marshal?'

'Do you not think that I can make my own decisions?'

'Very like you can and FitzMarshal has too much wit to forward such a foolish cause.' The Old King paused and seemed to be considering something. 'Maybe I should make him a grant of land and tear him from your side.'

Young Henry opened his mouth to protest, then shut it again as he perceived his father had bested him. 'Christ's bones,' he blasphemed under his breath and stormed out of the chamber.

It did not take long for almost every exchange between the Old and Young Kings to percolate throughout the Court. Ever since the Treaty of Montlouis the Old King had kept his heir beside him as he rode through his empire and most of that time they had been in England, Henry's French possessions being left in the hands of Duke Richard. Given the free-hand denied the Young Henry, Richard now ruled in his father's name with an impressive loyalty and although he was not fully trusted, the Old King knew that his son's love of war in such ungovernable country kept him devoted to the Old King's cause. Meanwhile the Young Henry had followed in the Old King's wake, unimpressed by his diplomacy and bored by the endless ceremonial, willing to load every word with contempt for those his father held in esteem. And with him went his mesnie and his own household, William among them.

It was during Lent 1176 when the two Kings were in London, in the White Tower, that the summons came to William after dark, secretly, borne by the Constable, who insisted William wore his hooded cloak. He was led to an upper chamber where Henry, the Old King, took a frugal supper alone, but for his hounds. After the Constable had been dismissed and told to wait without, King Henry himself refilled the goblet set before him with wine and pushed it across the table to William.

'My Lord King…?' William said uncertainly.

'Drink,' Henry commanded. 'I would have conference with you.' Henry paused while William took a draft from the goblet and laid it down again before the King. Henry indicated he should drink more and said: 'You will know that some weeks since my son, your master, did seek my leave to make pilgrimage to Santiago de Compostela, eh?'

'Aye, Sire.'

'And were you behind this request?'

Astonished, William shook his head. 'No, my Lord King, I was not!' William loaded his response with as much indignation as he dared.

'You would swear on the blood of Christ that you were not the evil courtier that I was informed urged my Lord Henry to this enterprise?'

'I would, Sire, without hesitation.' William thought fast. It was no mere fancy that brought him to this interrogation. Henry's

204

sword lay across the Lenten board and the Constable waited without. It even occurred to him that the goblet from which he drank had not been that from which the King supped, but one containing poison. He could be quietly murdered and thrown into the River of Thames and the act would whip the Young Henry into frightened compliance with his father's will once again.

'My Lord King, I will admit to remarking, perhaps injudiciously, that I should better like to spend my own time a tourneying but, since that is forbidden here in England...'

'Why? To make money?'

William shrugged. 'I have no lands, Sire, I am wholly devoted to your son's service.'

'Aye,' remarked Henry sarcastically, 'to my great disserve. But say, was this remark made in my son's hearing?'

William thought a moment. It was pointless to dissemble. 'No, my Lord King. I was in the company of Robert Tresgoz, Robert de Salignac, Adam d'Yquebeuf and Jean de Laon. It was no more than an expression of my private desire in my cups.'

'When you were gorging yourself upon crane, do doubt,' Henry remarked, indicating that he knew a great deal of what went on in his son's Court. 'And which of them, think you, may have suggested it to my son?'

'Sire?'

'Come, FitzMarshal,' you are not so modest a man as to think no-one thinks evil of you, nor would besmirch your honour were it to be useful to another's ends.'

William frowned. 'De Salignac I would trust with my life...'

'And Tresgoz?'

'Is close to the Young King...'

'And the Sieur Jean?'

205

William saw where the trail led and nodded. 'Is close to King Louis... as for D'Yquebeuf he does not love me.'

'Just so. What was an inconsequential remark of yours assumed a greater value than you intended. You should guard your tongue in the presence of such men. D'Yquebeuf and De Laon are of your own mesnie are they not?'

'D'Yquebeuf is of the Young King's, Sire, De Laon holds to me and I am aware of his loyalty. I keep him close that he may not draw closer to your son. The truth is that I had not thought the remark worthy of note any more than had I hoped for sunshine on the morrow.'

'But it seems that it may well have been.'

'Aye, my Lord King.' William was contrite.

'Well, no matter. There is something of greater importance I would speak of. There is unrest again in Angoulême and I would have Duke Richard reinforced. I would ease myself of an irksome son were I to send the Young King to his brother's assistance but I may only do this if I can vest the chief power held by the Young King elsewhere...in you, FitzMarshal. Both the Young King and Duke Richard respect you... You have ability in the field... You would have my blessing, and my leave to abandon them if they combine to foment trouble...'

William's head span. Here was a chalice bearing more potential poison that that of the King's goblet. But Curtmantle had not yet finished with him.

'You have sworn fealty to the Young Henry and the Young Henry has sworn fealty to me. There is no higher authority in my domains, FitzMarshal. This is no off-hand remark such as we have both made in our turn, but a matter of policy. Angoulême must be pacified and Richard must be helped. The Young King may garner some glory thereby and offer further proof of his loyalty to me. You may serve us both in equal measure, you understand?'

'I do, Sire.'

The Old King was silent for a moment, appraising William who felt his gaze keenly, like a burning brand searing his bent head. 'I do not blame you for what occurred at Chinon. In truth you had little choice, though Blund and Barre saw the danger, but they are both older men and not headstrong warriors.

'My Lord King is gracious.'

'Mmm,' Henry growled and held out his hand. 'You shall say nothing of my intentions, is that understood?'

'Aye, my Lord King.'

William knelt and kissed the ring that he wore, after which the Old King called for the Constable and William, his hood raised, returned to his own rude lodging.

*

It was after Easter that Henry revealed his intentions to his son, extracting a further oath of obedience and releasing Queen Marguerite into his company. The Young King was permitted by his father to visit Paris with his wife to relieve Louis' anxieties in his daughter's behalf. He was then to make for Poitiers to join Duke Richard, but to keep him on the leash the Old King had temporarily reduced his allowance. The Young King and his following crossed the Channel and arrived in Paris. Here, to William's consternation, the Young King threw off the traces. Leaving his wife in the care of his father and gathering his mesnie privée, he rode north, to the Court of Count Philippe of Flanders. Here he bemoaned his father's parsimony and cheerfully embraced Philippe's invitation to tourney. For three weeks Young Henry's mesnie excelled upon the field, compromising William. He was obliged to bend to the wind and did so not unwillingly and his personal success after so long an absence of opportunity somewhat restored his private coffers.

But they could not tarry long and William counselled departure. The Young King grew peevish and William feared the onset of a rage but good sense prevailed and the Young King was obliged to head south to establish his Court at Poitiers, where Robert de Salignac rejoined his mesnie and a brief conference was held with Duke Richard. Soon afterwards he took the field with William and De Salignac at his side. As he had sworn, William never mentioned a word of the Old King's confidence to Duke Richard, nor did Richard seek to give more than a hint of where he required his older brother's assistance, so that William wondered if he truly wanted it. Richard made war on his own terms and, as Duke of Aquitaine and Count of Poitou, the notion of submitting to his elder brother's orders was anathema to him. In the event the Young Henry and William were left to deal with pockets of resistance chiefly around the fateful town of Lusignan.

To William's frustration, this rather desultory and aimless warfare acted against the Old King's interest, for its undemanding nature and the presence of Marguerite drew the Young Henry back again and again to Poitiers. Within weeks the Young King was adding to his mesnie. To the great grief of Robert de Salignac, Robert Tresgoz and William himself, the Young Henry encouraged a score of knights known for their hostility to his father to join him. Led by Thomas de Coulonces, they were men whose adherence to Queen Eleanor had cost them heavily and their supplications to the Young King did not fall on deaf ears, renewing his outrage at his father's treatment of his mother. William, De Salignac and Tresgoz were not alone in their private condemnation of the Young Henry's actions, his Chancellor who – unbeknownst to William – had also been charged with a secret duty, was caught attempting to despatch the news to England.

William was beside himself with private anger: at the Old King, for not confiding that he had a spy planted in the Young Henry's household, at the Young King for his continued treachery and at the Chancellor for allowing himself to be discovered.

'God's bones! Are we to have no end of this intrigue?' he railed one evening in the company of De Salignac. 'We are both summoned to sit in judgement on this fool,' he said, pouring his friend wine.

'Aye…'

The following day the Young Henry had the man, named Adam Churchdiune, arraigned before a Court of Honour, which was obliged to sentence him to death. Only the intervention of the Bishop of Poitiers saved Churchdiune's life, though not his entire skin.

'He *shall* suffer for his treachery!' the Young King roared when the Bishop stood before him.

'But not with is life, I beg of you, my Lord King. He has the benefit of clergy; think what your father did to Thomas Becket. Would you have that stain upon your soul?'

Henry ground his teeth with anger. It seemed that every time he sought to rule as a King should rule he was thwarted! Adam Churchdiune had betrayed him under his very nose! And who else might there be in his household who had been planted by his thrice damned father?

'Show mercy, my Lord King,' beseeched the pleading Poitiers, going down on his knees, piously crossing himself.

'Mercy? Mercy? Was ever mercy shown me… or my mother, eh?'

'To be a King is not easy, Sire,' Poitiers continued, 'But to show mercy is to act as a true Christian King, in expectation of that mercy promised by our Lord Jesus Christ before the throne of God on the Day of Judgement…'

The Young Henry was breathing hard, the Bishop's appeal working upon him so that, in the end, he commanded Poitiers to rise. 'Very well, my Lord Bishop, I shall heed your wise counsel and I thank you for it.'

The Bishop of Poitiers rose, offered his ring for the Young Henry to kiss and withdrew, whereupon the King gave his final ruling to William.

'In the matter of Adam Churchiune. Have him whipped and, if he is flayed thereby, then that is God's will.'

William bowed and carried the order to the city's executioner. 'You need not kill him,' William said quietly, pressing ten marks into the man's filthy hand. The next day Adam Churchiune was very publicly whipped in the market square before being exiled to Normandy. Notwithstanding this act of clemency, it sent a message of renewed defiance to the Old King, for Churchdiune escaped to England where he revealed his back to Curtmantle. Henry flew into a furious passion, one of his greatest rages, not so much out of pity for Churchdiune, but out of fury over his son's continuing disloyalty and the fact that he himself had let his heir out of his own clutches.

As the winter approached the Young King left Poitiers to his brother Richard and led his household into Normandy to hold his Christmas Court at Bayeux. It was an act of provocation, of course, but one taken after some consideration. After Mass, at the great feast celebrating the birth of Christ, the Prince of Peace, the Young King's Court was made aware of the coming birth of another Prince, for Queen Marguerite was pregnant.

*

In the spring following, no recall came from England and the Young King expressed his anxiety that his father might soon land in Normandy, but the weeks dragged on. In the spring, at the Old King's behest, they rode out to quieten Berri, to the east of Poitiers, but it was a tame affair, the usual burnings, lootings, and a brief siege hardly worth remarking. On their return the Young Henry grew uxorious, for the dynastic implications of Marguerite's being brought to bed were considerable.

William could not tolerate the endless debates that seemed to entertain so many members of the Court. He nursed the private heresy that beyond a clear succession sanctified by the anointment of Holy Oil the members of a great house proved best their greatness by loyalty. It seemed a perfect system, ordained by God, that a man of wealth and power should be raised up to rule, to be duly consecrated by another man called by God to a spiritual life and thereafter to be acclaimed by his most immediate vassals, to whom those beneath owed fealty. He thought too that the Old King' divergence from this divinely simple succession, sanctioned by every precedent of church and state that William could think of since the Crucifixion of Christ, had led to so much misery for the people under the Angevins. The furious antagonism between Henry Curtmantle and his sons – most particularly the Young King – and the collapse of the Old King's marriage to Queen Eleanor, seemed a folly. True the Old King was a satyr, but William continually puzzled over the dynastic complications he had of himself constructed. They seemed so like the estrangement his own father had effected between himself and William, lacking in any quality of kingship, to cause William to wonder. Has it been truly wise to crown his heir before his own death? The King's action could only be thought sensible if seen to secure the succession but,

211

if his sons had proved as loyal as they should, it remained an unnecessary precaution, a following of the practice of the Capetian Kings of France.

Much of this sentiment arose from his own experience: the abandonment of his mother; his parent's heartlessness, his elder brother's demonstrable indifference and his lack of inheritance. The effect of such a casting-off had become visceral in William. All he could see about him appeared to lead to vast expenditure and ruin, and in the early months of the New Year he was much given to these thoughts, for the Young Henry had become uncharacteristically quiescent, often refusing the exercises of the tilt-yard and preferring to watch over his gravid wife as she grew rounder.

As for himself, beyond these bouts of introspection – near as bad in themselves as the gossip in the Young King's Court over the dynastic possibilities of not just the coming birth, but the fate of Queen Eleanor and the marriage prospects of Duke Richard and Count John – William maintained a rigid adherence to the knightly exercise. In this he was followed by only a handful of the mesnie so that it was remarked that in not following the new and languid fashion of Young Henry's Court, FitzMarshal was showing a dangerous arrogance.

The effect upon the Young King was that of reproach, inclining him to listen to the tittle-tattle of those envious of William's prowess, chiefly Adam d'Yquebeuf.

'Your friend would have us believe he is a great knight,' Young Henry remarked pointedly to Robert de Salignac one summer morning as the two of them watched William tilting at the quintain.

'My Lord King, he keeps himself in readiness to serve you,' De Salignac replied in defence of his friend.

'I am not sure that I need his service,' Young Henry replied darkly, turning away and leaving De Salignac staring after him. For two days De Salignac kept the Young King's remarks to himself and was on the verge of warning William when Queen Marguerite was brought to bed. But the tiny boy she brought forth into the world breathed for no more than a few moments before he gave up the ghost. The word spread quickly, helped by the mad rage into which the Young King descended.

'The mite took one look at the world and sensibly declined the blessings of life,' Robert de Salignac murmured to William, simultaneously crossing himself. The sardonic blasphemy drew a long sigh from William, who shook his head and followed De Salignac's gesture. ' 'Twill be a Requiem Mass now, I trow,' De Salignac added with a languid boredom before thinking that he ought to warn William of the Young King's disfavour. 'He is in a rare passion…' he began, but William seemed to have gathered himself up and, invested with resolution, made for the chamber door.

'William, there is something… Whither do you go?'

The noise of Young Henry's raving came in through the opened door and William paused on the threshold and turned. 'As you love me, Robert, arm, go into the tiltyard and raise the whole mesnie; tell Odo to make ready my destrier and pass word that the King's should be caparisoned. Blunt weapons for this day's work.'

'We are riding out?' De Salignac asked, puzzled. 'On such a day as this?' but William had gone. He stood for a moment watching the motes of dust dance in the sunlight where it entered the room like the shaft of an unstrung bow-staff and then did his friend's bidding.

William received no answer to his knocking on the Royal Chamber door. From within came noises like that of rutting beasts, rising and falling, punctuated by great sobs and indraughts of air. Two priests stood shivering with nerves and the squire on duty stared at him, wide-eyed and nervous.

As it appeared he would force the door the wretched squire protested: 'You cannot, my Lord Marshal! It is not seemly.'

'My Lord Marshal, it is we who should first console the King when he has ceased his blasphemies.' The priests looked too terrified to do anything.

'Then why to you not attend to the matter?' he said to the priests, 'I hear no blasphemies.' Then he turned to the squire. 'Stand aside, sir.'

'My Lord, I dare not…'

William opened the door. The Young King was on his knees beside his bed, gasping for breath. At first William supposed him at his devotions, until he saw the rent blankets and the torn palliasse below, the straw from which was crammed into the King's mouth. Then the roaring began again, though it subsided as he became aware of the presence of another in his private quarters.

The act of uninvited entry brought Henry to his feet. Fury at the cheating of God in the death of his heir changed to outrage at the enormity of the intrusion. William closed the door behind him as Henry, unable to articulate anything beyond a resumption of his leonine roaring with his mouth full of old straw, spat it out. When he had done so he vented all his ire on the intruder.

'You!' he shrieked, stumbling forward almost blinded by his wrath, his fists raised as if to strike William could he but bring him into focus. 'You! God rot your devilish soul, FitzMarshal. You have been the Devil's agent ever since the Queen my mother sent you to join my mesnie! Christ in Heaven, not one thing in my affairs has prospered since that moment! Do you know that?'

He was face-to-face with William, a few inches shorter and looking up, uttering his words with such vehemence that William felt the spittle on his face.

'And now…and now, in a moment of the most private grief, you burst into my chamber unannounced, unsummoned, un…' Young Henry could think of nothing to add and now began to strike William upon his breast, hammering with both fists. William braced himself against the blows and in the silence broken only by the dull thump-thump of Henry's assault gasped out 'My…Lord…King…you dishonour…me as…you dishonour yourself…'

'How dare you!' Henry stood back, his handsome face distorted with fury.

'This is not kingly conduct, my Lord!' William said steadily, breathing hard, for the pain in his bruised ribs was considerable.

'You sir, exceed yourself, God damn you to perdition!' Henry paused, gathering his wits. 'How do *I* dishonour *you*? Is there not a yawning cavern between us, FitzMarshal?'

'It was I who knighted you, Sire; dubbed and girded you, and I come as your loyal vassal to save you from yourself more readily than the two terrified and canting priests waiting without…'

'Priests? I have not sent for priests…'

'They come out of pity at your raving, my Lord King, and would give you the Host were you to take the straw out of your beard.'

Young Henry plucked at his mouth, over-swept by the sudden realisation of the fool he must look. To fill the void that threatened, William said quickly, 'my Lord King, we have more in common than you think.'

The Young Henry seemed to shrink. 'H…how can that be, you are a penniless knight; you owe all to me…'

'And you to your father, Sire, in that you are a Prince. But I was sent a hostage as a small boy, disowned, cut off from any inheritance since. I am not FitzMarshal, my Lord, but William Marshal, in the service of my Liege Lord and to that end I have ordered the mesnie made ready to ride out.'

As he strove to understand William's meaning the Young King partially calmed himself. 'You have *what*?'

'The person of the Queen is in no danger, I understand, and it would be better if we rode out and matched our mesnies. The day is perfect.'

'They will say...' Henry seemed uncertain what the world would say and hesitated.

'That your conduct was unseemly?'

'Yes.'

'Or that you recovered your manhood having seen the Queen comfortable. I warrant she will be sleeping. Word of all this,' William gestured round the chamber at the torn bedding and the strewn straw, 'will reach your father's ear. Better he hears otherwise, wouldn't you say?'

The Young Henry was still breathing heavily mastering his temper and staring hard at William. 'God's blood, William Marshal,' he said at last as he perceived something in William's proposal. Eventually he nodded. 'Very well. Go. I command you to make ready my mesnie privée. A red band upon their right arms and a white upon those who cleave to you.'

William made his obeisance and withdrew. Outside he dismissed the priests, who scuttled away with every appearance of deep contentment. To the Squire he said, 'The King will call you to arm him presently.'

Leaving the lad with a puzzled look upon his face William ran down the spiral steps and out into the tiltyard. The sunshine dazzled

216

him for a moment and then he saw the horsemen and felt the palpable atmosphere of disbelief and half-heartedness, as though they were set upon a fool's errand.

Kicking aside a small pig which had escaped enclosure, William shaded his eyes and raised his voice. 'The King's knights to arm with blunted weapons, a red cloth to be knotted about their sword-arms above the elbow! My own likewise with a white cloth! Go to it!'

There was a moment's hesitation as the import of the order sank in, then Robert de Salignac roared for his horse. 'Come lads, to horse! We cannot keep our Lord the King waiting!'

De Salignac had done his work and Odo, already in helm and hauberk, had William's own gear ready and his destrier saddled. William waved aside his surtout and lance Once caparisoned William put his left foot in Odo's joined hands and with a grunt from both men, flung himself into the saddle. Seeing his own men drawing up he rode along the line giving them a cursory inspection. Two of the knights wore their surtouts and William ordered them removed before returning to the head of the little column where De Salignac awaited him, his mount foaming at the chafe of the bit and pawing the gravel of the yard.

'We are somewhat outnumbered, Will,' he said drily.

'Aye, and we must lose, you and I especially. I would have the King win.'

'He comes,' De Salignac nodded and William turned his horse and walked it towards the Young Henry.

Leaning from the saddle, his helm on his saddle-bow he asked in a low vice, 'Does the Queen sleep, my Liege?'

Young Henry nodded.

'Then a game, my Lord King - for stakes,' he said, so that it was clear what lay between the two of them. 'Ten marks a life, to be

217

signified by the tearing off of our marks.' William touched the white woollen strip of blanket Odo had torn off for him and that now encircled his right arm. 'With blunt weapons.'

'Agreed,' Young Henry said curtly, adding, 'the flat and not the point or edge,' by which William knew the Young King's own sword was not for exercise. He bowed to pride.

'And with your permission my following to leave first since you have the advantage in numbers.'

'You would ambush me?' Henry's tone mellowed slightly, William thought, and a faint light of anticipation gleamed in his eyes.

'Since I lack a mesnie proper of mine own, Yes. Besides, only if you let me, my Lord King.'

'Then get you hence, William Marshal and do your damndest. I shall give you but half an hour by my own reckoning.'

William turned away, kicked his horse into a canter and led his own column out through the gate.

'What miracle have you wrought here?' De Salignac asked, riding up alongside him as they cleared the city and rode through open country.

'God knows, Robert, but I may be deader than a mere forfeit acknowledged by this day's end. I must pass word that each life is vested in our cloth token.'

'I have already done that.'

William turned and smiled at his companion. 'My thanks.' They rode on for a mile or two until they were passing through scrub and open woodland. Denser woods lay ahead of them and William held up his hand and drew rein.

'We cannot make this too easy for fear of further angering the King,' William said to De Salignac and his headmost knights as they gathered round, their mounts steaming from exertion in the sunshine. 'You shall all do your utmost; do you understand?'

They nodded or grunted and De Salignac asked, 'Do you intend we divide into two groups?'

'No, three. Two of eight lances; one of ten. The first eight under Robert de Salignac, then ten under the Sieur Jean and eight under my command. Jean, when we have chosen our ground do you conceal yourself and your party to the right of the road. Robert, yours to the left; you are to confront the head of the King's mesnie and as it turns to engage, Jean will fall upon them. You will be surrounded, their numbers will ensure this, but you should then break off the action and ride as if to escape. They will see it as a lure and break off their pursuit. That will be the point at which I fall upon their rear...'

'But my Lord Marshal we may well be too distant to come swiftly enough to your aid,' argued Jean de Laon.

'That is my intention. I shall pay the forfeits. It is the King's day for good sport, not ours. He has had enough grief already.' William looked around him, 'do you understand?' Again the nods and grunts of affirmation. 'Do not think he will not put me to the test,' he added, thinking of the King's sharpened sword. 'Now, let us choose our ground before we are caught in the open.'

They rode on into the woodland until, just beyond a slight bend, a glade opened up beyond which two low hummocks rose. The summer sun filtered through the canopy of leaves and the ground, thick with the rotting vegetation of last year, was dappled. William checked his horse and the column reined in. It would suit William's purpose and they had no time to linger. Indicating the slight rise to their left William nodded to Robert de Salignac.

'Lances low,' he said as De Salignac led his eight horsemen off. He only had to nod to Jean de Laon before turning to the remaining eight. 'Follow me…'

William turned about and rode back a bowshot along the way they had come. Having rounded a slight bend in the track he turned aside and drove into the woods until he judged the sunlight, shadow and interposing trees gave some concealment. He was lucky too, a slight dip in the ground added to their concealment. Ordering his men to dismount he handed his reins to Odo.

'Remount the instant you see my signal,' he ordered before walking back to lie beneath a tree from where he could command a view of the road.

They did not have long to wait. The still summer air carried the dull thunder of shod hooves and the faint jingle of harness a moment or so before he saw them, four out ahead and then the main body of fifty or so horsemen: odds of roughly two-to-one. It was going to prove an expensive day for himself, William thought ruefully. He waited until the Young King's mesnie was out of sight, rose and loped back to his waiting men. They mounted the second they saw him coming. Even as they did so they could hear the first shouts and clash of arms.

Holding up his hand, his heart beating, William led his men at a walk back to the road but once all were clear of the trees he waved them forward. Ahead of them they could hear the clang of arms and the shouts of exertion, then there was a sharp change, the noise of fighting ended and there were several loud shouts. William waited until they reached the bend, then kicked his horse into a fast canter. Having eschewed a lance he drew his sword.

Beyond the glade which opened up as they advanced they could see the swirl of indecision. The mêlée was over, but the Young King's mesnie had stalled and lost its cohesion. William had little

220

time to assess the matter, but it seemed to him that the men who faced about as someone shouted a warning of his own approach were not the full fifty he had seen ride past him earlier.

The shock of battle when it came bore both fear and exhilaration. It was only mock warfare but its intent was grim enough, to wrest from the enemy the coloured arm-bands by whatever means came to hand. Some tried the sword, others the fist, but the first was too clumsy and easily evaded and the latter required the removal of a gauntlet. Better by far to knock your opponent off his horse and have your own destrier, trained for the very task, to strike its hooves about the fallen foe to keep the fellow writhing in fear of their shattering effect until he submitted. William unseated two of Young Henry's men, a knight and his squire, before dismounting alongside them to cut off their arm-bands. Odo came up and grasped the destrier's reins as the beast stamped either side of the knight's torso until William called him off and completed his business. He saw the discomfited warrior was Adam d'Yquebeuf and wished it had been another. He could see the humiliation and fury in D'Yquebeuf's eyes as he tore off his helm in submission.

All about the two the swirl of the mêlée continued and this small triumph accomplished, William sought to remount, handing his trophies to Odo, when a great shout rent the air. William looked up and saw approaching what seemed to be the rest of Young Henry's mesnie, coming full-tilt after turning back from their pursuit of De Salignac and De Laon. At their head rode the Young King and he had identified William even without his surtout.

'He's mine!' he heard Young Henry bellow.

'Get clear!' William shouted to Odo, seeking room and digging his spurs into his destrier's flanks. He met the King at a half-gallop, parrying the blow aimed at his head and wheeling round just as the King did the same. But Henry did not return, instead he reined in his horse and William found himself surrounded by six or seven of the Young King's knights and four or five men on foot. He laid about himself with the flat of his sword, dealing several powerful blows and unseating two men before he felt a loss of control; one of the men on foot had severed his left stirrup strap and threw up his leg with a mighty heave, even as William's destrier turned its head and attempted to throw them off by biting them. For a moment they spun in a tight circle, then Henry rode forward again and was upon William. Wherever the Young King intended the blow to fall was uncertain, for the gyration of his quarry was so fast, but it struck William across his left shoulder and cheek as the King drove his own horse into the flank of William's. The great war-horse staggered sideways under the impact and might have fallen, throwing William and landing on top of him, but William's hours of training paid off. Somehow it skittered sideways and William heard Henry curse.

But he could achieve little with a lost stirrup and imperfect balance and he threw his leg over the destrier's shoulder, letting the horse dance clear as he slid to the ground to grapple with the two knights on foot, who had stood aside as their master rode in for the coup de grâce. William had denied them victory on their first clash, but policy dictated he did not long maintain his defiance, even though he felt the fight warming him. Notwithstanding his difficulties breathing, he could best these fellows, but this *must* be Henry's day.

He felled one of the foot-knights and went for his arm-band, deliberately exposing himself as Henry kicked his own destrier forward and caught him a mighty blow across his flank. William toppled sideways and fell, the second foot-knight at his throat in an instant, a gleamingly sharp dagger at his throat.

'Cry quarter, my Lord Marshal,' the knight hissed in his face, and William sensed he was enjoying himself enormously but then the man was sent sprawling and Henry stood over him.

'I said he's mine!'

'I submit…' William began but Henry stamped his right foot on William's already bruised breast and with the other flattened William's sword blade so that his hand was pinned by the hilt and sank into the leaf-mould and soft earth beneath. Henry bent and, with a quick insertion and twist of his sharp sword, severed the white cloth about William's upper arm.

'You are my prisoner, William Marshal, and my ransom for you is everything you have in this world.'

William was in some pain now, gasping for his breath, but the Young Henry's demand was as outrageous as it was dishonourable. He thought of the loss of his fine destrier which had fought with as much skill as he had trained it and panted: 'Ten marks…'

'Everything.'

*

That evening, after a Solemn Mass had been sung for the dead child, the Young King was in a middling mood. 'I have the making of another son,' he growled in William's hearing, brushing aside offered consolation in a chilling reminder of the words John the Marshal had once used about William himself. The day of mourning was considered by most of both mesnies to have been rescued from the priests, and the Young King's lost boy had been paid for by the mortal wounding of one of William's knights and the severe injuring of another. Both were held to be accidents, plain mischances that occurred from time-to-time in the tournament, but Robert de Salignac had word that not all the King's men had carried dull weapons and said so to William.

'Did you not expect some treachery?' William replied quietly. 'Do not let word of this pass elsewhere from your own lips, I beg you.'

De Salignac stared at his friend, then nodded. The day's events, extraordinary as they had been, had shown William to be a man of deeper understanding of more than the art of war for which he was already well known. This changing of the Young King's mood, thought Robert de Salignac, was prowess of an altogether different form.

Thus, although the tone of the feast that evening was muted to a degree, there was an under-lying sense that something had changed beyond the Young King's disappointment in his wife's failure to present him with an heir. It had not been the fault of His Grace, for sure, and while some might piously ascribe it to God's displeasure, there were others who thought it all the Queen's. By all that they held dear, the truth was that it has been a good day.

After the submission of William Marshal, the herald Young Henry had had in his retinue had blown his horn for a cessation of the tournament. It had been, after all, nothing, much more than a game to most of them: friends against friends. This and the wine established a rich source of anecdote and the King's men acknowledged that, for an outnumbered force, the Marshal's men had executed a good plan with great cunning. But they had lost, had they not?

And the Marshal's men toasted their own valour and coolness, and raised their goblets to their chief who sat in the post of honour at the Young King's right hand. Henry beamed and joined the toast to William. He had said nothing to the Marshal throughout the meal, not even after William had first called upon his own following to acknowledge the King's victory, but as he made to rise from the board, Young Henry leaned towards William.

224

'Do not think I owe you anything by this day's work,' he said in a low voice. 'And do not forget that all your horses and equipage are mine, even while you have the use of them. And now I am to my Lady that I may explain my absence was because of you.'

William re-seated himself in the wake of the Young King's retiring, whereupon the noise of chatter in the great hall at Poitiers rose. In the hubbub Robert de Salignac leaned across the board towards William. William inclined towards him, cupping one ear.

'You had made an enemy of him before this day, William,' De Salignac said. 'I had been minded to warn you, but the moment did not seem right until now.'

William shrugged resignedly and stared directly at De Salignac. 'He repudiated our agreement over forfeits as regards myself. He has everything I own by way of arms…'

'God's blood,' swore D Salignac. 'I should have warned you sooner.'

'Perhaps, but he is, like all his brood, capricious,' William replied quietly. 'He may change his mind in a week or two…'

'Or may seem to.'

William smiled at his friend and rose. 'I need air Robert…'

'Shall I…?'

'No, I would rather be alone until I sleep, but thank you for your thoughtfulness.'

Robert de Salignac watched the powerful figure leave the hall unaware that William was having difficulty breathing from the bruising and battering the Young Henry had given him earlier in the privacy of his chamber.

The Court went into formal mourning for three weeks at the end of which the Young King could stand it no longer and sent for Robert de Salignac. At the end of their conference De Salignac sought out William, a rueful smile upon his face. William was with

Odo in the castle smithy where new sword blades were being forged for William and his squire. William looked up, seeing the expression upon De Salignac's face.

'I am commanded by my Lord the King to inform you that we go hawking tomorrow.'

'What's that to me? I have no hawk. 'Tis now the King's.'

'But I see you have your own sword,' remarked De Salignac drily, nodding at the white-hot blade just then being drawn from the forge.

'I must needs have something of my own for my own defence,' William's tone was grim.

'But there is another matter that I am charged with.' De Salignac gestured with his head and William nodded at Odo, the smith and his armourer, to continue with their work and withdrew alongside his friend.

'Well?'

'In all humility His Grace acknowledges the will of God as made manifest in the death of his son. It is not God's purpose that he should yet have a son and he marks this as guidance to withdraw from all dynastic disputes, leaving these to his brothers. He believes, or is persuaded,' De Salignac said sardonically, 'that God in His infinite wisdom charges him to eschew all challenges to his father in his father's lifetime and to better prepare himself for his own time by…guess what?'

'Robert, I have played enough games with this King…'

'We remain in Aquitaine until the turn of the year and then, my friend, we move to Normandy and the Vexin and go a-tourneying.'

'What?' scoffed William, 'until the Old King's demise?'

'Presumably,' responded De Salignac lightly. 'A Holy mission. Our Lord King is contrite. In the death of his child and the sparing of his Queen, he is seized by a realisation of his own mortality and that for years past he has imperilled his soul by disobedience.'

'The priests have been at him.'

'Very likely. But the best news comes last.'

'Oh, and what is that?'

'That we – or rather you as his Marshal – make the most perfect preparations for his mesnie over the coming months that he, we, may enter the lists as though new; that he wishes as a mark of his great favour that you combine your mesnie with his own...'

'Is that not already the case?' protested William heatedly. 'God's blood! But I have no mesnie, never have had beyond commanding a handful of friends like you. Besides he *owns* me and all that I have: my hawks, my horses, my...'

But De Salignac was holding his hand up for quiet, his eyes twinkling. 'And that you be restored to all your possessions, hawks, horses, harness, the lot. He asks not one mark more in your forfeits. There! What say you to that? Shall you pole-axe the messenger, eh?'

William stared at De Salignac. 'Huh, not one mark more, eh? He already has ten marks for every man he took, a dozen in number, one hundred and twenty in all.'

'But none from you, eh?' De Salignac guyed him. 'Why Will, you are better at your numbers than heretofore.'

'The destrier and the peregrine would have been hard to replace,' he mused quietly.

'Come, Will, are you not cheered by this news?' De Salignac was puzzled at his friend's slow acceptance at this change of fortune. The tournament offered a great opportunity for personal enrichment and, with an uneasy peace upon the land, they might have time to treat King Louis' knights roughly.

'I am wondering how long the whim will last, my friend.'

227

'Well, a season might see us make up for the expenses of these last years of campaigning.'

'True,' responded William ruminatively. 'And if it is God's will one might expect a little longer, don't you think?'

'I think at the very least we shall have a span of time long enough for the Queen to be again impregnated and bring forth a sturdy son. Surely that would be God's will.'

William nodded agreement and both men crossed themselves. 'Yes, that would seem like God's will made manifest.'

'Then we must pray for it, and if not,' added De Salignac mischievously, 'perhaps another season until the Almighty makes his true purpose known'.

*

The Divine purpose was not revealed for three years during which the augmented mesnie of the Young King Henry and his Marshal acquired all the glory that a growing interest in the tournament could confer. These years were marked by large meets of the great magnates to assay their valour and luck, catching the fragile mood of the moment, earning the sanction of the Pope and the support of Kings, for prowess accrued in the tournament was a currency by which prestige was measured and dynastic settlements might be proposed and arranged. Vast tracts of the border marches between counties were taken over for these war-games, and the encampments of the opposing parties attracted even greater gatherings of humanity than earlier occasions. The fortunes of whole towns were often transformed by the sudden commerce of such large bodies of wealthy noblemen, though occasionally things got out of hand, the fighting spilling through the streets themselves. But it was the fortunes of the participants that formed the core of the matter and whilst the Young Henry threw himself into the tournament with enthusiasm, matters quickly went awry.

228

The Old King's generous provision for his heir enabled his son to put into the field a splendid and well-equipped mesnie which created a magnificent impression when it arrived in the lists from whence the parties dispersed. Unfortunately it soon proved no match for the hardened exponents of the noble game, mostly the Flemish and French knights who fought under the banners of Louis of France or Philippe of Flanders. At an early encounter William, desperate to make captures and earn a useful share of the booty, led a violent charge during which he far outran the Young King. It was only when he rounded-to having cut off and savaged a portion of the enemy, that he realised he was himself isolated and had to fight his way out to rejoin Henry's banner.

Humiliated by chagrin, he was obliged to submit to a public haranguing from the Young King in front of the mesnie as, deflated by defeat, it licked its wounds and counted the cost of failure.

'It should not be for me to advise you that you should cleave to me, Marshal,' Henry fumed. Nor did it help that Adam d'Yquebeuf stood beside the Young Henry barely concealing the smirk on his face and it was some days later that De Salignac quietly informed him that he suspected D'Yquebeuf of delaying the charge of the Young King, exposing William.

'Why would he do that? The whole mesnie loses thereby…'

'But D'Yquebeuf appeared the wiser man, for by not supporting you the King was bested. Had the King fallen in with your impetuosity without delay things might have fallen out differently. They are saying that D'Yquebeuf pointed out you were arrogant in leading the charge, that your station was subordinate to the King…'

'He is right,' William interrupted, 'though I would it were not so. I had thought the King rode hard by me and took no thought of him lagging behind…'

'D'Yquebeuf would oust you if he could,' De Salignac said.

229

'Even to the detriment of his own fortune?' William was incredulous.

'If he has persuaded the Young King that without you he would do better, then aye. He plays a long game, William, you must watch him. He has not forgotten the encounter outside Poitiers and is, in any case, jealous of you.'

'If you are right, he could ruin me quickly,' responded William, quite at a loss. 'And there is little I can do about it.'

'I will speak with him…'

'No, I cannot allow you to do that.'

'You cannot afford not to.'

'No, Robert,' William said, perceiving a way of out-witting D'Yquebeuf. 'I will cleave to the King. Let the achievements be Henry's alone; I too can play a long game.'

'Very well,' De Salignac nodded.

*

It was at Anet that providence changed in William's favour, and changed through farce. Since that first humiliation William had kept close to the King, aware that the careful planning he had successfully employed in his earlier ambushes rarely worked in the wide-ranging mêlées as engaged in by Norman-French chivalry. Not that the performance of the Young King's mesnie improved in any way, but William did not expose himself to folly or ridicule until the mesnie entered the lists at Anet. The chosen ground lay close to the confluence of the Rivers Eure and Vesgre, to the south of the Vexin and at the assembly at the lists there was a good deal of abuse from the French knights against whom Henry's mesnie was arraigned. Whether or not it was over confidence on the part of their opponents, or the caution urged upon the Young King by William and Ranulf FitzStephen, but Henry held his forces back until a propitious moment offered.

William stayed his hand, deliberately cautious, watching both the Young King and Adam d'Yquebeuf who, gladdened by William's apparent passivity beside the King, was eager to prove his own valour. It was Henry who gave the order to charge and William followed the King as they thundered downhill, couching their lances and driving right through the main body of the French so that they broke up and as they checked their horses to wheel about and set about the broken force to make their captures, the French fled in a precipitate rout, making directly for Anet and the crossing of the Eure .

With howls of frustration and cries of anger, most of Henry's knights put spurs to their destriers and made after the French, sensible to the fact that if they did not do so then they were going to lose the best opportunity they had had all season of redeeming their heavy losses. Having seen D'Yquebeuf among their number, William attended to the securing of three or four prisoners and, with Odo at his side, rejoined the Young King. Henry, torn between two courses of action, wheeled his destrier round and round.

'We must support them, my Lord King!' William called.

'Let us ride then!'

William, De Salignac and half a dozen others, including Odo, spurred their horses and made after the pursuit, clattering into the main street of Anet which had been deserted by its citizens for fear of inciting further outrage and damage from the warring parties. A few stalls in the market place still stood, the majority had been flattened as the running fight had passed through the town. There was a desultory struggle between a French knight and one of Henry's squires, and a wounded horse was trying to regain its feet as they briefly checked their pace before Henry, his blood up, urged them forward.

At a half gallop they swung round a corner beyond the square and came face-to-face with a mounted French knight, his brace of squires and a contingent of foot-soldiers. They wore the colours of Simon de Neuphle.

Henry checked his mount a touch, allowing the others to come up with him, whereupon he shouted: 'We shall not pass them, yet we cannot retire…'

'So help me God,' roared William, 'let us charge them!'

And with barely a second's hesitation the lance points were lowered again and couched. Then, their destrier's eyes ablaze and thunder of their hooves shaking the beaten mud of Anet, they rode the infantry down. The foot-soldiers fled, opening up to allow the handful of knights a way through, but as Henry struck sideways at one of the squires, who immediately gave ground and was followed by his companion, William dropped his lance and rode directly at the solitary knight, checking his destrier so that it caracoled, sitting back on its haunches, its sharply shod front hooves pawing the air in the face of Simon de Neauphle. Thrusting aside the lowered lance point with his gauntlet William leaned forward, the signal to his mount to lower his front legs, then reached out and caught the right-hand rein of his opponent, tugged the head of De Neauphle's destrier round. Its head thus viciously jerked, the horse followed as William spurred his own horse onwards.

Clinging onto the reins of De Neauphle with all his strength he dragged the Frenchman after him, chasing the others as they fled from Anet. The going got easier after a few seconds and William quickly came up with his fellows who had drawn breath half a mile clear of the town to regroup. Here a number of the mesne who had gone in hot pursuit of the broken French were coming in to rejoin Henry's banner just as William came up to the Young King who was flushed with the excitement of their escape.

Seeing Odo, William commanded, 'secure this knight, sirrah!'

At this point the gathering of knights and squires burst out laughing and Young Henry asked to which knight William referred. William turned to see the destrier's saddle empty; there was no sign of Simon de Neauphle who had jumped clear soon after William had grabbed his mount's reins.

'But I have a horse, my Lord King,' William said, joining in the laughter and reviewing the animal's caparison. 'And some harness of value, I think,' he added as he passed the reins into the hands of a grinning Odo.

The Young Henry rode alongside him and clapped him on the shoulder. 'By God, William,' the King said with a sudden flare of warm familiarity, 'but that was nobly done for all you lost your quarry!'

And as the mesnie gathered its own and returned to the lists, the Young King and his entourage were in high spirits.

*

'May I have private conference with you, Sire?' William asked one day. The relationship between William and the Young King, and indeed the fortunes of the Young King's mesnie, had changed after Anet. Ever capricious, the Young Henry turned again to the man who showed him loyalty and, as far as it was possible for a landless knight, a friendship the Young King was much in need of. That evening the two men came together.

'What would you say to me?'

'My Lord King, I have word that there is a tourney to be held at Pleurs... The whole of French chivalry will be there...'

' 'Tis too far, William, the expense of the baggage train is such that...' Henry broke off and shrugged. ' 'Tis too far.'

'I have thought of that, Sire. But would you permit me to suggest something: deception.'

'What? As practised by Count Philippe?' the Young Henry asked, referring to the practice of Philippe of Flanders arriving at the lists with his mesnie to rule out a contest and declare himself a spectator, only to throw himself and his companions into the field when both parties engaged were exhausted. 'How would that help? I have told you it is the distance…'

'No, no, Sire,' William interrupted, presuming upon the Young King's amity. 'What I am proposing is that you permit me to attend with some among my following. We would wear no device, just plain surtouts. We would travel light and, should we be successful, profits shall be as if you were in our company.

As Henry perceived the guile in William's proposal his face broke into a grin. 'Perhaps I should accompany you in disguise.'

William smiled back. 'As you wish, Sire, but if the affair miscarries and your presence became known I should not wish you to be thought of as a losengier.'

'Well, being a deceiver in the tourney does not seem to trouble Count Philippe,' Henry countered wryly.

'True, Sire, but he is not a King.'

'No…' The King thought for a moment or two and then said. 'But if you wished to deceive by your plain surtouts, a mesnie would be too conspicuous. What say you entered the lists with one other knight and each with a squire? Such a small party would rouse no suspicions en route and should secure you anonymity. Should you prove your prowess, half the profits to my Treasury.

William did not hesitate. 'My Lord King, I go as you command.'

'In secret, William.'

'Aye, Sire, in secret.'

That night William spent on his knees and the following morning approached Robert de Salignac. 'I would have words with you, my friend, but before I do I require an oath of secrecy. The

234

matter which I wish to discuss I have only spoken about with my Lord King.'

'Not, I hope, a plot against his father, William. Surely you have not sunk so low,' De Salignac responded sardonically. 'Or is it a challenge to Adam d'Yquebeuf, for you have him half out of the saddle, now you might give him the coup de grâce.' Here De Salignac feigned a sword blow.

'No, but I have two choices as regards yourself.' William told De Salignac what he had proposed and the Young King approved.

'Well, I can see one choice you have as regards myself and that is whether I accompany you or not. What, pray is the other?'

'That you remain here and keep my place and I take another.'

'Huh. Who would you take?'

William shrugged. I had not thought of it. FitzStephen, perhaps, even D'Yquebeuf to heal the rift between us.'

De Salignac shook his head. 'Too risky; D'Yquebeuf would see you ruined by capture and count it no dishonour… No, by God, William, leave FitzStephen in your room and I shall go with you. When do we leave?'

'Ten days hence.'

*

The grand tourney at Pleurs in the Champagne was a splendid affair attended by a myriad nobles including Count Philippe of Flanders, Theobald of Blois, Hugh of Burgundy, Jacques d'Avesnes and Guillaume des Barres among a host of other gallants. William and Robert rode in, each accompanied by a squire and with an armourer and smith between them. The four followers had been given five marks each to stop their mouths and promised more pending the verdict of fortune. They had been told, if asked, that they served William ap Gwyn and Robert de Morlaix, Breton knights and was these pseudonyms that they entered at the lists. Neither wore any device, but both bore surtouts of plain black.

'To whose mesnie do you belong?' they were asked by the heralds.

'We venture our fortunes as free-lances,' William replied for them both, amused at the sceptical stares this bold assertion drew from the heralds and those within earshot.

William's imposing frame sitting upon his obviously well-trained destrier sparked a rumour that gained currency with every passing hour: he was a great nobleman come to tourney for the love of it; he must be great for without wealth no man would venture to enter the lists; without a mesnie he would gain great prowess if he achieved anything. By morning all were certain they knew William's identity: he was Duke Richard of Aquitaine and had dyed his beard to fool them all. But who would take on such a formidable foe? No-one in single combat, but he had no mesnie and might be trapped. Duke Richard would fetch a handsome ransom...

The two free-lances entered the lists late. Across the countryside the fighting swirled in a riot of colour and fury but once in the field William and Robert made their presence felt. Leaving their squires to await the outcome of the day's events they both headed for the main mêlée and drove the contending parties asunder in the fury of their onslaught. They passed clean through the fight, leaving the body of horsemen like a partridge struck by a falcon, spinning headless to earth surrounded by a cloud of whirling feathers.

Unlike a stooping falcon they did not stop, but checked their horses a little and rode on until they encountered another group of tussling men. Riding out from behind a clump of bushes, they struck in the flank, bowling over horse and man with such success that they left it to others to capture the unhorsed, even though, but a moment before, they had been losing.

Five times they struck thus, like thunderbolts out of the blue, causing consternation as they eschewed the spoils they had earned in a formidable display of prowess such that it could only result in one outcome, a combination forming against them.

Having broken out of their fifth encounter with little more than a few bruises, they dismounted and watered their horses beside a stream. Taking off their helms they knelt and scooped water into their own mouths, grinning at each other.

'They will combine,' De Salignac said blowing out his cheeks, resuming his feet and flexing his body.

'Of course they will, though they have yet to find us.'

'That will not take them long.'

'Well, since they must, let us ride directly back towards the lists if we…'

'I hear…' But De Salignac said no more, both men were up in their saddles thanks to a fallen tree than the stream had undermined in last winter's floods.

'Good fortune, my friend. Stay close.'

They rode back onto rising ground and began to trot across open country. Rolling grassland and scrub, gorse and bramble bushes failed to conceal them from hostile eyes and it was not long before a large body of horsemen broke out of woodland to the north and begun to gallop towards them.

'I do not fancy a chase,' William called to De Salignac.

'Nor I. They cannot all fight us at once.'

'Quite so,' said William, 'let us make for that eminence and let them wind their horses and then…'

With every appearance of panicked flight, the two free-lances dug spurs into the flanks of their mounts and the fear of their escape caused their pursuers to redouble their efforts to catch them. Then, to the astonishment of the pursuers, at the top of a small hill they saw one of the strangers rein in his destrier. William tugging the animal's head round to meet the oncoming chivalry and De Salignac followed him; both hefted their shields and drew their swords for close fighting.

'Shall we take them back to back?' De Salignac queried.

'Only when they surround us or we are on foot...'

Perhaps it was the rising ground or perhaps it was something else that caused the attackers to check their onward race, but the sight of the two isolated and lonely knights stemmed their enthusiasm until a man on a gorgeously caparisoned horse broke free of the others who were at the same time spreading ominously around the two black figures.

' 'Tis Jacques d'Avesnes,' said William recognising that knight's device. 'I shall take him and then do you charge the thinnest part of their line...' William brought his destrier's head round to confront D'Avesnes as he covered the last few yards, his lance lowered. It was one of William's most favoured moves, but he exposed his right breast and kept his sword vertical and at the precise moment swung his right arm in a wide arc, carrying the lance point clear of his body. The instant it was clear, using his immense strength, he swung his sword back, dropping the blade and catching his foe a fearful blow right across his breast so that he sprawled back in the saddle. Then D'Avesnes was past and William stared at his following. There was a moment of hesitation and then another knight rode forward and waved them all on. A second later and William was fighting for his honour if not his life, for the effrontery of the two black clad free-lances had angered many there present.

The blows fell thick and fast, but William, skilfully using his destrier's hooves, kept himself in the saddle and fought off that first onslaught. He caught sight of De Salignac, equally hard-pressed, but holding his own until a dismounted knight ran in under his horse's belly and severed the girth strap. It was a concerted attack and the next thing William knew as he warded off three mounted men, was that De Salignac was on foot and his horse was being dragged away.

William's destrier despatched one of his assailants, a shod hoof breaking the man's shoulder; a second was laid out by a sword-blow across his helmet and then the third made the mistake of leaning forward to seize William's reins, shouting: 'You are outnumbered and my prisoner!'

William flattened the helm about his head so that his ears rang for three days afterwards. This apparent invincibility caused the attackers to draw off for a few moments and another knight rode forward and shouted: 'You cannot win, Sirs! Your conduct does you honour, but you cannot win!'

While they waited for the expected capitulation, William backed his horse to cover De Salignac, but the knight saw what he was doing and rode forward with a shout of 'God's blood, but I shall make him mine, stand clear!'

For fear of interrupting, the remainder stood where they were and William faced the oncoming threat. The knight bore a mace and first feinted and then dodged William's parry, bringing the mace across his helm with a sound like the striking of a cracked bell. William reeled from the blow but, his own ears now ringing, he caught the next swing on his shield and thumped the pommel of his sword into the ribs of his enemy, hearing the gasp of distress as, out of instinct, the knight wheeled his destrier aside.

'Robert! Mount up!' William threw down his shield, clutched both reins and sword and reached down, swinging De Salignac up behind him. Then he rode at the astonished ring of armed men who, in acknowledgement of their extreme prowess, made way for them.

That evening the fires burned beside the tents and the most distinguished knights met in conclave to determine the division of the spoils and send their stewards about the business of negotiating promissory notes of ransom. There was too the usual debate about who had earned the accolade of the worthiest warrior and while there was much talk of the two strange free-lances, not everyone had witnessed the extraordinary nature of their deeds. Hearing these stories, several knights who had among their train numerous prisoners awaiting ransom, declined the honour out of modesty and curiosity, among them Count Philippe of Flanders who set about finding the strangers.

Having returned to their squires, both William and De Salignac had divested themselves of their black surtouts, but William was unable to remove his helm and it was only by accident that someone recognised in the firelight William's destrier. As the man looked about him he saw two men, attended by two squires and an armourer. He sent word to the Count of Flanders who, with a train of knights arrived to find William kneeling on the ground, his head on an anvil while the rivets of his helm were carefully sheered by a sharp chisel. De Salignac looked up to see in the half dark a ring of figures sporting the heraldic devices of half the nobility of France and Flanders that waited for the revelation.

In those few moments there were those who maintained that it would be Richard of Aquitaine whose head would rise from the anvil unencumbered by the battered helm.

'Who are you?' Philippe of Flanders asked, coming forward and addressing De Salignac.

'Robert de Salignac,' my Lord Count.

'And who is he?' asked Philippe impatiently, pointing at the still prone figure from whom the severed helmet was even then being lifted clear.

'William Marshal,' said De Salignac as William, his ears ringing painfully, rose unsteadily to his feet.

Philippe of Flanders peered into his face. 'By the Rood, so it is! Well, by the Lord of Hosts, you and your companion in arms have done some fine execution this day, William Marshal.' He looked about him, seeking approval. 'Yours shall be the accolade, I trow,' and turning to De Salignac, he said, 'and you, sirrah, shall have your horse back free of ransom upon my word.'

*

The tournament at Pleurs marked a turning point in William's life, establishing his reputation for prowess which, as he said to De Salignac, had perforce to stand in the place of land. However, his failure to secure booty or ransom raised eyebrows in the Young King's mesnie, and while Young Henry remained friendly, D'Yquebeuf began again to manoeuvre against William. William might have avoided trouble had he heeded his master's advice to cleave to him both on the field and off it, but William's head was turned by sundry invitations to attend the Courts of others and, at first Henry indulged him. After a string of lucrative tourneys in Henry's mesnie and on the eve of another, William was invited to dine in the company of Count Theobald of Blois at his lodgings in the town of Épernon. The evening was drawing to a bibulous close when shouts of alarm rang out and everyone feared some piece of treachery.

Characteristically, William was first on his feet and taking no leave of his host ran outside to see Odo, his head streaming blood, reeling, as from a blow.

'Your destrier, my Lord…'

'God's blood!' Out of pride William had ridden into Épernon on his war-horse, leaving it in the care of Odo and Odo, it was clear, had lost the great beast to a thief.

'That way…' gasped the barely conscious squire and with a great bellow, William set off after his stolen mount. The narrow streets, slimy with dew and excrement inhibited a speedy escape and William could hear the clatter of hooves in the night. Hesitating briefly at one corner as he recovered himself from a slither in shit, William bethought himself; it was his trained war-horse that he pursued and he whistled, a piercing shriek of command. Someone threw open a casement, shouted a protest and flung the contents of a chamber-pot into the night. The body of the contents missed him, but he felt droplets of piss and cursed the fellow that dared to so embarrass him as to take his horse.

'I'll pay no ransom…' he thought as he redoubled his effort to catch up and then, beneath a cart loaded with brushwood standing idle before a warehouse and awaiting the morning light for discharge, he caught sight of movement. The destrier's restless hooves, oiled by Odo, caught the weak starlight and he heard the snort of the beast, objecting to the mauling of the unfamiliar rider as the wretch sawed at the bit of the near-ungovernable beast.

Unarmed, William, grabbing the end of a piece of wood, drew it from the cart and dodged round the thing.

'Hola! Hup! Hup!' The destrier, wild-eyed, foam flying from its mouth, obeyed the familiar voice and reared in the caracole. Stepping clear of the pawing hooves, with a swipe of the brushwood, William completed what the horse had begun and swept the thief backwards over the rump of the great horse. The destrier, freed of its torment, made off and William, raising the branch so that the brushwood stuck up above his right shoulder,

242

brought the cut stump down upon the half-seen head of the man who tried to roll away under the shelter of the cart behind which he had hoped to escape detection.

William felt the blow go home in the darkness, accompanied by the cry of pain. He straightened up, threw down the branch and went in search of the destrier, making a low crooning noise. The entire street was awake now and bellows of annoyance flew about his head as others from Count Theobald's feast caught up with the affray. By the time William had his horse by the reins his companions had the thief by the hair and had dragged him out into the convenient candle-lit doorway of an offended citizen, who stood complaining at the disturbance. He was, he declared, a merchant of some importance in Épernon, and would make his protest at the ribaldry to Count Theobald in due course.

'Messire,' someone explained politely, ' 'Tis William the Marshal who recovers a stolen destrier, not a parcel of drunks…'

'My God! The Marshal is here?' the man said, touched by William's celebrity.

'Aye fellow, and we have apprehended a thief who will, I think trouble no man again.'

The wretched fellow was dragged into the parallelogram of light and the merchant looked upon a face covered in blood, and saw one eye hanging down on the thief's cheek. Then, as the man lifted his eyes from the horror, there was a new presence, a tall man leading a great horse who regarded his night's handiwork with a mixture of disgust and pity.

'My Lord Marshal…?' the merchant said in an awed tone, 'will you come in and take wine?'

William shook his head and thanked the merchant. 'I thank you, but I have wine enough at my Lord Theobald's board.' Smiling the great man made off, surrounded by his dinner companions, two of whom had haltered the thief and led him, stumbling and whimpering in their wake.

Returning to the hall and recounting the incident, Theobald called for a hanging in the morning. Épernon was under his governance but William pleaded for mercy.

'He has lost an eye and will not forget this night. Brand him the better that he may serve as an example to others.'

While such an incident added to William's growing reputation for chivalry, his successes in the tournament enabled him to accrue wealth. He, Robert de Salignac and a Flemish knight named Roger de Jouy, all formidable warriors, formed a syndicate to fight together. They perfected techniques of horsemanship, weapon-skill, speed and strength which were almost guaranteed to catch the unwary at a disadvantage, at the same time deterring most of those who had experience of fighting them from attempting it again. In this way they unseated, fought, captured and ransomed over one hundred opponents one spring. To ensure the Young King benefitted from their valour, they employed Wigain, Clerk to the Kitchen of the Young King to act as a disinterested tally-clerk, to keep their accounts and render to Henry's treasury their Lord's rake-off.

Matters did not always go William's way. In a moment of inattention at another tournament fought over the familiar ground between Anet and Sorel, William was cornered by a determined group of six knights who separated him from his companions-in-arms and, in a simultaneous onslaught, unhorsed him. Satisfied with the capture of his destrier they rode off bellowing with triumph, leaving William dismounted and in a foul temper. At the end of the day he accosted Pierre de Leschans who, on behalf of the six knights, sought a ransom of forty pounds for the destrier, claiming they might have had the Marshal himself but that they wished to spare him the humiliation.

William gave way to a rare temper, a display of ruthless and pressing cunning rather than an Angevin rage. The temperamental outburst drew admiration from many, particularly the Young Henry, who looked on with some pride as his friend verbally fought his way out of the corner. De Leschans's uncle, Guillaume des Barres, a knight with a reputation as formidable as William's and an old contestant in the tourney at Anet was scathing at William's conduct. He was not the only one; even De Salignac was ambiguous about his friend's behaviour, though Roger de Jouy openly encouraged the mitigation of the syndicate's loss.

Relentlessly brow-beating De Leschans, William wore down the ransom demand from forty pounds first to twenty and then to ten in a gruelling negotiation lasting hours and depriving both men from attending that night's feasting. In this way De Leschans was also denied the accolade of the day for assisting in the unhorsing of the Marshal. In the end William shook hands on a mere seven pounds, his manner conveying the impression that he had done De Leschans a great favour.

'I could not lose that horse,' he growled at De Salignac afterwards.

'You did not have to, Will. A mere forty pounds…'

'You have not known poverty, my friend,' William said firmly, closing the conversation.

But De Salignac had seen D'Yquebeuf commiserating with young De Leschans and could have sworn he read from D'Yquebeuf's lips the words 'grown arrogant…' The incident troubled De Salignac. William had no need to worry about money; besides his own swelling coffers, the Young King now maintained his mesnie with a degree of largesse that contributed to his own reputation. The days of being laughed into the lists had long passed; now their appearance was greeted with apprehension, even fear at what might be lost in ransom money, harness, weapons or horses. As time passed the Young Henry gathered about him one of the grandest mesnies in Europe, success attracting the successful. Thanks to the bankers of Bruges and his father's generous allowance, Young Henry made provision for every want of his following, gaining for himself great renown.

Cheated of his ambition to rule a part of the Kingdom that would be his in due course, the Young King gained power and influence by means of the tournament. Opposed to tourneying in England, the Old King restored land and revenues to him, almost revelling in the reflected glory his son brought him throughout Europe, an achievement in contrast to the dark days of filial rebellion and of the obloquy following the martyrdom of Becket. Such was the diplomatic impact of his heir's glory that in the spring of 1179 the Old King invited the Young Henry to attend his Easter Court at Winchester.

It seemed a complete reconciliation. The twin monarchs splendid in their accord, their glittering households united to mark at this Holy and Blessed time the extent and magnificence of the Angevin Empire. The Old King, Henry Curtmantle, grizzled yet striking, brim-full still of energy, careless of his appearance as only the truly powerful could be among the rapacious Anglo-Norman barons, was complemented by the Young Henry whose almost angelically handsome features and bedazzling person seemed to embody the emerging virtues enshrined in the notion of chivalry. He was likened to Iskander the Great, or by the English knights who had increasingly flocked to his standard to tourney in the Vexin, as a reincarnation of the legendary Arthur.

And all the while at his side rode a man of near equal stature and mighty prowess, a man whose name had become almost as well-known, for all that he wore his master's coat-of-arms - William Marshal.

CHAPTER TEN: THE FALL FROM GRACE 1179 - 1182

King Louis VII lay on his death-bed. Ever since the star of Henry Curtmantle had seemed to wax, that of Louis Capet had waned. It was as if Divine Providence, having held out the promise of his seizing the lands of his great rival and enlarging the Domain of France, had withdrawn its favour. A further shaking of King Louis' faith quickly followed. That summer his young heir, Philippe, had fallen sick after having been lost for hours during a boar-hunt. The youth had contracted a fever and become so ill that his life was feared for.

The already ailing Louis had taken the unprecedented step of crossing the Channel and making a pilgrimage to the tomb of the martyred Becket at Canterbury. And although he thereby saved his son's life, on his return to Paris Louis had been taken by a seizure of such violence that it left him almost immobile. For the most part Louis lay, half paralysed, a drooling wreck, surrounded by the priests and monks whose company he had long ago left to become a King. To ensure the succession, and prevent the meddling of Henry of England and Normandy, it was essential that Louis' heir, Philippe, was crowned for a second time without delay in the ancient and royal city of Rheims, lying in the Champagne country north-east of Paris between the Rivers Aisne and Marne.

Here, on 1 November 1179, gathered all the chivalry of Christendom to witness the anointing of Philippe II of France. As the greatest vassal present, the Young Henry bore the French crown ahead of Philippe in the procession as it entered the cathedral for the coronation. And after this great and magnificent solemnization, came an equally great feasting and tourneying.

But there was more than the valour to be entered into in all this; there was now that of diplomacy as Hugh of Burgundy, Philippe of Flanders, Theobald of Blois and the Young Henry vied for political influence over the new and youthful King Philippe of France.

The assembly of knights, great and small, at Lagny-sur-Marne was unprecedented in its magnificence. The mesnies and their supporting entourages made a great and colourful throng, spread out in their encampments across the countryside, banners a-flutter, cooking fires and forges a-glow and a roistering company laying wagers, feasting and drinking.

Young Henry attended with eighty knights, fifteen of whom were knights banneret, each with his separate mesnie of a dozen knights, heralds and men-at-arms and each with his distinctive device and banner. Such additions to his own mesnie privée added to the Young King's prestige and he had included William among his knights banneret. For William, still a landless knight, despite the money he had accrued in the tourney, it was an especial honour. For the first time William bore his own device: a lion rampant, blood red as the Old King had charged him and as God – not the Devil - had marked him at birth. He was by now certain of this, able to entirely throw off the dark shadows of his boyhood. Nicholas de Sarum had been right to put his trust in God; so too had Angharad ap Gwyn, for there was something of the Old Ways in this predestination that filled William with a strong sense of both humility and pride. At Lagny-sur-Marne he glimpsed what he might yet achieve, a sense that he was favoured by God but that he could – and must – assume and maintain a proper modesty.

And yet it was difficult. As William rode into the lists at Lagny, his ensanguined lion upon a ground vertically divided: half green, for the colour of the lance pennons of his first opponents in the tourney, and half yellow, pale gold for the patron under whose

249

colours he had triumphed, old Roger de Vaux, he felt a surge of pride at the men who rode in his train: *his* train. With him rode Robert de Salignac, now the chief knight in William's mesnie and his closest friend, who showed no sign of the jealousy that disfigured the countenances of others, men like D'Yquebeuf who also rode as a knight banneret but who could not forget that William FitzMarshal was a landless *Englishman* with a coiled tail in his breeches who stood higher in the esteem of the mighty than he did himself. Nor did it help that William had acquired a bumptious herald named Henry, a man who claimed to be half English and whom William had engaged on a whim. This fellow, known to the mesnie as Harry the Northman had a habit of blowing his master's trumpet both metaphorically and literally, adding fuel to the fire of his rivals' resentments.

Besides the envious Adam d'Yquebeuf, among William's fellow knights banneret rode Simon de Marisco, Thomas de Coulonces and Robert de Tresgoz, and Baldwin de Béthune, a man with whom William had developed a friendship. They were but a fraction of the three thousand men said to have flung themselves into the fray in the great mêlée at Lagny-sur-Marne; a chaotic, whirling business of a short autumn day's duration in which the Young Henry came close to being bested.

Surrounded by opponents eager to seize him for a prodigious ransom, Henry fought valiantly, lost his helm in the struggle and had to be rescued by a gallant charge by William and his own mesnie. As they charged to the relief of the hard-pressed King, William's knights raised the battle-cry of 'God for the Marshal!'

Despite this timely intervention, there were many who afterwards held that such a rousing call to the deity was, in displacing Henry's name, a treasonable act. William had not ordered the battle-cry, though he gloried in it, not least, for its spontaneity. But if the day

250

was adjudged something of a 'great confusion,' William's part only added to his reputation. However, his moment of crowning glory at the tourney was marred by God's warning to humble himself before pride consumed him: young Odo was mortally wounded by an unfortunate lance thrust that – intended to unhorse him and compel William to come to his aid – slid over Odo's shoulder between his coat of mail and his chain coif. His carotid artery pumped blood for a quarter of an hour before he gave up the ghost and it was only that November evening, when the smoke of the bivouacs was sharp in William's nostrils and the invigorations of the day elevated his spirits with a glorious exhilaration, that he saw his squire's body brought in from the field of combat.

*

Within months of this spectacle Louis of France was dead, young Philippe was on the throne and at his side, wielding influence, stood his namesake, the Count of Flanders, seeking a new sphere of influence. The new French monarch promised little: a sickly creature who lent upon the unscrupulous and ambitious Flemish nobleman which precipitated a short but vicious campaign in which the Young Henry took the field against men who had hitherto been friends and no more hostile than rivals in the lists. The result of the swift chevauchée recommended by William Marshal against Philippe of Flanders and Hugh, Duke of Burgundy, was their outwitting. This was followed by a quickly concluded peace.

Thereafter the Young Henry forsook William's advice and, hand-in-hand with Marguerite, rode into Paris, though it took two unhappy years for him to make up his mind to do so. If the Young King's appearance at Lagny-sur-Marne had been a manifestation of the Old King's indulgence, and his swift victory over Hugh of Burgundy and Philippe of Flanders earned him the Old King's full forgiveness and even admiration, his conduct in Paris threatened everything. At Lagny the Young Henry bestrode Europe like a titan; in the short but brilliant campaign that followed he seemed to strike with the speed and blaze of a meteor. In Paris, by contrast to his sickly host, he was every inch the superior, titular heir to a vast empire that put the domain of France to shame. In his greeting to his feudal lord, the Young Henry was almost condescending in his vassal status to Philippe.

But that was the rub; he was but a vassal and as long as his father lived, a vassal inferior to even his younger brothers who held fiefdoms in their hands, not like a promissory note! Richard in particular was hacking out a formidable reputation as a warrior and a ruling Duke of ruthless competence. Men called him 'Richard Yea-or-Nay' and half-admired and half-hated him as he suppressed successive rebellions that his cruelty and wickedness stirred up. In Richard's eyes no man might stand against him and he subjected his fiefdoms to an iron fist of his governance. Should they have the temerity to rise against him, he fell upon them with a terrible savagery, seizing their lands, castle, tenants and villeins and abducting and raping their women, even casting their ravished wives to his soldiery.

Envious of his sibling's reputation for feared savagery, admirable in their father's eyes, but full too of the pride and the splendour of his own achievements, the Young Henry was persuaded that, faced with the pallid boy-king in Paris, he might over-awe the youth and renew his plea for the Duchy of Normandy from his father. He could not fall from such a summit as he had achieved: men called him the 'Father of Chivalry,' the 'Glory of Christendom.' Great things were expected of him – now, not later. What should he do? For two years the Young Henry writhed upon the horns of his dilemma as the glory of the tourney palled and the supply of money coming from England ebbed away. What alternative had he but to take his French-born Queen, sister to Philippe, to her brother's Court and first weaken his father's hold on Normandy?

Beneath this act of over-weening pride lay an appalling economic truth. The Old King's indulgence of his eldest son had bled his treasury almost dry. England groaned under taxation frittered away in the marcher lands of the Vexin between the French Île de France and Normandy as those two more years of tourneying leached vast sums in expenditure. Whispers of the Young King's excessive extravagance, of the unwarrantable demands of his expectant mesnie circulated the Old King's Court, while a slow desperation for revenue gripped the exchequer of his son's. That he might stand upon his own two feet, maintain his state, his household, his mesnie and his entourage, the Young King demanded of his father a province able to support him. Once again the Old King turned him down, though he increased taxation throughout England, raising the number of Young Henry's mesnie to one hundred and increased his allowance.

'He puts me off with baubles!' the Young King exclaimed, grinding his teeth in anger and in this renewed hostility with his father, men other than William Marshal increasingly gained Young Henry's ear. Some, like Adam D'Yquebeuf, did so by a direct discrediting of William as the chief among the Young King's counsellors, maintaining that the Marshal had out-grown his place, that the battle-cry of 'God for the Marshal!' was evidence of a dangerous ambition. It was a subtle enough ploy, for it played into the Young King's own paranoid anxieties, and while William brushed aside the intrigue, Robert de Salignac constantly warned him of the increasing danger he was in.

'What have I to fear from D'Yquebeuf?' William had asked one night as they lingered in William's chamber over wine, unwilling to confront the problem.

De Salignac was incredulous. 'Why everything, William! It is true you now have wealth, but you have no land and do you not see the influence of Duke Richard? Knowing his father's good opinion rested only upon the Young King's good showing as his surrogate – exactly the part the Old King cast him in – our Henry fears that upon his father's death he will lose Aquitaine to Richard…'

'But he gave fiefs to Henry…'

'Paltry stuff, you have to admit; chewed bones to a bitch, nothing more. Richard is stamping what he calls order across the whole of Aquitaine, Geoffrey does likewise in Brittany, Normandy is under Old Henry's thumb, as is what is, nominally at least, young John's. D'Yquebeuf fosters a growing resentment in Young Henry that will find him close to this pathetic creature on the throne in Paris. Who will benefit from such an unholy alliance I shudder to think but it will not, most assuredly, be Young Henry or, God have mercy on you, you yourself.'

William glowered at his wine for a long while, then took a deep draught and looked at his friend. 'You have a subtle mind, Robert,' he growled.

'Can you see a hole in my reasoning?'

William shook his head. 'No, by God, I cannot.' The two men relapsed into a long silence and then William asked rhetorically, 'what would you do now in Henry's circumstances? He fears the loss of prestige that his father's continuing refusal will bring about his head once it is generally known, and he has ensured that by his pilgrimage to suck at King Philippe's tit in Paris. What one act would outflank the Old King and his brother Richard? Do you know, my clever friend?'

'Why,' responded a smiling De Salignac, warming to the game, 'of course. The Holy Land… Why William, 'tis not I who have the subtle mind…'

And both men laughed into their cups.

*

The Young Henry's announcement that he would carry his mesnie by sea to the aid of his distant kinsman, Baldwin IV, King of Jerusalem, proved the two men correct. This wretched man, a leper from child-hood, was increasingly menaced by Muslim forces intent on ousting the Frankish enclave and the Old King's desire to come to Baldwin's relief had been diverted by the rebellion of his sons. That the Young Henry should pick up the gauntlet and surpass his father would not only strike a blow at the old man's pride, but gain Papal merit which might be swung in the son's favour in the reconsideration of the question of Normandy. Beyond that, it might secure the crown of the Kingdom of Jerusalem for himself, for Baldwin the Leper had no heir of his body. Such a prize was beyond equal and, remarked Robert de Salignac drily, 'a thing worth tilting at'.

And then, with this magnificent and Holy policy raised, the Young Henry was lured away, seduced by an opportunity nearer home: to undermine brother Richard and loosen his grip on Aquitaine.

Thanks to his ruthless cruelties and outrages against them, both real and imagined, many of the lesser nobility in the western duchy had again risen against their overlord. Anxious, the Old King crossed the Channel and marched south to his son Richard's aid, summoning the Young King who was ordered to join them at the rendezvous in Périgord where the Angevin loyalists were besieging the castle of Puy-St-Font. On 1 July the two Henrys were united with every appearance of amity. Within weeks the rebellion collapsed and the Angevin armies dispersed. The Young King lingered, making slow progress north, dispensing largesse among

255

the nobles and, with his elegant appearance and easy charm, casually offering them an alternative to his vicious brother.

The ploy worked. That autumn Richard's rule was again openly defied and the Young Henry was receiving secret pleas for help from Aquitaine. A duchy lay within his grasp

*

'Well William? What is the state of our high project?'

The Young Henry had assembled his Court and retinue at Evreux where his mesnie awaited the order to advance into Aquitaine. Among the assembled knights banneret that sat as counsellors in the matter that morning the mood was one of mixed expectations. On the one hand, despite Duke Richard's formidable reputation, they had all convinced themselves that the appearance of the Young King at the head of his own prestigious war-host would suborn the majority of the vassal lords of Aquitaine, from north to south. They had been assured this would be the case and all waited the word to mount up and ride. There was, however, a problem beyond the dynastic evil of one brother making war upon another, and it centred upon the man to whom the Young King now turned for confirmation that the mesnie was ready for war. Without precisely knowing its cause, Henry had caught something of the cautious hesitation of these knights and had called them to his board to thrash out the matter and help overcome his own residual doubts.

William, the Young King's closest military confidant, retained his post as Marshal; he had no lands, was unmarried and therefore had neither distraction nor reason not to act as the Young Henry's chief counsellor for war. Besides, he was exceptionally able in the matter of assembling a siege train and the requisite horses, men and forage. Thanks to his high standing in Young Henry's opinion, the King had delegated responsibility to William to muster, arm and review the foot-soldiers and mounted men-at-arms committed by the Young Henry's vassals. And whilst these qualities commended him to the King and brought forward Young Henry's political aims, making of them a reality, neither endeared him to many in Henry's wider mesnie.

Ever since Lagny-sur-Marne a faction had been growing within the Young King's household that sought first the displacement and then the downfall of a man they thought unworthy of the heights to which prowess and renown in the field had brought him. He was an unlanded upstart, an Englishman to boot, an outsider, some said a bastard (his lack of land proved *that*); others kept up the old canard of his being bewitched, the Devil's spawn. How else, they argued, could such a man rise so spectacularly? By such means did the jealous acquit themselves of accusations of sin? And now there was something else; it was popularly held by men such as D'Yquebeuf, whose animosity towards William had become psychotic, that William had himself fomented this new interest in Aquitaine, that he had poisoned the Young King's mind and diverted him from his Holy intention of going on a crusade. It was a novel notion and found favour among the clerks in Holy orders to whom these knights turned for their spiritual guidance and soon it became clear that William must be rooted out of the Young King's Court altogether, for – it was now obvious - he imperilled their master's soul.

'He is too ready to find fault...' D'Yquebeuf was fond of grumbling, sounding out the opinion of those about him.

'Or picking it where none exists...' echoed Thomas de Coulonces, who was firmly of D'Yquebeuf's opinion and stood at his right shoulder.

'He would not be so particular had he lands of his own and felt his own coffers draining dry...' added Jean de Laon.

Robert de Salignac knew of the intrigue and constantly warned William.

'De Laon…'

'Who we both know to be a French spy, Robert, and who will shift his allegiance when he is told to do so,' William interrupted, brushing his friend's anxieties to one side. It was inconceivable to William that anything substantial enough could be brought to the Young King's ear to discredit him. Indeed the very arguments that persuaded his enemies that he was dangerous, for William indicated his helplessness. He had no land and therefor lacked a base for his power; he was wholly dependent upon the largesse of the Young King. And such a lack of distraction surely made it logical that, if Henry required a disinterested friend, then William's amity – a matter of proven loyalty – was to be preferred. Besides his prowess and wider martial skills, no-one but Henry knew that William had rescued him from the rage that had threatened to destroy him after the death of his short-lived son. And the Young King knew William never sought to capitalise upon this incident. True, Henry had felt touched by humiliation when William had had to rescue him at Lagny, but of all his knights he would rather it had been William than any other. And what man better fitted than to keep his mesnie fit for purpose and to see the money bestowed upon his companions-in-arms was properly used?

William rose at the Young King's question, placed both hands flat upon the table and leaned forward to sum up the state of the war-host.

'My Lord King, we are all assembled and are in tolerably good order. I would recommend we await the arrival of Ranulf FitzStephen who is late to the muster but, should Your Grace wish to proceed and not lose this fine weather,' and here William

258

gestured towards the shafts of sunlight pouring through the casements, 'then we may move within two days…'

'Why not tomorrow?' asked the Young King pointedly.

'I would remuster one mesnie, Sire, it was wanting some bowmen who are said to be hurrying hence…'

'One mesnie? You mean one among those here assembled, that of a knight banneret?'

'Aye, Sire…'

'To whom do you refer?'

'My Lord King, I, er…'

'Do not evade the query, William,' the Young King said, his voice warm.

'I do not evade…'

'Then whose, sir, whose?' The Young King glared round the table as William hesitated. 'Well, one of you must know. Which of you is it?'

Thomas de Coulonces raised his hand. 'I believe the Marshal refers to me, Sire. I have a want of bowmen and bow-staves despite a requisition to my Lord Marshal for the latter…'

The Young King looked from De Coulonces to William. 'You have been squabbling over the matter?'

William shrugged coolly. 'The bow-staves await the men, my Lord King; I would have saved the worthy Thomas the embarrassment of this. The matter will be swiftly concluded…'

'But I wish to march tomorrow,' said Henry, suddenly resolute. 'My mind is fixed upon the matter.'

'Then we march without the bow-men, my Lord King and carry the bow-staves with us in anticipation of the archers following us. Ranulf FitzStephen may take them under his wing and bring them forward.'

'Very well.'

259

And there the matter rested, though William afterwards deplored the matter as a nonsensical farce to Robert de Salignac.

' 'Tis a pity it was De Coulonces's mesnie,' De Salignac mused, 'but who else's would it be other than Adam D'Yquebeuf's. Did you see how he coloured at his friend's discomfiture?'

'No, I saw only De Coulonces anger. They are such damnable hotheads…'

'It would not surprise me if De Coulonces had delayed bringing forward his men to catch you out and that the thing went against him only caused him a mortification.'

'Surely it was no more than a discomfiture,' William remarked, 'not a matter for choler, surely.'

'As you yourself say, my friend,' De Salignac observed, 'they are such damnable hotheads.'

William shrugged again. 'Well,' he said resignedly, 'there the matter must rest.'

*

Would that it had.

During the rest of that day Evreux buzzed with the hurrying forward of the war-host as the order went out for the expected march to commence on the morrow and all the knights looked to their own equipages, harness, weapons, horse and men. For William the hours passed speedily and he was quite unaware of any consequences from the morning's council-of-war. It was only as the knights fore-gathered in the great hall to dine that evening that Robert de Salignac told him that the castle had been disturbed that afternoon by the noise of the Young King falling into one of his Angevin rages.

'What has upset him?' William asked, surprised.

'I have no idea, but I hear that he was put out of countenance by this morning's council and later by something said by Queen Marguerite, or one of her women. Anyhap, here he comes…'

The Young King swept into the great hall and took his seat at board. Taking his own place William shot a glance at him and saw him composed, but of that high colour that William knew of old presaged ill-temper.

After some moments Henry leaned over and asked: 'What would you say if our departure were to be postponed to await the arrival of FitzStephen and De Coulonces' men?'

William thought a moment, then responded. 'We are poised to move, Sire, a further delay might signal irresolution.'

'But I would have the host together in all its puissance when we enter Aquitaine, surely you can see that? FitzStephen's mesnie is second only to your own.'

'Would you have me send someone to meet FitzStephen and hurry him?' William asked with a suggestion to ease the Young King's obvious fretfulness.

It was the Young King's turn to consider. He shook his head. 'No, place your own mesnie under Robert de Salignac and wait here yourself until FitzStephen musters. You are best fitted to urge a forced march and will surely catch us up by the time we reach Alençon.'

William nodded agreement. Privately he deplored Henry's too evident anxiety, FitzStephen would take the matter badly and it would require William to provide a soothing balm to a wounded spirit, but Ranulf had been lately in Eu and had had a long march.

'Whatever happens, William,' Young Henry said, 'I want you at my side by the time we leave Alençon and I cannot afford to break my march there for more than a day, or word of our coming will reach my brother.'

261

William nodded. So that was it; now the matter had ceased to be a dream, the long shadow of brother Richard was thrown across the threshold of Aquitaine. 'Do not fear my Lord King,' he said reassuringly, 'both FitzStephen and I will be with you 'ere you cross into Maine.'

The following morning William rode up and down the length of the column as it passed through the town gate and headed south and west. He saw his own mesnie ride out under his own banner, the red lion rampant upon its field of pale gold and green, led by Robert de Salignac who saluted him. He watched his following, all with his emblazoned surtout, led by his bumptious herald, Henry the Northerner, whose pompous flourish made William chuckle. Last, he watched as the Young King mounted his own white palfrey, a horse as handsome as any destrier, and led his own retinue clattering out of Evreux on the road to Alençon.

' 'Till we meet again, William!' the Young Henry called, in high good humour now that all matters were settled and he was on the move. 'God speed you to my side!'

'God's will be done, my Lord King!' William shouted in response as the cavalcade passed and a slow and anticlimactic silence fell upon the town.

With the Young King's army on the march William returned to the castle and ordered his own affairs. He had held back two squires and a dozen men-at-arms for an escort and earlier that day he had sent one of the squires to ride in quest of Ranulf FitzStephen. As for his person, he had retained only a body servant, a lad named Adalbert, and a single groom to look after his own preparations. The castle seemed empty and silent, even though populated by a garrison consisting of some fifty men under the Constable of Evreux and the Court of Queen Marguerite numbering some one hundred souls of differing ranks. Most of the men therefore wore the leopards of the Angevins and it came as some surprise to run into a knight wearing the colours of Thomas de Coulonces.

'What do you here?' William asked out of curiosity.

'I am left by the Lord Thomas to await the arrival of his archers, Lord Marshal.'

'Do you know when they are expected?' William asked.

'In two or three days. Four at the most.

'Good, for I would not have it longer, nor would I wish to linger once they arrive, but march immediately.'

The man nodded. 'They are my own orders, Sieur Marshal.'

William nodded with satisfaction. 'What is your name?'

'I am called Eustace, my Lord.'

That evening, after a solitary meal in his chamber, William went as was his wont in moments of quiet to pray. The chapel was empty, it being William's habit to avoid the offices of the church that he might give to God his own time. Vespers had long been sung and beyond a pallid sunset shining through the east window, there was only the glim of the reserved sacrament to light the Holy place. He was lost in prayer when he felt a light touch upon his shoulder and started with surprise. A hooded figure stood behind him and although dimly lit by the dying light he knew immediately who it was and dropped to one knee.

'Madam…'

'Forgive my disturbing you at your devotions, my Lord Marshal, but I would have conference with you.'

'Madam, I am yours to command,' he responded uneasily, rising.

'Not here, in this sacred place,' she said, 'come…'

William followed, his heart sinking. He had no wish to become embroiled with Marguerite and had always studiously avoided all contact with both her and any of the ladies of her Court, two of whom had attempted his seduction at various times. He preferred

263

to take his pleasure in less complicated places, preferably in the chaotic aftermath of a tournament and then only upon occasion.

'Madam,' he began a protest as it became clear that the Queen sought to confer with him in her own apartments. 'Madam, is this wise?' But all she did was turn and bid him be silent. There was no guard on the door to her apartments, nor any lady-in-waiting in the ante-chamber within; he was drawn into her presence like a fly into a spider's web, unresisting as they passed into her private quarters.

'Madam,' he said again as she flung off her cloak and turned towards him, slim and elegant, her blonde hair caught up in braids, her face uncoifed, sculpted by the imperfect light of a solitary sconce. 'Madam, I should not be here. What is it you want of me?'

'Comfort, my Lord Marshal, comfort...' She sat on a settle covered with furs beyond which lay a huge chest and a bed. She indicated a small table set with a flagon of wine and rare crystal glasses – two of them. She had planned this and others knew of it. William felt his heart thump. 'Pray pour some wine and be seated.' She patted the furs next to her.

Knowing the folly of the act he filled two glasses, handed one to her and sat beside her. 'Madam, this is not wise...'

'You took my husband from me the day my child was born and died, FitzMarshal, and yet I cannot find it in my heart to condemn you for it for I do not love Henry...' Her accent was decidedly French, sharp and precise, lacking the robust and rounder forms of the corrupter Norman tongue.

'You should not say such things to me...'

'Nor do I care about him or his want of a son,' she continued as though he had not spoken. 'He barely notices me unless he wants me as a pawn in his diplomacy.' She sighed. 'It is the lot of women, to be so used, even a Queen.'

'I would stop my ears,' William said, rising.

264

'Sit!' she said sharply and then in a softer tone, 'must I command you to sit? Or will pleading be sufficient. You are a knight of great renown, FitzMarshal, Henry speaks so often of your prowess and the lustre you add to his mesnie that I grow jealous of his affection for you.'

William was lost for words, a man swimming in a fast flowing river, out of his depth and aware that he might, in the next few minutes, begin to drown. She sensed this uncertainty and gently took the glass of wine from him and set it down, retaining her grip upon his hand. Then she drew his hand towards her and placed it upon her breast. 'For God's sake William, show me some pity for I am nothing.'

William drew back his hand. She sighed and said, 'see here,' and turned her head so that the light from the single flare fell on the right side of her face hitherto in shadow. He saw the bruises and the cut ear, encrusted with a scab.

'His ring…?'

'And his rage. There is more. Here,' she touched her right-hand ribs, 'and here,' she touched her left rib-cage.

'Madam…'

'Marguerite…'

William shook his head. 'I cannot,' he said unhappily.

The Queen seemed to choke, then rose, compelling William to leap to his feet. 'No! Sit!' she said as she refilled both glasses and handed his back to William. 'Then you must talk. I command it and you shall not gainsay me! Tell me, was it you who dissuaded my husband from his crusade?'

The question astonished William. 'God's bones! From whence did that notion arise?'

She shrugged. 'It is common gossip that I took for common knowledge.'

'The thought never entered my head…' The warnings of Robert de Salignac swam into William's mind.

'You would swear to that upon the bones of saints?'

'Upon my very life, Madam, did I not hold it cheap for my Lord King's service?'

Perhaps it was the wine but the Queen seemed more resolute now, holding herself as she ought as she reseated herself, half turned towards William, but regally upright. 'And you have ambition for yourself?'

'What ambition should I have, Madam? I lack land and am the King's servant in all things…'

'But not mine,' she said as a matter of fact, suddenly flirtatious.

'Madam, you toy with me…'

'Would that I did, FitzMarshal, would that I discovered where it is you keep your tail, in your breeches behind you or….' She lowered a hand and, with her fingers, drummed it upon his thigh, 'or here, in front.' Then she withdrew her hand and gave a half giggle before turning serious again. 'When he does not ignore me he treats me worse than one of his hounds. He loves his hawks more…' She trailed off as her voice cracked with bitterness, dropping her eyes. He sat, not drinking but unmoving; not daring to compromise himself in any way; eager to leave yet flattered into staying. Without looking up and in a voice so quiet he could barely hear she asked, 'could you not love me, FitzMarshal? Even a little, the little that one night might encompass?'

'Such love might encompass more than this night,' he responded, suddenly moved by her plight and reaching out a hand to hers. 'You to a nunnery and I to a flogging and then some death that would forever dishonour me…'

'You are thinking of Walter de Fontanes and his love for Isabelle de Vermandois?'

266

'I am thinking of the vengeance taken by Phillippe of Flanders for the cuckold's horns De Fontanes placed upon his brow, and how the Count had him ducked in a sewer until he drowned,' replied William pragmatically. 'Was the Lady Isabelle's brief consolation worth that end for her lover?'

'Count Philippe was covered in shame for his act,' she said, 'and went for his penance to the Holy Land.'

'Aye, Madam,' William riposted, 'and De Fontanes was covered in shit and went to Hell for his mortal sin.' He began to recover himself and although still holding her hand, went on: 'Let them not say you plucked me from my prayers to bed me in the heat of lust the instant your husband was absent. Let them not say that William Marshal lacked both lands *and* honour. Do they who come from the northlands not say that you may take my sheep, my arms, my gold and all my goods and chattels, but leave me my reputation?'

Again she sighed and William drew her hand to his lips and kissed it. 'In that I am the King's servant, Marguerite, I am yours,' he said with quiet sincerity. 'To that I am pledged by solemn oath. I am sorry for your plight and if he persists in using you ill you may, I think, retire to your brother's Court and seek a separation. More than my counsel I cannot in all conscience give you.'

She looked at him, her eyes full of tears and squeezing his hand detached her own. Still regarding him she nodded and then put out her hand and touched his cheek. 'You have given me great comfort, and I thank you for your courtesy.'

Slowly he stood up and stepped away from the couch, unable to throw off her steady gaze. For a long moment it seemed as though both might throw caution to the winds and bow to the imperative of lust but the chapel bell rang for Compline and, with a sharp intake of breath William made his obeisance and withdrew.

The empty ante-chamber made him shiver; something was awry. The two glasses indicated premeditation and the absence of any attendant would not go unnoticed, if only by those who had been dismissed from that duty. He thought again of the warnings of De Salignac. William swore and stood stock still. Jesu Christ, but he had been such a fool! No sound came from the Queen's chamber and it struck him that the silence hanging over Evreux was preternatural. But this, he thought to himself as he pulled his wits together, was but a reaction to the noise and bustle of the last weeks. Then he heard the rising chant of the priests in the castle chapel and went to the door to pass from the ante-chamber and so to his own quarters.

To his relief no one waited outside, though at the very least a page should have been in attendance. Should he summon someone? He did not have to pretend a concern for the Queen's safety, but to do so would reveal his knowledge of her exposed situation. Then the problem was solved for him, for out of the shadows came the man he knew as Eustace.

'You are not on duty here,' William said, unconsciously giving voice to the fact that Eustace was of De Coulonces mesnie, not a member of the garrison.

'No, my Lord Marshal, I was merely passing…'

'Where is the Queen's guard?' he asked. Eustace shrugged. 'Do you inform the Constable that he is in dereliction of his duty and the King shall hear of it unless he rights the matter without delay.'

'Aye, my Lord Marshal'.

*

Ranulf FitzStephen rode into Evreux the following afternoon and brought with him the bow-men of Coulonces. 'I found them encamped not half a day's march from here, William,' FitzStephen told him after expressing his astonishment at finding William almost alone at Evreux and saw the look of puzzlement that crossed the Marshall's face.

'Make yourself comfortable, Ranulf. Shall you be fit to march on the morrow. I have orders to rejoin the King at Alençon and there is little time for delay.'

'Aye William, we shall be ready.'

William went in search of Eustace to inform him of the arrival of his bow-men and to quiz him as to their presence so close to Evreux. But Eustace was nowhere to be found and when asked, the sergeant of the watch the previous night told William that he had been bullied into opening the bailey gate to allow an armed knight and his squire leave with a message for the King. On further enquiry the town watch confirmed that the gate on the road to Alençon and Le Mans had been opened to allow a knight and a man-at-arms to pass 'with despatches for the King from my Lord Marshal.'

'And at what time?' William had pressed, his heart thumping in his breast.

'Perhaps an hour after Compline,' came the reply.

*

William slept but fitfully that night and when he did it was to dream of an encirclement of serpents. At dawn Adalbert, sticky with sleep, found his master dressed and pacing his chamber. Despite leaving orders for an early start, William let FitzStephen depart without him, promising that he would catch up, since FitzStephen would be slowed by the archers. As soon as it was decent to do so, William sent for the Queen's Confessor. When the priest arrived William scrutinised him carefully, trying to seek out any sign that the man knew anything disreputable or suggested he felt awkward in the presence of the Marshal.

'Before my departure I would have audience with Her Grace, Father,' he asked. 'Would you be kind enough to pass this request?'

While he waited for permission to attend Marguerite, William continued to pace his chamber, his head hot from lack of sleep. When at last he was in the Queen's presence he made his obeisance and loudly asked if she was content that he follow her husband. As he did so the priest withdrew, and as soon as he was out of the room, William fell onto one knee.

'Madam,' he said, his voice low, tense and urgent in its tone. 'I beseech your forgiveness for my impropriety, but did anyone suggest that you sought my help last night?'

She looked as astonished as he had done when she had asked if it was him that diverted her husband from his avowed crusade. 'No!'

'Then I fear there may be evil consequences from our brief intimacy. You may rely upon my discretion,' he added rising, 'and forgive me that I must follow after His Grace directly, but to delay further would compound what mischief others have already made.'

'Why, what is amiss?'

'I was seen leaving your chamber...' It was clear that she was shocked. 'But, Madam, the two glasses, the absence of any page, guard, or lady-in-waiting...you purposed our... encounter.'

'I sought you out in the chapel, having observed it to be your habit on occasion to pray. I had been waiting the opportunity for some time...'

William nodded, then shook his head. 'I fear...' he broke off.

'The sewer?' she asked, half smiling, as if she welcomed the incipient scandal, if only to wound her husband.

'God's blood, no! I should not let them do that to me, but you...'

She shrugged. 'I am Louis Capet's daughter and sister to the King of France, William Marshal,' she said, drawing herself up so

270

that he might, just then, have fallen at her feet. 'Please go,' she said her tone suddenly haughty, so that he was chastened, whipped like a cur. But before he left the chamber, she called him back. 'Go, William,' she said in a softer voice, 'and with my blessing.'

Five minutes later he was on the road to Alençon with his small retinue, hard on the heels of Ranulf FitzStephen and the archers of Thomas de Coulonces.

*

Marching on foot, De Coulonces' archers delayed the column led by William and FitzStephen so that it was at Alençon itself that they caught-up with the Young King. The first man of note to greet them was Baldwin de Béthune, who drew William aside, his face anxious.

'We have heard strange rumours, William. De Salignac is beside himself, suspecting treachery… Pray God he is right, but the King is in a strange mood and we do not know whether we shall continue the campaign…'

'I am half-expecting this…' William began, interrupting his friend, but here De Béthune stopped him. 'I do not think the King will see you.'

'*What*? He must!'

'See Robert de Salignac, William, he stands loudest in your defence.'

'And who are my accusers?'

'D'Yquebeuf…'

'And De Coulonces.' William finished the sentence.

'Those are chief among them, yes…' but Baldwin de Béthune got no further for a bellow rang out across the yard, announcing the presence of the Young King who, hearing of the arrival of FitzStephen and William Marshal, had come out to prove De Béthune wrong.

'FitzMarshal,' cried the Young Henry, 'attend me!'

'If you love me, my Lord Baldwin,' William said, handing the reins of his horse to his friend, 'see my horse fed and watered, this may take some time.'

Once within the castle the King cleared the great hall and led into a chamber, slamming shut the door behind William before turning upon him. William had expected rage, red and dangerous, but there was something worse in about the cold fury in Henry's blue eyes.

'You have cuckolded me! Made a fool of me the instant my back was turned! You! You of all people! You that I loved better than any brother and favoured better than any other knight! You William Marshal, spawn of the Devil and bastard of an English whore…'

'My Lord King…'

'Do not seek to…'

'My Lord King, whatever I am, and I am no adulterer, my mother was not a whore nor am I bastard, nor Devil's spawn. You have been misinformed…'

'No, sirrah! I have not! You spent an hour in my Lady's private chamber; you dismissed the guards, her ladies…'

'I spent an hour in Her Grace's chamber at her own request. *She* dismissed her attendants and I am the victim of a conspiracy by those who seek to harm both you and me. Our enemies have waited a long time to use such circumstances as presented themselves at Evreux.'

'And what in God's name did my Lady want with you if it was not…' the King could not quite bring himself to say it, did not want to say what was being said throughout the war-host, throughout Evreux, Alençon and would soon ring throughout Christendom.

'My Lady, The Queen, was in distress, Sire,' William said in a low voice. 'She showed me the cut about her ear and told he there was more.

'And you consoled her,' sneered Henry, taken aback. 'and then fell for her and fucked…'

'I did nothing more than take her hand, Henry,' William replied, possessed now by a cold anger to match the Young King's.

'How *dare* you. That is lese majestie! That is treason, like bedding my wife.'

'Since your accusations make us equals as regards your wife, my Lord…'

'You are *not* my equal…'

'No, Sire, I am not, and I should not presume to take the place in my Lady Marguerite's bed that is yours either, but since you consider me capable of such an act I must act as an equal to get justice. Come, Sire, I am content to lay the matter before Almighty God and engage in single combat: lance against lance; sword against sword and body against body! That or seek the answer from Her Grace the Queen herself.' William paused a moment. There was something so uncharacteristic about the King's lack of tempestuous passion that he half-divined it: Henry had no wish to believe what he had been told, but he had uttered the accusation and William would rather hazard his flesh than have his honour compromised. What else had he to lose? Sensing Henry vacillated, William plunged on. 'And my Lord King if you should not wish to engage me yourself – for I am not your equal and your own honour is as sacred to you as is mine to me – appoint one of my accusers as your champion. Who are they? Adam de'Yquebeuf? Thomas de Coulonces? Jean de Laon? Jealous men who have plotted against me and would have me detached from your mesnie that they might bask in your esteem as they encompass my ruin.'

273

The Young King had opened his mouth to speak but the three names stopped him and he turned aside to fill a goblet with a shaking hand. As he again confronted William he found the Marshal in his knees.

'My Lord King, I swear on the Holy Body and Blood of Christ I did no dishonour to Your Grace.'

He could see the conflict plainly in Henry's eyes now. 'But the world thinks you did and the world will listen to that which best appeals to its low appetites…' Henry sighed, extended his right hand and allowed William to kiss his ring. 'I must banish you, send you into exile if only to signal my disapproval and your disgrace.'

'I understand, my Liege,' replied William rising.

'You cannot remain under my roof but must be gone tomorrow.'

William thought fast. The majority of his mesnie were rested, having arrived with the Young King. There was nothing beyond his own fatigue to keep him in Alençon. 'I will depart within the hour, Sire.'

The King nodded and turned away. 'I will make way in my mesnie for yours. They are men sworn to me through yourself.'

Silently William made his obeisance and left the presence chamber, a hand of cold ice about his heart.

As soon as he had seen to the stabling of William's palfrey, Baldwin de Béthune had passed word to Robert de Salignac that William had been called to conference with the Young King. And presciently De Salignac had called the knights of William's mesnie to a meet in the inn stables he had taken over in the Marshal's name, quartering the men in the adjacent pension. Thereafter De Salignac had awaited William's emergence from his audience and met his friend with a single interrogative.

'Well?'

'I did not bed the Queen, Robert, you have my word on that, but I am banished that the King may be seen to disapprove of me.'

' 'Tis the work of D'Yquebeuf and…'

'I know, I know…'

'Shall you challenge them?'

'Not now. Where are…?'

But De Salignac forestalled William, 'I have your mesnie assembled in the stables, come…'

They were all there, wearing long faces in the gloom, for the place was barely lit by the sunlight of late afternoon. At the appearance of William and his friend they fell silent after a brief gasp of astonishment that William remained at liberty, and the only noise was the snickering of their horses in the stalls.

'My Lords and gentlemen you have heard of the conduct imputed to me and the treason which I am supposed to have committed. Think you that I should have done such a thing out of lust? Think you that I should have done such a thing to so dishonour my name? Think you that I should have done such a thing as to wreck my fortune? No. But to preserve the honour of our Lord the King I am banished…'

The news was met by a rising clamour of incredulity. Raising his hand William waited until this had subsided.

'I thank you for your service to me. You are at perfect liberty to go where you will and His Grace the King reminds you that as sworn to him through me, you are but a part of his own mesnie where you will find welcome. I ride out before sunset.'

William spun on his heel, clapped De Salignac on his shoulder and left the stables for the brief comfort of the adjacent inn. Behind him he left a moment's silence which suddenly erupted into a clamour of debate and fury. He heard it only as a muffled anger. Ever since he had had his helm knocked off at Pleurs his hearing

275

had been impaired and he failed to distinguish the rallying shout of Harry the Northman: 'God for the Marshal!'

Ten minutes later Robert de Salignac found William staring glumly into thin air and called for wine. 'All but two will come with us, Will,' De Salignac exclaimed, his eyes dancing with excitement.

'Us? What do you mean...?'

'You have men loyal to you, William. No, better than that you have men devoted to you.'

'And you? Will you hazard everything?'

'Do you have to ask? I am a younger son; my parcel of land is small; enough but small and if the King disinherits me I should not wish to be better placed than you.'

'No, no,' Robert. 'You must not follow me. You warned me often enough.' William straightened up. 'Nor must the others; tell them that. Tell them that I thank them for their service...'

'You have already done that.'

'Then tell them that I cannot countenance their accompanying me.' William rose, suddenly resolute; De Salignac remained seated, looking up at his tall companion. 'I shall go now, at once. Do me one last service, my friend, and summon my horses, squire, page and armourer.'

'Where will you go? Not to Richard?'

William scoffed. 'No, that *would* be treason, thought the temptation is sore. To be truthful I do not know.'

'Go to Count Philippe...'

'Why would I do that?' William asked, laughing bitterly. 'Have you not heard what he does to adulterers?'

William held out his hand but De Salignac refused to take it. Instead he too rose and strode out of the inn. William looked down at his out-stretched hand and felt the folly of the day in its palm.

276

Dropping it to his side he saw the inn-keeper and his wife staring at him and he sat down again. He must give De Salignac a moment to ready his horses and he needed a moment's quiet to order his thoughts. He took a deep draught of the wine and opened his pouch to find gold to pay for the quartering of his mesnie. Perhaps he should have confronted D'Yquebeuf and his miserable followers and challenged them to mortal combat. But that would embarrass Young Henry and seem like further arrogance. No: it was better that he assumed the sentence of banishment dutifully and in all humility. He would go first to Bruges and settle his affairs with the bankers there and then pass over into England with what remained of his fortune after making arrangements to pay his mesnie.

He rose again, throwing gold upon the scored and worn boards of the table to the gasping joy of the landlord who feared a decampment without payment. The whole of Alençon knew of the disgrace of William Marshal and the jubilation of being chosen to accommodate so noble a knight had evaporated rapidly with the arrival of the knight Eustace.

Outside the westering sun shone directly down the narrow street and after the gloom of the pension rendered William almost blind. His palfrey held by Adalbert was ready for him, and Adalbert's own horse was followed by William's destrier on its long rein. The pack-horses too were loaded and there were his two squires. One bore William's banner which hung listlessly in the still and fetid air. He felt a twinge of pity for them having to follow him into exile and resolved to give them their freedom in a day or two, once they had passed Aumale into Ponthieu on the road to Flanders.

Nodding to Adalbert he took the palfrey's reins, mounted and kicked the horse's flank. The shamed and insignificant cavalcade clattered up the street, watched by the curious citizens. They turned the corner towards the northern gate and trotted into the town square.

Here he ran into several ranks of mounted knights and it took his a moment to realise that they were his own mesnie, not some intimidating muster ordered by Young Henry or – worse still – his enemies. He ordered his banner lowered in salute to this last mark of respect but even as the squire dipped the bloody lion, Robert de Salignac kicked his horse forward, grasped the banner and lifted it vertically again, stationing himself at the haunch of William's palfrey. Then, to William's astonishment, Harry the Northman blew his trumpet and sang out: 'God for the Marshal!' and as he passed, William, with tears in his eyes, heard the clatter of hooves on cobbles as his mesnie fell-in behind him. They were approaching the northern gate and the sergeant of the guard fell back allowing the cavalcade to pass and, as it did so, echoing from the ramparts and the tightly clustered houses within the walls there went up a terrible roar of 'God for the Marshal!'

Almost blinded by emotion, William did not see the long shadow cast by the town gate, nor those of the figures who, alerted to the imminent departure of their enemy, watched from a-top the barbican.

'What hauteur!' Adam d'Yquebeuf exclaimed, his hatred yet unsatiated.

'He is gone,' said his companion, Thomas de Coulonces, feeling the warmth of the setting sun upon his back.

'But whither does he go?' asked D'Yquebeuf, 'to Philippe of France, or Philippe of Flanders, for he takes the road north?'

'To England, perhaps,' suggested De Coulonces. 'That is where he comes from and at least he does not go to join Duke Richard.'

'Wherever he goes,' added De Laon, 'if it is not to Duke Richard then it is sure that our own advance will end here.'

278

'Think you that?' D'Yquebeuf asked, surprised.

Jean de Laon nodded. 'Without him our Henry will not go to war against his brother…' But De Laon was not giving much thought to Duke Richard; he was more concerned with the impact of William Marshal's departure upon the politics of his own secret master. King Philippe of France was proving less the callow and pallid youth of his coronation and, for all his disdain of bodily cleanliness, was revealing an astute and scheming mind.

As the walls and faubourgs of Alençon fell behind them William's head cleared. He half turned in his saddle and Robert de Salignac rode up alongside him. He had returned the banner to its squire and wore a smile. He reached out his right hand.

'Thank you, my friend,' William said, reaching out and clasping Robert's fist. 'Now tell me, was Jean de Laon among the knights that left my mesnie?'

'Aye, Will.'

William nodded and stared ahead to where the road led north and east and the world rolled into night.

CHAPTER ELEVEN: AN END TO AMBITION 1182 – 1183

The presence of his loyal mesnie persuaded William not to pass through Aumale, but to cross the Seine at Rouen and head for Eu, a more direct route to Flanders which avoided Evreux. However, he was in no hurry and the mood of the mesnie improved with every day that passed, so that when they reached Bec, to the south-west of Rouen, they were all imbued with a sense of freedom. William had not yet decided to cross the Channel to England, where the tourney was forbidden. There was a lingering regret that he had left D'Yquebeuf and his cronies triumphant and this wore on his spirit. He was veering towards remaining in Flanders where, with Count Philippe's permission, he might maintain himself and his retinue. Somewhere at the back of his mind he hoped for the chance to better prove his innocence and his thirst for vengeance did not diminish, politic though it had been at Alençon to act otherwise.

Then, out of the blue, a few hours before their arrival at Eu, as dark clouds roiled up from the west, a courier came galloping up from the south-west. It proved to be one of Young Henry's heralds and he drew rein alongside William with a flourish. 'My Lord Marshal, I have orders from my Lord King.'

'You have ridden hard,' William observed drily, giving the newcomer's steaming mount a cursory glance before staring ahead and maintaining the pace of his palfrey. He was eager to reach Eu before nightfall.

'A message, sir, I am commanded to deliver a message,' insisted the herald.

'Then deliver it,' William responded curtly. Beyond Eu lay the border of the Angevin dominions and he was now keen to shake the dust of his old master's provinces off his horses' hooves.

'The Young King, our master requires your presence at the forthcoming tournament. The lists will be opened between Gournay and Ressons.'

'Is not the Young King *your* master campaigning in Aquitaine?'

'No, my Lord Marshal.'

'And why not?'

'The decision was made not to proceed following your departure.'

William sat his horse in silence then motioned to De Salignac. 'Did you hear that, Robert?' De Salignac nodded. 'What think you of it?'

'That you must obey, William.'

William nodded, turning to the herald. 'Gournay and Ressons, you say.'

'Aye my Lord, north-west of Paris...'

'I know that. Tell His Grace I shall wait upon him with my mesnie there.'

'I will, my Lord.'

'And give him my greeting... But stay, there is bad weather coming, you will ride to Eu with us and shelter for the night.'

That night William learned from the gossip disseminated by the herald in his cups and brought to him by De Salignac that Queen Marguerite had been ordered by her husband to proceed to Limoges. 'Is that for fear of you?' De Salignac asked drolly, or are the Angevin leopards about to fall out again?'

*

The tournament that autumn of 1182, fought between Gournay and Ressons was an ill-tempered affair. William's mesnie received

281

no welcome from the Young Henry's and the evident rupture between the two leaders was plain for all to see. If the Young King's knights shunned those of the Marshal, William's got their own revenge by too frequent a use of the battle-cry 'God for the Marshal!'

William had attempted to curb this near-treasonable excess but he could not suppress it, and the capture of knights in D'Yquebeuf's mesnie only added to the ill-feeling and resentment. Although William resisted the temptation, saving the moment for a later date, De Salignac's several assaults failed to take either D'Yquebeuf himself, or Thomas de Coulonces. Predictably, Jean de Laon was not present.

Despite having been summoned to tourney by the Young King, it dawned upon William that Young Henry's motives were dishonourable, borne of the darker and raging facet of the King's character, designed not for reconciliation but for a display of displeasure and estrangement. Indeed, the palpable divide between the two prompted the pragmatic Count of Flanders to publicly remonstrate with Young Henry, warning him that he was acting like a peevish youth to throw off the support of so staunch and able a warrior. It was even rumoured that in private the two men had argued over the alleged adultery.

'He may go over into England and lay his sword at your father's feet, or join your brothers,' Philippe argued, 'and appear in the field against you with vengeance in his heart, for I hear he did not bed the Lady Marguerite, though others imagined he did.'

Henry, it was said, had confronted Philippe with his own conduct when he had caught Isabelle de Vermandois with her lover. It was the only thing that unscrupulous nobleman felt any prick of conscience over. Stung, he told the Young Henry he deserved to lose his wife and should have brought her to bed of a second child long since.

But William was oblivious to all this, just as he was oblivious to the intrigues and under-currents of diplomacy that were obvious to others that Christmas. After the unsatisfactory encounter at Gournay-cum-Ressons, William received a secret emissary from the Old King, passed by way of Guillaume de Tancarville. He was to attend King Henry II's Court at Caen, part of the most magnificent gathering ever seen in that part of the world, an assembly of over one thousand nobles and knights, including the Old King's four sons. Indeed, it was remarked behind hands held to mouths that the only personage of note that was missing was Queen Eleanor. She remained, everyone thought, a peripatetic prisoner in England.

Flushed with wine and confidence, basking in the glorious company and especially in that of his cousin-german Guillaume de Tancarville, bolstered by the fact that it been the Old King who had surreptitiously invited him and stung by the Young King's disregard of his obeisance as the Young Henry passed him as he went to Mass, William forgot himself.

It was a tradition after the great feast for the Lord of Normandy to hear and redress grievances. William sat and heard Guillaume de Tancarville lay before the Old King some arguments as to his loss of powers and privileges as Chamberlain of Normandy. After Henry had handed down his judgement William, still starting from the snub he had received from the son and banking on exploiting the fragile affection of the father, jumped to his feet and appealed to the Old King. The whole Court, all of whom recognised William and scented a gross impropriety to add to the scandal of his alleged cuckolding of the Young King, fell deathly silent.

'My Liege I plead a case of injustice,' William said. The Old King waved him to proceed, his face flushing as William blundered on. 'My Liege, certain allegations have been laid against me that impugn my honour. I know my accusers and would have them meet me in mortal combat one-at-a-time that Almighty God may strengthen my arm for a just result. Moreover, my Liege…'

'How many men do you propose to fight, FitzMarshal?' the Old King asked. The sound of supressed laughter could be heard.

'Three, Sire.'

'Name them.'

'Adam d'Yquebeuf, Thomas de Coulonces and Jean de Laon, my Liege.'

'And do these three accuse you?'

'Not directly, Sire, no, but it is they who…'

'Who accuses you?' The Old King's question was made amid total silence. Even the hounds seemed to await William's response and it was only then that he realised that he had walked into an ambush. He shifted his gaze to the Young King Henry, sitting at his father's right hand and swallowed hard, trying to clear his head of the wine.

'I do not know, my Liege,' he answered and it seemed the whole Court expelled its breath as one. 'I only know I stand accused and was banished from the presence of the Young King on the words of others.' It was a clever ploy and the curl of admiration might have been seen on the Old King's mouth until William over-reached himself. 'And my Liege, I would fight with these men with one finger of my right hand cut off to seal my defeat if they are bested.'

All eyes turned to the Old King. Most who knew him had already noticed his gathering ill-humour. He leaned over towards the

Young King and then turned his steely blue eyes upon the suddenly hapless and exposed plaintive.

'You mock my justice, FitzMarshal, and you mock my son by your presence here. As your Suzerain I confirm the sentence of banishment.'

William stood stock-still for a moment. Had not this very man ordered his presence at Caen? Was not the purpose of this Court to dispense justice? What was the evidence against him? He felt a plucking at his sleeve and looked round to see De Salignac's hand.

'Get out! Go!' bellowed the Old King, drowning his friend's advice to withdraw.

*

William rode north-east, back to Eu and over the border into Ponthieu and Flanders beyond. In Bruges Count Philippe of Flanders offered him five hundred English pounds if he conjoined his mesnie with his own. Within a sennight Hugh of Burgundy sent him an equal offer and, but days later, his old friend Baldwin de Béthune offered one thousand pounds and the hand of his daughter, a renowned beauty.

Angry and humiliated, William turned his back on such blandishments. Later, in the New Year he accepted an income from one quarter of the rents raised from the Count of Flanders' ownership on the town of St Omer, whither he withdrew under Philippe's protection. That spring, in the closed season for tourneys, he embarked upon a Lenten pilgrimage to Cologne in the company of Jacques d'Avesnes where he knelt in contrition at the tombs of the Three Magi and prayed for humility and peace of mind. But not even the offers of support, money and opportunity, nor the refuge provided by the Count of Flanders, nor the conspicuous friendship of so great a knight as Jacques d'Avesnes, not even penitential prayer before the Holy Shrine of the Magi could assuage the deep feeling of wounded pride and seething injustice that wracked his soul with endless torment.

God had deserted him, or had raised him just high enough for pride to cause his fall. Perhaps, after all, he *was* the Devil's spawn, a mere plaything of Kings, a Court fool. Only the steadfast friendship of De Salignac and the firm affirmation that there were those who, like Jacques d'Avesnes and Count Philippe, considered him ill-used and kept him from dismissing his mesnie, though even that had shrunk after Caen.

'The wheel will turn,' De Salignac remarked consolingly one night on the return journey from Cologne to St Omer, 'just as the wind changes eventually.'

'I have seen thirty-five summers, Robert,' William said miserably. 'I am already old and all I have is one quarter of my Lord Philippe's rents in St Omer. Why 'tis less than you lay claim to and you claim only poverty keeps you cleaving to me.'

'That and a small thing called love and regard, William,' said De Salignac sardonically. 'Besides the bankers of Bruges still greet you like a Prince.'

William stared hard at his friend. 'Forgive me,' he said quickly, 'that was unpardonable. You know I value your love and loyalty…'

De Salignac brushed William's apology aside. ' 'Tis nothing. Your spirits are low but tomorrow they may take a turn for the better.'

'I cannot for the life of me see why you should think that,' William said, chuckling despite himself.

'Because I feel it in my piss-water,' De Salignac said, rising to relieve himself. 'It is never wrong,' he threw back over his shoulder as he went out into the darkness to relieve himself.

*

'Who comes here?' De Salignac asked rhetorically.

Ahead of the mesnie the vanguard had first arrested and then allowed to pass a solitary horseman who now spurred headlong towards them.

'Some fellow bound upon his own business, Robert,' William said dismissively. He stared ahead at the long road as it ran over the low open country north of Amiens as they made their way at the head of the mesnie south towards Aumale in expectation of a tournament.

'No, no, he is for us, William!' Robert exclaimed cheerfully, making his horse rear in the caracole. 'I told you so!'

' 'Twill not be good news. That is for sure.'

A moment later the horseman, an unarmed knight by the look of him, drew rein and turned his horse alongside that of William.

'I know you,' said William puzzled, 'you are Ralph FitzGodfrey, Chamberlain to the Young King. What in the name of God do you here?'

'My Lord Marshal I am sent by the Lord Henry to find you and have spent many days on the road. I heard you were at Aumale, then St Omer…but no matter, the purpose of my quest is of the greatest importance. My Lord the Young King has great need of you and,' FitzGodfrey looked round and nodded at the bobbing horsemen trailing behind, 'and of your mesnie.'

'*What*?' William could not conceal his fury and pulled his horse up short. 'I am falsely accused, cast out, repudiated, humiliated, banished and now summoned! By the Holy Blood, would you treat a hound like this? Eh?'

'William, shall I ride on,' suggested De Salignac, as the column of horsemen came to an untidy halt. William nodded and drew FitzGodfrey off the road to allow the mesnie to continue. The men stared at the newcomer curiously and those that recognised him passed word of his identity among the retinue.

287

'My Lord Marshal I understand your anger but I am charged to tell you Thomas de Coulonces has confessed your disgrace the result of a conspiracy; that he and D'Yquebeuf sought any means by which to discredit you and charged their followers to report any detail. That of the knight Eustace condemned you, for they could not have wished for a better means by which to accomplish your downfall.' FitzGodfrey delivered the substance of his message in almost as quick a pace as he had driven his steaming mount.

'What of D'Yquebeuf?'

'He is in disgrace.'

' 'Tis a pity I had no hand in the matter. And now?' asked William, scarcely believing this sudden change in his fortunes. The entrusting of the summons to a Court official of such high rank as the Young Henry's Chamberlain attested to its gravity.

'And now, my Lord, to Aquitaine with all despatch.'

'Aquitaine?'

'Aye, my Lord Marshal. All is chaos there and the Young King would have you at his side.'

'You will ride with us, FitzGodfrey, and appraise us of the matter in hand this evening in Aumale.'

William spurred his horse after the column and ordered a new horse be supplied for FitzGodfrey from among the remounts.

'We are for Aquitaine and war, Robert. All is forgiven. De Coulonces has confessed, D'Yquebeuf is disgraced and the Young Henry has work for us.'

'Then your pilgrimage was not in vain,' De Salignac remarked cheerfully.

'I did not pray for war, Robert, I prayed for humility.'

'And God has answered you, William, in returning your lance to the Young King's service.'

*

288

'And I was fool enough not to see it,' William remarked, picking meat out of his teeth. 'I suppose *you* knew,' he said to De Salignac, referring to FitzGodfrey's opening explanation that a full blown conflict had erupted in Aquitaine.

De Salignac shrugged. 'I think the hounds at Caen sniffed something unpleasant in the wind. Most of the combined Courts did, did they not FitzGodfrey?'

The Chamberlain shrugged, feeling awkward among the company of these outspoken and obviously close friends.

'You may speak freely here, my friend,' William said kindly, pouring more wine as they sat over the wreckage of a good meal. 'Now, how did this come about?'

'Shortly after your unfortunate departure from Caen, my Lord Marshal, my Lord Henry the Old King moved to Le Mans where he proposed a settlement of his realms and possessions in favour of a peace among his sons and in anticipation,' here FitzGodfrey paused and crossed himself, 'of his own death in God's good time.

'Duke Richard and Count Geoffrey were to pay homage to the Young King and hold their lands in fief of their brother. Count Geoffrey did so, as did Richard after a remonstration. However, Duke Richard insisted that he retain full rights of governance and revenue throughout Aquitaine in perpetuity in his own name, whereupon the Young King my master, calling for a copy of the Holy Gospels, swore that as God was his witness he would cleave to his father, but he had already pledged to support the nobility of Aquitaine who refused Richard's unholy rule and acknowledged the Young King, my master, as the rightful Duke of Aquitaine.'

'God's blood,' remarked De Salignac, imagining the scene. 'And what of Richard?'

'I thought he might draw upon his brother but the Old King held him back and ordered heels to kick until a second meet was held at

289

Angers, assuaging Duke Richard with promises of private colloquy with his heir. I do not know what passed between them but I gained the impression that having taken so public an oath it would have been a blasphemy for the Young King to give ground. At Angers the Old King was obliged to support his natural successor with the consequence that Duke Richard fell into a great rage.

'The rift defied any further healing. Plans for further conference fell apart. The Young King sent Queen Marguerite from Limoges to Paris before she was taken hostage…'

'The Old King washed his hands of them?' De Salignac queried impatiently.

'In part. 'Tis said he despaired of any peace between them, especially betwixt the Young Henry and Duke Richard, and would wait upon the outcome.'

'Let them tear themselves apart and back the victor,' observed De Salignac wryly. 'God's Blood, no wonder the Young Henry wants you at his side if he is to cross swords with brother Richard.'

'That is the sum of it, is it?' William asked.

'Oh no, my Lord,' FitzGodfrey shook his head. 'There is much more. They have already crossed swords…'

'Go on.'

'The Young King lay at Limoges in the company of a gathering war-host. Count Geoffrey joined with him and has called his levies out of Brittany, as did the Viscount Aimery of Limoges who summoned men from Gascony and the south. Geoffrey of Luisgnan came into the Young King's camp…'

'He that had a hand in the murder of my uncle,' William remarked quietly, shaking his head. 'And what of Richard?'

' 'Tis all of Richard: he mustered his force at Poitiers and struck north, destroying the men from Brittany and putting those who were not dead to the sword. Then by a forced march south-east of

290

two days and nights he cut up the Viscount Aimery's Gascons at Gorre before retiring with his prisoners to the castle of Aixe …'

'Along the Vienne?' queried De Salignac, who knew the country.

FitzGodfrey nodded. 'Here he put out the eyes, threw into the river or simply cut down those Gascons unfortunate enough to be alive.'

'And when was this?' William asked.

'Some two months since.'

'Go on.'

FitzGodfrey sighed. 'The Old King came to Limoges, riding under the leopards and intending, I suppose, to intervene, but someone ordered his party fired upon and, had the King's horse not reared up and taken the cross-bow bolt in its belly, my Lord the Old King would be dead.

De Salignac whistled through his teeth. 'God's blood!' he blasphemed softly, looking at William.

'And he went to join Richard,' queried William.

'Aye my Lord, at Aixe, whither my Lord the Young King went to parley and apologise for the error. He was not believed, especially since he had neglected to deal with the man responsible for loosing his cross-bow and he returned to Limoges fearful of an assault by Richard and the Old King.'

FitzGodfrey paused to take wine and scratched his forehead. 'I cannot with certainty say what happened next. There was talk of a parley, of a crusade, of the expense of the forces raised in the Young King's name, but the continuing bad weather of late February delayed any offensive until early March when the combined forces of my Lord the Old King and Duke Richard appeared before Limoges. We had some hopes that the gales and rain than showed no sign of easing would hamper them, but our own spirits were failing. Duke Richard's methods promised little if

291

the garrison fell apart and there were intimations that he would not countenance ransom among the nobility. There was much attending Mass in the Abbey Church of St Martial and, upon the eve of his defection to the Old King, Thomas de Coulonces called for me and confessed the plot against you, my Lord Marshal. It clearly weighed heavily upon his mind and he asked me that I waited until morning before acquainting the Young King. I had no idea of his treacherous intention, judging him to be of unsound mind. Indeed, I had informed His Grace before we heard that he had passed to the enemy. I was immediately charged to slip that night through the lines and ride in quest of your Lordship.'

'That is quite a tale' William said, breaking the silence that followed FitzGodfrey's account. 'Then tomorrow we must ride towards Limoges and discover how affairs now lie upon our way.'

*

William and his mesnie rode south along the border with the Angevin lands. FitzGodfrey and De Salignac had rendered signal service by securing safe-conduct passes from King Philippe and Theobald of Blois, allowing them to travel unmolested. William was eager for news. There was plenty of it, but what there was seemed contradictory, carried by merchants, tinkers and pedlars, all manner of itinerant persons who had skirted the scene of the fighting and had their information at third or fourth hand. The Young King was out of money, had escaped Limoges and was looting abbeys hither-and-yon; the barons of Aquitaine were wavering in their desire to have the Young King as their overlord; the barons of Aquitaine were content to have Young Henry as Duke; Geoffrey of Brittany had changed sides; no, he remained in Limoges with Geoffrey of Lusignan; Limoges held out against the Old King and Duke Richard; Duke Richard was unwell and Raymond of Toulouse was on the march to the relief of the city.

William crossed the River Cher and headed for Limoges. Glorious spring weather accompanied them as May swept across France. Roads were open, trade revived and word of his coming reached the camp of the Old King. Shortly after leaving Châteauroux he received an emissary, one if Henry Curtmantle's heralds charging him with securing Old Henry's son's submission and giving him a pass to enter the besieged city with a small escort.

But the Young King was not there. Only the twin Geoffreys: he of Lusignan who had murdered William's mother's brother, Earl Patrick of Salisbury, and the Count of Brittany. William would have no truck with the former and misliked the latter, recalling the words of Robert de Salignac that Count Geoffrey was not to be trusted.

'My Lord Brother,' Geoffrey informed him loftily, 'has been about the country raising money and prosecuting the war in his just cause, FitzMarshal. I last had word that he was at Aixe.'

The castle of Aixe, on the Vienne, had been abandoned by Richard on his investment of Limoges and, returning to his mesnie, William rode hard for Aixe, lying to the south-west of Limoges. All about them were the signs of war, mostly the ruthless stamp of Richard's fell handiwork: burnt villages, mutilated and rotting corpses from which their approach disturbed the crows and ravens. Aixe was empty of all but a small garrison who refused them entry but held a parley over the ramparts. Upon William riding forward with his standard-bearer, following Harry the Northman, who made a formal declaration for the Young King, the Constable said only that his master had gone south upon a pilgrimage.

Returning to his anxiously waiting retinue – they had all heard of the Old King's lucky escape from death at the hands of one of the Young King's cross-bow-men under the walls of Limoges – William conferred with his principal knights.

'They say he has gone upon a pilgrimage,' he reported, puzzled.

'To Rocamadour,' De Salignac suggested. 'His father was wont to go there. Would he pillage such a Holy Spot?' At the uttering of the blasphemous thought they crossed themselves.

'It seems he has been plundering other Holy places,' William put in ruminatively, having hear of this when in Limoges, 'for he is desperate for money. What say you FitzGodfrey. You know your master's mind.'

'Little better than you, my Lord Marshal, but I judge you correct.'

'Well, if he has gone south he would have made first for Uzerche and then Martel,' De Salignac advised. This was the countryside of his youth and it was clear to William that if he was to find the Young King soon he must press on.

'Very well. Onward to Martel.'

At Uzerche there was positive news: the Young Henry had been there on the 26th May. He had been unwell but had moved on towards Martel and was indeed said to be heading for Rocamadour.

'What day is it?' William asked, for, unlike many of his peers, he was barely literate and had difficulty reading a calendar. The headmost of his knights began debating the issue.

'We think the second of June, my Lord,' FitzGodfrey advised him after their colloquy.

That evening they came in sight of the castle of Martel and William sent on ahead FitzGodfrey and his herald, Harry the Northman. Even before either returned they observed Young Henry's leopards lazily lifted in the softly moving summer air and moments later, just as his herald rejoined the mesnie, they clattered into the castle.

It was at once evident that something was wrong. 'My Lord King is a-bed with fever,' Harry announced and, as William dismounted,

FitzGodfrey ran out of the keep to meet him. His face bore an expression of grave concern.

'He is taken by the bloody flux, my Lord Marshal, and his life is feared for.'

'Christ have mercy,' William crossed himself. 'Are there priests with him?'

'Aye my Lord. His chaplains and some from the Holy Shrine of Rocamadour.'

'Did he do damage there?' William asked anxiously for fear the Young Henry had further compromised his soul.

FitzGodfrey nodded. 'He took all the plate and valuable votive offerings…'

'And the Black Madonna?' broke in De Salignac, his voice infused with outrage.

'I do not know, I had no time to ask…'

'We shall soon learn,' placated William. 'I must go to him. He must know that I am here and that I answered his summons.'

The castle of Martel was not large; neither were its chambers and within the grandest above the hall he found the Young Henry in a parlous state. Even before he entered the presence of the Young King, William's nostrils encountered the stink of excrement sharper than that habitually thrown onto the midden. Within, the room was dark, but for four candles standing at the four corners of the bed. To one side a priest kneeled at a prié-dieu; two more sat silently watching their charge, while two knights, Simon de Marisco and Robert de Tresgoz, stood in attendance.

As William's bulk filled the doorway, all looked up and, catching De Marisco's eye, William knew, even in the gloom, that there was no hope. He moved towards the bed and was shocked at what he saw. The Young Henry's golden hair lay dank upon a wet pillow, his cheeks had fallen in and his closed eyes were sunk in their sockets so deeply that he might have been one of the victims of his brother Richard's savagery. Perhaps he was, thought William, his heart moved by the pathetic creature that had once been the most glorious and Puissant prince in Christendom. Now his pallid skin was stretched tight across his skull, the hollows under his collar-bones seemed pools of darkness, showing above the thin and sweaty fabric of his night-shirt as his chest heaved with the labour of breathing. They had laid his hands crossed upon his breast and placed a crucifix in them.

'My Lord King,' William murmured, kneeling and crossing himself. 'God's good Grace has brought me to your side.'

For a long moment there was no response and then William saw, through the film of his own tears, the King's eyes open.

'William…? Is it truly you?'

'Aye, my Lord King.'

A hand fell off Henry's breast alongside his body and the fingers moved as through clawing their way towards William and the King's mouth seemed to essay a smile. William seized the hand. It was pitifully thin; he felt the bones and tendons under the dry skin and kissed the ring that had gashed the ear of Queen Marguerite.

William felt the hand twist and eased his over-passionate grip. Slowly turned palm uppermost, William felt it curl in summons and rose, to bend over the King's mouth.

'Forgive me, William,' the murmur was barely audible to William's poor hearing but the odour of disease and death was on Henry's breath.

'There is nothing to forgive, My Lord…'

'There is much to forgive… Do you stay with me, Will, stay to the end…I beseech you do not…abandon me to make…your peace.'

'I am yours to command…you have always known that…'

'Aye,' breathed the King in a long and foetid exhalation, 'it is I who lacked loyalty…'

'Put such thoughts from you, Sire, the priests…'

But Henry had his own desperate agenda. 'Have you a man to trust?'

'Aye…'

'Then send him to my father… Ask that… he come… that we may end all hostility. Do it now.'

The King closed his eyes and seemed to sink back into a comatose state and William rose. Nodding to De Marisco and De Tresgoz he said: 'He wishes me to request his father's presence.' Both men nodded. 'I shall send De Salignac.'

'A wise choice, Will,' murmured De Marisco.

Quitting the chamber William sought De Salignac who had just completed the quartering of the mesnie. 'There is scarcely room here for the Young King's retinue, let alone our own,' he began before William cut him short.

'Robert, I wish you to take my herald and an escort. Remount yourselves; take fresh horses from the King's mesnie if you wish. Ride to the lines of Limoges and determine the whereabouts of the Old King and tell him his son is dying and would have him here beside him.'

'In the name of Jesu.' De Salignac crossed himself.

'I would not send you but that I need a man to trust and you know the lie of the land hereabouts.'

'Of course, Will, of course. I will take a bite to eat and leave before sundown.'

'My thanks.'

'One thing, Will.'

'What is that?'

'A pass, a letter from you?'

297

William shook his head. 'You know I have no hand in these things and it will take too long for me to fashion the words for a letter and dictate it to a clerk…'

'I am able to write,' De Salignac put in.

'And you can speak with greater eloquence than I can dictate. No, go at once. Tell the Old King that his heir… God, not his heir for Henry a-bed is no heir to any earthly thing,' William said as the political import of what he was now central-to impinged upon his mind. 'Tell him his son is contrite and would make his peace with his father and his God.'

'Very well.' Both men crossed themselves.

Good as his word, less than an hour later Robert de Salignac rode north with Harry the Northman, two knights and six men-at-arms, a string of remounts on long reins trailing behind them.

*

He was back in four days and his countenance told William he had failed in his mission.

'He will not come, William,' De Salignac reported as he dropped from his hard-breathing horse and eased his aching muscles.

'*What*? Why? In God's name…' expostulated William.

'He sends a ring,' De Saliganc adopted his sardonic tone and patted his midriff, 'a ring of peace. He says he fears treachery as he was exposed to at Limoges. Without a letter of accreditation…'

'Ahh. Then I am at fault.' William cast his eyes down.

'No, no, William,' De Salignac put a hand on his friend's arm. 'You are not to blame. These leopards are continually at each other's throats, not content until they have, one way or another, torn themselves to pieces. While Henry Curtmantle showed every sign of mortification short of ordering his horses saddled and his escort readied, the Duke Richard was silently drinking to his good

298

fortune. They say he was already in close contact with the Count of Brittany.' De Salignac shrugged. 'No, you are not to blame.'

'Come, you must attend me,' William ordered De Salignac and the two men ascended the stairs.

The Young King now lay in his death chamber, the floor of which was bestrewed with ashes. The smell of incense partially masked that of the dysenteric discharge that flowed from the sick and dying man, leaching fluid and life out of his body so that he seemed to shrink by the hour. What remained of the Young King's spirit now inhabited the frail shell of a man far older than Henry's twenty-eight years so that, to William and others, the soubriquet 'Young King' seemed a cruel irony.

When William knelt again at the King's bed-side, Henry turned his head and smiled wanly. He seemed to have revived somewhat and it pained William to be the bearer of bad tidings.

'You have heard…from my father?'

'Aye Your Grace, he sends this ring of peace…' William laid the ring brought by De Salignac upon the King's breast as watched as Henry's hand fluttered from the crucifix to clasp it, like a sparrow wounded by a cat.

'But he…does not come…himself.' It was a statement, not a question.

'No, Your Grace.'

And Henry emitted a long and foul sigh of resignation.

The following day, the 7th June 1183, Henry was tenderly lifted out of bed and, stripped of his night-shirt, laid upon the floor of his chamber in the presence of the Bishop of Cahors. He was naked but for a soiled loin-cloth. The Bishop placed his crucifix before Henry's prostrate body as all his attendants left the room so that the King might make his confession in private. After this he received the Holy Sacrament at the Mass.

Early on the 11th William and the other senior nobles and knights were summoned while, barely audible but recorded by a clerk-in-Holy-Orders, Henry repeated his confession, publicly threw over his pretensions to the Duchy of Aquitaine and dictated his last Testamentary statement.

He wished to be laid to rest in the Norman cathedral at Rouen; he begged his father to show mercy to his mother, Queen Eleanor, to his Queen, Marguerite of France, and to those who stood loyally in his mesnie.

William was singled out and called again to the royal bedside. Again the fluttering hand beckoned him close. 'Wilt do…some…last service for me?' Henry's hand edged towards William, who took it. It was dry and thin as a sheet of parchment.

'Anything,' he breathed, half choking with emotion.

'Take…my cloak…lay it…take it…Holy Sepulchre…Jerusalem…pay…debts…to God.'

William nodded, his voice catching in his throat. 'Aye, my Most Gracious Lord King.' And he felt the slightest pressure on his fingers, as though the parchment was being rolled carefully about them. Then all fell slack.

William stood, shaking his head. The Bishop of Cahors came forward and absolved Henry from all his sins, administering Holy Unction as the attending priests chanted. It was clear to all that Henry was giving up the ghost and the priests took over. The bed clothes were removed, the King's night-shirt cut away and a hair shirt laid over his emaciated body. A rope halter of penitence was placed round the King's neck and by this crude means he was eased to the floor and laid out, stone blocks at his head and feet. William, the attendant knights and priests kneeled about him.

For a long moment no-one moved. The priests chanted the Rite and then the King's head fell slightly to one side, the mouth dropped open half open and death rattled in his throat. Again there was a long wait until the corpse vented air, revealing the sordes within. The Bishop of Cahors rose and, stepping forward to bend over the corpse, motioned for the priests to stop the seven orifices to prevent the ingress of the Devil while he opened the single casement to permit the escape of the soul.

A gust of fresh air blew into the stifling chamber and three of the candles went out.

*

'To Jerusalem…'

'Aye.'

'You will need company.'

'I do not go to fight, Robert, I go on a pilgrimage.'

'But you will need company,' De Salignac insisted.

'I am pressed to pay his debts. It will ruin me. I must go alone but for a servant or two for I can no longer support the mesnie. His charge is an end to all ambition…'

'But you cannot go alone and I can support you with a small following. We shall go together, you and I and cast off the dust of this accursed Aquitaine…'

'But it is your country, Robert…'

'Ach, I have no deep roots here. Truth to tell I despise the place since its nobles quarrel so. There is no peace to be had and as for ambition… poof! The wine is good but I hear the wine of the Lebanon is as fine…' De Salignac paused, chuckling.

'What?'

'I hear that already they are saying miracles are being attributed to him and we have yet to get his corpse to Rouen…'

It was true. They had marched slowly north, a cortege draped in purple and black, banners furled, through towns and villages where even the peasants, who had privately cursed the House of Anjou,

301

came out to watch them pass. Henry the Young King had never ruled an acre and was by this sanctified as an ideal King; the King who never was and now never could be, called to God before his old father and ruthless brothers Richard and Geoffrey. His own misdeeds, his plunderings of their lands and abbeys was set aside, lepers and scrofulants asked to touch the bier; cripples cried for mercy and new limbs. At night a shaft of light was said to fall upon the coffin where it rested; others claimed it glowed from a Holy light within.

They continued towards Normandy and such was the scrimmage at Le Mans that the incumbent Bishop ordered the body interred in the cathedral, next to the Young Henry's grandfather Geoffrey. The Bishop claimed the near-riots in the streets were unseemly, blasphemous and disrespectful.

'Ha!' laughed De Salignac, 'the old fox would have Le Mans a centre of pilgrimage for the benefit of his own Bishopric!'

It was at Le Mans that the Old King made his presence felt. He was said to have fallen into a paroxysm of grief and rage at the news of his heir's death, and later to be infuriated by the mystical cult that had grown so swiftly around the corpse of the dead monarch.

'He is jealous,' remarked De Salignac wryly.

Hearing of the action of the Bishop and Chapter of Le Mans, he ordered his son's body disinterred and the progress to Rouen resumed. Now was heard a great lament for the dead Henry, written by the troubadour Bertrand de Born, and at last, after a great Requiem Mass, the Young King was finally laid to rest.

It was at Rouen that William finally agreed that Robert de Salignac should accompany him to carry Henry's cloak to the Holy Sepulchre at Jerusalem.

'When will you leave?'

302

'With the King's permission I shall go first into England. There is some need to order my affairs with my brother John…'

'You are not thinking of quitting the field and taking up Holy Orders, are you? I have marked the effect this death has had upon you. You could join the mesnie of Count Philippe, or, should you wish, the service of our Lord Henry the Second; Baldwin de Béthune, among others, has transferred his allegiance… this,' De Salignac gestured, 'this need not be an end to all ambition…'

'It is a sacred charge, Robert. Do you go where you will and I will meet you where? Limoges? In September?' William held out his hand as Robert nodded and grasped it.

'Until then.'

'Until then.'

*

'So FitzMarshal, you are for the Holy Land.' The Old King held out his hand and William knelt and kissed the King's ring. 'I am charged to…'

'So I hear.'

'And seek my Liege's permission to venture there in the company of Robert de Salignac.'

Henry sat back and stroked his beard. It was grey and 'Old' suited him even more now. He motioned William to rise and gazed upon him. 'You shall take the cross?'

William nodded. 'Aye, My Lord.'

'And are determined upon this path?'

'Sire, I am bound in honour to your late son.'

Henry grunted and made a gesture and a small leather pouch was brought forward. Taking it, he threw it casually at William who instinctively caught it, causing Henry to smile. 'You were ever good at catching money, FitzMarshal.'

'You judge me too harshly, my Lord King.'

303

'Do I indeed?'

'That for your expenses since you travel in my son's name.'

William sought some manifestation of grief at mention of the Young King, but Henry had put mourning behind him. Death had claimed a troublesome heir for whom, by his own lights, he had done everything, and his mantle must now fall upon Richard, a man of proven ruthlessness like his father. All that was clear to William, though he laid it aside for the moment; this was no time for such speculations.

'My Liege is most gracious,' he said.

'And what shall you do when, and if, you return from your pilgrimage?'

William had given the matter little thought. The immediate preoccupations of paying off the Basque mercenaries which the Young Henry had employed and who had importuned William for money the instant they knew of the death of their pay-master, and then the troublesome journey escorting the corpse north, had left him little opportunity to consider much else. The discharge of his final obligation to the Young King was all that loomed beyond this moment and it weighed heavily; that and the darker shadows of mortality that the death of the Young Henry had cast over him.

The King moved in his seat as though impatient to be done. 'You have two fine destriers, have you not?' he asked matter-of-factly. 'You will have no need of them as a pilgrim. You may leave them in my care. If either lives upon your return, you may claim your place upon its back in my mesnie. Now go.'

William felt no gratitude, made his obeisance and left. Outside he opened the purse and counted the gold. It was half what his destriers were worth. He bit his lip, stung by the King's accusation of cupidity only to find he had been cheated. De Salignac would appreciate the irony, but it was typical of the shifting morals of the

304

House of Anjou. He stood stock still in the warm sunshine, slightly bemused, reflecting upon the reality of the loss of his great war-horses. Their training had taken weeks and they exemplified the chivalric preoccupations of almost his entire adult life. But now his obligation to the Young King made him nothing greater than any other pilgrim and he thought of how, long ago he had been nothing when he had been in imminent peril of being thrown as a missile from a catapult. Somehow the worldly glories of the tournament, his feats of arms, his prowess, his money, even the ensanguined banner that he had had carried so proudly as a mark of his presence in the field as a knight banneret, had all been a sham.

It struck him that, had he been shot against the walls of his father's castle at Newbury castle as a child, his life would have been better spent. He stirred himself and headed for the stables where his destriers were quartered. The service of Kings, he concluded, was a thing that yielded little. Honour perhaps, perchance a name, but soon forgotten; and after that, as he had seen at Martel, death to end all ambition – King or Commoner.

He remembered the prophetic words of the old Welshman FitzHubert of Guent at the coronation feast of the Young King; and Angharad ap Gwyn who had the second sight, loved him and knew the Old Ways. He recalled too Nicholas de Sarum, and King Stephen who had advised him to cleave to the crown. Aye, but which crown? Which crown? William shook his head at the confusion of it all. He remembered, with a sharp twinge of reproach, the precocious pride that had caused him to confront his father and throw a noose over the beam in the hall of Hamstead Marshal. And it had been an over-weening pride that had compelled him to seek justice before Henry Curtmantle so conspicuously during the great Christmas Court at Caen.

But he thought most of the little boy who – had King Stephen not vacillated – would have been shot from a mangonel to briefly join the birds of the air before dashing his brains out against the wooden palisade of Newbury castle. Aye, it would indeed have been better to have died as a child, innocent of any sin. Had he done so there would not be this giving-up of his mesnie and his war-horses, nor the looming of this long and hazardous journey to the Holy Land, undertaken at the behest of a fickle Prince who laid a death-bed burden upon him like a cross.

Perhaps he might find some peace in Jerusalem, far from the turbulence of the Old Angevin King and his devilish brood. Perhaps.

*

To be concluded by
PART TWO:
GUARDIAN OF THE REALM

Printed in Great Britain
by Amazon